Growing Up American

Growing Up American
Schooling and the Survival of Community

Alan Peshkin

The
University
of
Chicago
Press

*Chicago and
London*

For Maryann: *At the heart of my community*

ALAN PESHKIN is chairman of the Department of Educational Policy Studies and professor of comparative education at the University of Illinois at Urbana. He is the author of *Kanuri School Children: Education and Social Mobilization in Nigeria.*

The University of Chicago Press, Chicago 60637
The University of Chicago Press, Ltd., London

© 1978 by The University of Chicago
All rights reserved. Published 1978
Printed in the United States of America
94 93 92 91 90 89 88 87 86 85   6 5 4 3 2

Library of Congress Cataloging in Publication Data

Peshkin, Alan.
    Growing up American.

    Includes bibliographical references and index.
    1. Community and school—United States.
2. Rural schools—United States. 3. Education,
Secondary—United States. I. Title.
LC217.P47   373.73   78-5849
ISBN 0-226-66196-2 (cloth)
ISBN 0-226-66197-0 (paper)

Contents

WITHDRAWN

Acknowledgments

A collective expression of gratitude to the people of Mansfield whose generosity and cooperation made possible this study does not do justice to the many special kind hearts who gave me hours and hours of their lives. I hope they will understand that I cannot record them all by name and that they remain very special to me. Another collective expression of thanks to my family—Maryann, Nancy, David, and Julie—who help me in more ways than they know.

Going to Mansfield, rather than to other possible sites for my study, was facilitated by Van Miller and Bob Burnham, but most especially by Gordon Hoke, himself a rural American and continuing student of rural life. For the years of my work in Mansfield, Gordon was a port of call for me, a tireless listener and supporter. Gordon, as booster, was joined by Mike and Ann Atkin and Nancy Weinberg and Steve Asher, who listened to my weekend anecdotes and communicated that quality of interest which encouraged me to think that I was learning something of value in Mansfield.

More than booster, Steve Asher joins the group who read my manuscript as it evolved through various titles. His counsel of patience and his assurance that I would have to fight off the publishers who would scramble for my words is greatly appreciated. Steve and Wally Feinberg and Bill Maxwell read my early drafts and were helpfully critical. Finally, my latest draft was read and edited with great insight and sensitivity by Mike Agone and Fred Jaher. The manuscript benefited enormously from their efforts. May they all be blessed with an endless supply of chocolate cake. My friend Elliot Eisner helped me overcome a persistent problem with some of the chapters, but more than this must be acknowledged to him. For the idea of this study evolved through discussions with him over weeks of leisurely treks along mountain meadows and paths in Colorado. I am fortunate to have such friends.

I was joined in my fieldwork in Mansfield by a competent group of research assistants—Sandy Getz, Joel Altschul, Larry Shirley, Marcia Harms, Sue Parker, Bruce Stewart, Dick Feldman, and Marion Metzow. Back-up library research was very ably done by John Kennedy and Stanley Wellington. Marion Metzow deserves special thanks for her uncanny ability to be everywhere in Mansfield High School, noting and recording and thus providing me with an exceptionally rich record of student and teacher life at school.

I received financial support from several sources. I am grateful for this aid, it was indispensable, and I hope they feel rewarded by the work that resulted from their generosity. Within the University of Illinois, funds were provided by the College of Education (with the help of Mike Atkin and Arden Groteluschen), the College of Agriculture (with the help of Fritz Fliegel and Steve Sanderson), and the University Research Board (in whose debt I have been since I came to the University of Illinois in 1967). In addition to this support, I received a one-year fellowship from the John Simon Guggenheim Memorial Foundation. The encouragement this fellowship provides is significant beyond the ample funding it offers.

Over the course of many drafts, enduring my pinned inserts and abbreviations, typists Barbara Franklin and Linda Roberts served me well. I'm especially pleased with the help and dedication of Denise Hoffman who stuck earphones to her head for one year and transformed tapes into transcripts.

In fact, most persons acknowledged here did more than what I specifically expressed my gratitude to them for doing. Thank you, as well, for the other things. And my apologies to those whose support I have inadvertently overlooked acknowledging.

1

Getting Started in Mansfield

It is clear what kind of work farmers and factory workers do; in any event, it is clear to the residents of Mansfield, the site of this study of school and community, because most of them have such jobs. But what do professors do? My host, friend, and well-wisher in Mansfield, Don McNally, wondered. Actually, he did not so much wonder what professors did as whether I got paid during my time in Mansfield, incredulous that anyone could get a salary for attending meetings or football games, and for going everywhere with a notebook and a tape recorder. We became friends, the professor and this eighty-four-year-old Scottish immigrant, former coal miner, and farmer, who laughed when I shoveled rather than scooped snow, and sharply challenged my views on Viet Nam, Nixon, and Watergate during my stay with him from 1972 to 1974. More personally, however, he doubted whether there was anything to study in Mansfield, and, if there was, why it would take two years to do it. Nevertheless, accepting me, he accepted my work, as did his fellow Mansfielders who demonstrated that it mattered little, and then only at first, what I said I had come to Mansfield to do. What mattered significantly more was that by local standards I was OK. That I was Jewish, of urban background, and a professor, and thus in important ways different from everyone else in Mansfield, did not automatically place me beyond the boundaries of their acceptance. To be honest, accepting, and capable of speaking to and not down to people is to advance markedly toward acceptance in Mansfield. And more than merely discreetly quiet about the wonders of the larger society outside Mansfield, I marveled at the village community Mansfielder's words conjured up, a community which for many actually exists. I think my marvel showed. Finally, other things being equal, I believe it is difficult not to welcome a person who is infinitely and uncritically interested in everything you say, who listens attentively and then adds, "Please tell me more. What you say is important." The details of the person I announced myself to be at the start of my work in Mansfield were of less consequence than the person I demonstrated I was. Once accepted, I was trusted; among many other things, Mansfield taught me about trust.

1

As a professor of comparative education, I ordinarily go abroad for my research, having specialized in two geographic areas, the Indian subcontinent and Nigeria. Accordingly, I should explain how I came to study an American village.

I can see, in retrospect, that I arrived at Mansfield both by way of my neighborhood in Chicago and by way of Jalaripet, a village on the east coast of India. I can also see now that a single thread connects Chicago, Jalaripet, and Mansfield: it is community survival. While dimly aware of this thread at the start of fieldwork in Mansfield, I nonetheless felt I had embarked on a journey without a map, on an adventure whose plot might remain unknown until the study was complete.

From my birth until midway through college I lived on the same street in two adjacent apartment buildings. My neighbors and the merchants who operated the little stores that served us in those pre-supermarket days remained virtually unchanged during this nineteen-year period. Most of these people were Jewish, first- or second-generation immigrants, and they enjoyed a stability, a continuity, and a sense of belonging, that small-town people do not believe exist in the city. I can still visualize every building, every backyard, and every store in the square block that contained my immediate neighborhood community.

Around 1950 the trickle of migrants from this neighborhood and many others to the outskirts of the city and its suburbs became a torrent. New persons arrived. Soon, urban renewal programs and new mass transportation systems transformed and destroyed still intact communities. Thousands of people were involuntarily uprooted, their pain difficult to imagine by those of us who move freely to seek opportunity. The point is that I had experienced community life, notwithstanding its locale in a city of four million, and I have always been saddened by the displacement of unwilling urban groups. I personally missed a sense of community when I joined the throng of moving Americans, and I missed it vicariously for those urbanites forced to abandon their homes.

Another important autobiographical event applies here. In 1970 I went to India to prepare to study modern and traditional values. I sought a sample of villagers to interview in Jalaripet, home of a fishing caste who live literally in the shadow of a growing seaport city of 250,000. As I waited for our informants to locate interviewees, I visited Jalaripet's only school, a thatch-sided, tin-roofed, one-room building in which a single teacher taught grades one to five. Once past the courtesies extended to all visitors, I learned that of the approximately forty-five enrolled students, only five were in the fifth grade and that more than half were in the first grade. Apparently, the villagers were unable or unwilling to use the school as a stepping stone to advanced education and new job opportunities, and most stopped their schooling short of becoming literate. Nor did the villager's fishing practices, moreover, promote success in their traditional occupation. While they went to sea with nets and dugout canoes and refused to fish more than a mile from shore, non–fishing-caste fishermen from the city used modern equipment and power boats. Thus in their response both to education and to work the people of Jalaripet appeared curiously shortsighted. I intended to study Jalaripet's seemingly imminent decline, but I had to abandon my plans when diplomatic relations between India and the United States became strained by the Pakistan-Bangladesh conflict. Thinking it unlikely I could soon conduct such a study in India, I sought a comparable setting at home.

I began to search for an American village. They abound in the Midwest, and many people think their future is in doubt.[1] At that time, as though to confirm my intention to organize such a study, a newspaper article warned, "The problem of the small town in its simplest terms is the quiet acquiescence of a pending reality—its decline. Perhaps, without help, its death." I looked for a town that contained a high school, since I planned to study both school and community; one that was rural, with agriculture a dominant factor in its life; small, so that in time I could understand fairly well all the aspects of its community life; comparatively isolated—that is, not a suburb or so located as to be engulfed by an expanding city; without an industry or showing promise of the type of expansion that industry portends; and agreeable to my conducting a study in its midst.

The formal issue of agreeability only holds for the school. Generally, one cannot be prevented from entering a town, attending church, meeting people, and the like. Entering a school, however, requires explicit consent. And entering for a long period of time requires a superintendent of a special sort, one who can appreciate your research goals, adequately reassure his teachers and school board, and be comfortable with the daily presence of outsiders from a university. Mr. Tate of Mansfield High School was such a man, and the village of Mansfield was the type of place I was looking for.[2] At no time have I doubted that I made the right choice. Many places could satisfy the first five criteria; I am less certain about the last one. Mr. Tate was a very special man, the right one for Mansfield and the right one for me.

Mansfield school district, the unit of my study, contains approximately 2,200 persons and somewhat over 500 students in a kindergarten-through-twelfth-grade system. This enrollment places it in a category (see table 1) with 13.8 percent of the other school systems in the United States, which together contain only 2.3 percent of the country's total public school students.[3]

I began formal work in Mansfield on the first day of school in August

1972. To allay the expected anxiety of teachers toward a stranger who visits their classrooms, I assured them I did not plan to evaluate their instruction—and, of course, this was and remains true. Nor did I plan to evaluate the community and make recommendations for its improvement. In short, reform was not my goal. I proposed, rather, to portray the nature of the high school experience and to investigate the relationship between the high school and its host community. I hoped to learn how, if at all, they served each other.

Believing that after graduation rural youth migrated to urban areas, I wondered which reality Mansfield's high school reflected—that of its own rural outlook or that of the city life to which its youth surely were attracted. If it were the latter, then the needs of Mansfield would be slighted, but if it were the former, then its youth would be ill equipped for their post-Mansfield lives. In any event, without an overriding central issue or perspective to guide the study, I cast my net widely, committing myself to exploring all aspects of the community and its school, slowly, patiently, and exhaustively. Though each proposal I wrote seeking funds for the project reassured me, at least momentarily, that I knew what I was doing, I was still often disconcerted by the accumulating mass of information, fearing it might perversely remain as nearly amorphous as the form in which it was received.

I lived in Mansfield off and on for one year and for most of a second year, employed several research assistants, and as much as possible became involved in the daily life of the community. In this two-year period, my assistants and I were participant-observers, conducted interviews and a questionnaire survey, and obtained many documents from the school and community. We moved slowly to become "part of the woodwork," to have our presence so taken for granted that in time students and educators would behave naturally, taking no account of us.

Although it was not requested, I assured anonymity to the school, the town, and all those we interviewed and observed or who wrote diaries for us. Anonymity is not an easy burden for the researcher. While Mansfielders cannot be identified by non-Mansfielders, they can certainly identify each other. Thus, I have made modifications in what usually are verbatim transcripts (prepared from handwritten notes the first year and tape recordings the second year) in order to obscure identity. All names and places are pseudonyms. The biographies of teachers and school board members characterize composite persons; the background facts presented to describe a person, facts that could reveal his or her identity, are never attached to the statements of opinion that person uttered. Moreover, when necessary, identifying features were either changed or omitted. I trust, of course, that real people remain in my study. That they are synthetic in some way should be of less moment than the fact that every opinion included was spoken or written by some Mansfielder in the exact language recorded here (and transcribed without the use of "sic" to call attention to misspellings and other blemishes).

One statement in my questionnaire survey asked adults to indicate whether or not persons like themselves were accepted in Mansfield. Of 239 respondents, 12.1 percent stated they were not accepted, 68.1 percent said they were, and 18.4 percent were indecisive. Given this information, and allowing for the possible bias of those who chose to return the questionnaire, I estimate that approximately 70 percent of the population comprise Mansfield's mainstream. My study is about this group. The remaining group, the "outsiders," are of consequence as human beings, but they are not the major actors in my story; the relationship I see between school and community in Mansfield is not defined in their terms.[4] This is not to say that mainstream Mansfield consists exclusively of the rich and the well-born; it includes large and small farm families, highly skilled and unskilled factory workers, college graduates and high school dropouts, Florida vacationers and those who vacation close to home. Overriding the group's class and status distinctions is their attachment to Mansfield. For all of them, Mansfield is a special place.

The mainstream contains a sizable subgroup with exceptional affinity for their community. Of the 239 respondents, 52 percent agreed they feel more at home in Mansfield than they ever could outside the Mansfield community; 28 percent disagreed; and 19 percent were indecisive. So phrased, the question selects out those who identify with Mansfield. This 52 percent is *at the very least* the proportion of Mansfielders who strongly feel they belong. They are epitomized by farmer Paul Erdlund who said he would not go to Florida for a winter vacation unless his wife insisted. It's vacation enough, he explained, just to stay right in town and meet his friends every day at the restaurant where farmers congregate, drink coffee, tease the waitresses, and jaw with the men they have known all their lives. They are further epitomized by Erdlund's friends in the Brethren Men's Fellowship who asked me, at the end of my fieldwork, if I wasn't sorry I had grown up in Chicago now that I had learned about the joy of growing up in Mansfield.[5]

The outsiders are no more homogeneous than the mainstreamers. They are often poorer persons or newcomers, but the mainstream includes both groups. If a person is poor, a newcomer, and nonparticipant in any community associations, from the Merry Stitchers to the Church of the Brethren, then he is likely to feel distinctly "outside." Mansfield, however, though not readily welcoming everyone, does not consistently reject any existing group identifiable by a single criterion, such as national origin, religion, or wealth.[6] Some persons may feel they more thoroughly belong in Mansfield, but its embrace reaches persons of diverse occupations, interests, and backgrounds who are comforted by its intimacy, call everyone by his first name, and are sufficiently accepted to think twice about moving elsewhere.

Perhaps at this point it is necessary to sort out several terms used almost interchangeably in the book. They are *school district, community, Mansfield, support community, mainstream Mansfielder,* and *subgroup*. The *school district* is the legal unit establishing the boundaries for attendance and for financial support of Mansfield High School. Because of the importance of schools to rural people, the school district also is coterminous with the *community* of Mansfield, not only in legal terms, but also in psychological terms, where a sense of community exists. Thus community is defined as an "*awareness* of sharing a way of life as well as the common earth" (MacIver and Page, 1949:10).[7] *Mansfield* is the village which is encompassed by and gives its name to the school district, the community, and one of the townships included within the school district. *Support community* refers to the people living within a school district who feel attached to a school,[8] for whom the school is important both in personal and community maintenance terms; the support community both supports and is supported by its school. There are persons within a school district, however, who have financial obligations to the school through the property tax but who do not feel part of either the community or support community. Support community is therefore a more limited concept than the body of taxpayers. In fact, a person's children may attend a school and still he may not be counted by others or himself as part of the school's support community. When the school is perceived as contributory to the maintenance of a person's valued community, then he is part of the support community. The entire case study has been prepared from the standpoint of the numerically, politically, and socially dominant *mainstream Mansfielder* whose interests, sense of belonging, and outlook make them a subgroup, that is, a collectivity whose members share "some common quality that makes them distinguishable from other members of a group to which they belong" (*Webster's Third New International Dictionary*). Mansfield and its schools prepare their children for membership in a subgroup; the children grow up American but in a particular way.

The referents of community, support community, and subgroup are virtually identical in Mansfield. In other settings, where the population is more diverse and less stable, a school's support community may not encompass a subgroup. And no general sense of community may unite those who are linked through their taxpayer's connection to the school.

When, however, there is an identity among these three groupings, then a school system has a critical, sensitive relationship with some set of adults.[9]

Since I value intimacy and a sense of community, it follows that I came to admire Mansfield's school and community for their contribution of these qualities to their student and adult members. This admiration may well affect my objectivity. The transient researcher can afford to be distant from the people he studies, but I intended, on the contrary, to remove as much of the distance as I could. As a result, I soon felt a strain between my commitment to objectivity and my increasing involvement with the local people. As such involvement grows, one's objectivity erodes, and as I wrote this book I was nagged by the question, "How will this read in Mansfield?" Of course, this "confession" does not free me from the obligation to have written as carefully and honestly as I could. I trust, however, that what passed through my subjective filters constitutes a credible and comprehensive picture of the nature of school and community in Mansfield.

One reads and selects one's data, and reads and selects again and again, knowing that the dangers of misrepresentation are high, but also knowing that there would be little chance of consensus, except, perhaps, on the most obvious points, if one invited the opinions of others about what to include. At the risk of explaining the obvious, therefore, I must state that the school and community portrayed in these pages are *my* Mansfield and *my* Mansfield High School, both artifacts of *my* outsider's vision. Who could possibly add enough facts and qualifications to his observations to satisfy any group of Saturday morning shoppers in Black's Supermarket? I, too, shopped at Black's and idled through the one checkout line where customers exchanged greetings and messages with the friendly, knowledgeable cashier. I also went to church, attended school board and village board meetings, cheered at football games, ate dinner with the Senior Citizens (my favorite meal) and supper with the Kiwanians, paid my telephone bill at the locally owned telephone company, kept a checking account at the local bank, and regularly read the *Mansfield Times*. Still, I am not a Mansfielder; I had to depend on extensive observing, listening, and reading to uncover the life of the people, personally experiencing as much as I could, but always, in the end, remaining an outsider who was in Mansfield for a particular purpose. (I didn't tell them that when I attended the University of Illinois at Urbana, I thought I was entering southern Illinois on passing Chicago's city limits. In fact, the unfamiliar accent of downstate Illinoisans convinced me that outside Chicago I was on the edge of the American South.) Given other purposes—or even other researchers with my purpose—different events, emphases, relationships, and char-

acterizations would follow. The point I wish to emphasize (specially to
my friends in Mansfield) is that I do not see and write as a Mansfielder,
but as a researcher whose observations and conclusions may be different
from theirs but still valid.

The heart of this book is a case study which responds essentially to
the question, What is an American high school like? Given local control, this nation's schools are highly diverse, so the answer my study
offers to this question may not encompass the nature of many suburban
and large urban schools. Yet, in my discussion of the classroom experience, the vast extracurricular program, the money-raising activities, the
student diaries, and the reflections of seniors on their school days, I
hope to have captured, in the special way outsiders often can, the reality of school life in many American communities. I would like students of American schools to read this study and say, "So this is the
way it is," and contemporary participants in American schools to say,
"So this is the way we are!" More than a case study of a school, however, the book is intended to portray the integral relationship between
school and community in a rural area. This portrayal, guided by very
general purposes in the initial phase of my study, was eventually shaped
by a central idea which orders the mass of data I collected: this idea
is the survival of community.

2

Belonging, Nurturance, and Intimacy:
The Community of Mansfield

Introduction

Mansfield is located in Mansfield Township, Cunningham County. It is the locus of the mercantile, religious, organizational, social, and educational agencies of the community. The community embraces not only the village but also the surrounding countryside, and it is the countryside that provides the distinctive flavor to this section of the state, for farming places its stamp on all local citizens. Since farmers historically have been the area's most stable group, nonfarmers cannot be unaware of the cycle and demands of agricultural activity. Corn and soybean fields make an island of Mansfield village, shaping the countryside just as they shape the lives of Mansfield children and adults.

To understand the world of Mansfield High School one must experience its encompassing community, and not merely because our tradition of local control is possibly most intact in the stable, smaller school districts of the country. More than this: the school is located in a particular place, serves a particular clientele, and therefore takes on the flavor of that place, shaped by those who hire the educators, prepare student lunches, and cheer at football games. Thus each school is based not only in the notions of its educators, but often also in a community with its own history of aspirations and commitments broader than, though most decidedly embracing, education. This may even be true in the stable, generally homogeneous neighborhood communities of cities.

Who are the Mansfielders, these 2,172 people who live in the school district? They can be characterized in several ways. Of the 2,172, 2,023 are native Americans, most of them born within the state to white, English-speaking parents. Nearly 30 percent are of school age, 5 to 21 (see table 2). Fifteen percent of the population are 65 or over, a large portion of whom are widows (in the state as a whole this same age group comprises only 9.7 percent of the population). Mansfield's youth grow up conscious of the full continuum of ages. Indeed, the ubiquity of the elderly heightens all Mansfielders' awareness of a group that tends to require continuing concern and attention.

Of all persons 14 and over,[1] 69 percent are married; 16.9 percent were never married; 10 percent are widowed; and 3.1 percent are separated, divorced, or living with spouse absent. Thus Mansfield is basically a place of intact families.

The levels of education achieved by the district's 1,258 persons 25 or over are not striking (see table 3). The several women who did not complete first grade undoubtedly matured at a time when schooling was less available for females. Fewer than half the males (269 of 601) and a slightly higher proportion of females (309 of 657) completed high school. Though approximately 50 percent of the high school graduates attend post-secondary institutions and many live in the Mansfield area (see chap. 3), only 9.6 percent of the males and 10 percent of the females over 25 now living in the school district have attended college. The median number of years completed for both males and females is approximately 10.5, compared with 12.1 for white males and females in the United States, and 11.7 for rural persons of both sexes in the United States.

The salary distribution for Mansfielders shown in table 4 details the income of 624 families. The median family income in 1970 was $9,500. Since family income includes the earnings and income of *all* persons in a family, these figures are more modest than they appear, though somewhat above average compared with the following state medians: overall—$8,914; urban—$9,089; rural nonfarm—$8,251; and rural farm—$7,877. Based on the 1970 census definition of poverty as family income below $3,000, 5.6 percent of Mansfield's families are below the poverty level. The need for a second income is reflected in the fact that more than 400 women 14 or over work at least part of the year.

Of the approximately 360 full-time working men who live in Mansfield Township, 240 hold factory jobs, while 90 work in agriculture and 33 in business. These data mostly reflect the job picture of the men who live in town. If these occupational figures included the 300 persons who live in the school district but outside the township, the agriculture total would rise considerably. Of the approximately 190 full-time working women who live in Mansfield Township, 62 are in clerical positions, 61 have factory jobs, and another 70 are secretaries, sales clerks, and the like.

A slight majority of the approximately 700 persons 14 and older who were employed work in Cunningham County;[2] full-time male workers outnumber full-time female workers almost 3 to 1. The community provides employment for about 175 persons, most of them on a full-time basis. The largest single employer is the school district, with its 50 workers, mostly teachers. This is a significant feature of the school's role in maintaining the community.

In physical terms, Mansfield is on a plain 680 feet above sea level, with glacial drift of 130 to 150 feet underlying it. The average annual rainfall is 41 inches. The effects of these several qualities are visible from any direction: this flat, almost treeless land of remarkably black soil produces an abundance of corn and soybeans, as well as some winter wheat. Here and there trees have grown up along the ditches that are essential to draining off the surface water which otherwise would create large swampy areas. Most former stands of timber have been transformed into fields, except along the narrow Mansfield River which winds through the countryside.

Two minor hard roads enter the village, one of them coming to a dead end at its southern edge. Relatively little nonlocal automobile traffic passes through town. Because of its somewhat out-of-the-way location, Mansfield gets few casual visitors. Two sets of railroad tracks cut through town; one carries one train a day and the other is out of service. Weeds grow tall along these tracks, and the Junior Women's Club has debated whether to organize a beautification program along the section within the village.

Mansfield is a good commonplace town. The houses are old, mostly of frame construction and ordinary in design, though well maintained. Vegetable gardens and well-trimmed lawns are common. The space around and between houses suffices to prevent the claustrophobia small-town people believe they would develop if they lived in a city. More elaborate architectural style appears only in the former homes of two bankers, one building now a funeral parlor and the other a shelter-care home for mentally retarded and senile persons. Two subdivisions, built in the last ten years, and two small housing units for the aged, developed with federal assistance, represent the organized efforts to upgrade the community's residential potential. Houses seldom are offered for rent or sale, and recent zoning regulations discourage moving trailers and mobile homes onto town lots.

As the map of Mansfield shows, the village consists mostly of short streets. The business section is on Main Street between the Saginaw railroad tracks and County Street and to a lesser extent on County and Fairlane. Over the years, many stores have been renovated inside and out, though it is clear from the nature of the still-exposed brickwork and the painted cornices that the buildings are old. New sidewalks and trees are further signs of a progressive spirit, of a retreat from the recent past when nobody cared enough to "prevent the village from going to seed." Yet closed stores—permanently closed from all appearances—attest both to the seedy phase and to the feeling that Mansfield has seen better days.

For a small town the business section is fairly intact, though gloomy forecasts are often heard, even from the most capable shopkeepers. The soundest stores have external affiliations: Rexall for the drugstore, Bi-

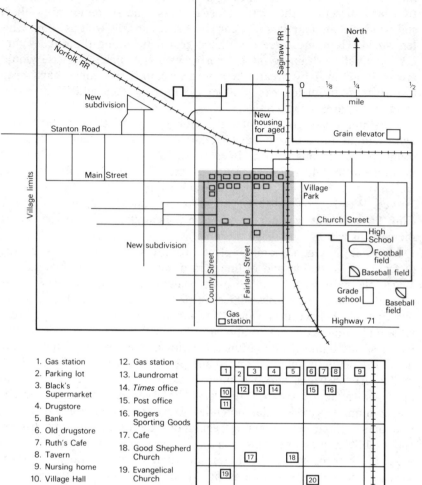

1. Gas station
2. Parking lot
3. Black's Supermarket
4. Drugstore
5. Bank
6. Old drugstore
7. Ruth's Cafe
8. Tavern
9. Nursing home
10. Village Hall
11. Bennie's Garage
12. Gas station
13. Laundromat
14. *Times* office
15. Post office
16. Rogers Sporting Goods
17. Cafe
18. Good Shepherd Church
19. Evangelical Church
20. Funeral parlor

Business section and adjacent areas

The Village of Mansfield

Rite for the grocery store, and True Value for the hardware store. Several others, another grocery store and a dry goods store, are wholly local and suffer the consequent purchasing disadvantages of buying in small volume at higher prices and therefore charging more. Shopping patterns and recreational pursuits are strongly oriented to Stanton, an industrial center about twenty-five miles to the north, and to Auburn, the county seat located ten miles to the east. Other than the park, the schools, and a community-sponsored center for senior citizens, Mansfield has no other recreational facilities. Residents still complain about the loss years ago of its movie house, roller skating rink, and bowling alley.

At the principal business intersection of Main and Fairlane stand Mansfield's bank and its post office, both important informal meeting places. One of the village's two restaurants, Ruth's Cafe, is near this corner. Two back tables at Ruth's always are pushed together to accommodate the farmers who traditionally claim this spot as their own. Ruth's is one of the major loafing centers for both males and females. With the exception of the Laundromat, the drugstore, and the *Mansfield Times* business office, most other such centers are reserved for men, including Roger's Sporting Goods, the gas stations, the grain elevator, Bennie's Garage, and the bench outside the bank. Women and students stop and chat in the good, small library that occupies an old Main Street store. The business section, referred to as "uptown," is always busiest when the town's two doctors have office hours, since they attract people from beyond the community. Anyone expecting to see a doctor must come to his office, register with his nurse, and wait. No appointments are accepted, though both doctors will make house calls. The waiting room is another place in town to talk.

One does not in fact always see clusters of people chatting idly during the day, but village life is comparatively unhurried, and people expect to converse with the women in charge of the post office, bank tellers, waitresses, and merchants. It is unfriendly not to pause to talk, and even motorists stop in the middle of the street and converse from their cars.

Mansfield's cooperative grain elevator, the skyscraper of the prairie, overlooks the village. Its four steel storage bins and one very tall elevator stand at the edge of town where the village joins its fertile fields, symbolizing the linkage between country and village life. The late editor of the *Mansfield Times*, Ben Matthews, mostly ignored the hard times of the countryside. Were he alive today, he probably would still urge the townspeople to get moving, concerned about the farmer, to be sure, but focusing his attention on the well-being of the village. Then, as now, the future of the village was uncertain. The land, on the contrary, is

more fertile than ever, its products urgently demanded by a hungry
world.

The Heritage I

In the beginning there was the prairie flatland and some Indians. It was
the early 1830s. Then came the farmers and the preachers and the
traders from Ohio, Virginia, and Kentucky, descended from forebears
who originated mostly in the British Isles. They cut down the tall
grasses, laid tile so the land would drain properly, worshiped and taught
their children in rough-hewn cabins, and established settlements which
in time evolved into a town and community. They had large families
and many children died before reaching adulthood; as late as 1896,
Mansfield citizens were sick with malaria, typhoid fever, and diphtheria.
The later settlers came mostly from Ohio, Tennessee, and Kentucky;
many of the southerners came north with a persisting antipathy for
the black American.

Settled in 1850 and incorporated in 1873, Mansfield had 767 residents by 1890. The township, however, contained about 1,500 additional persons. This proportion reflects the then dominant fact of American agriculture—the small family farm. The statistics of table 5 clearly
reveal the move away from such farms as these 1,500 rural living persons in 1890 (calculated by subtracting the village from the township
figures) decline to slightly more than 500 in 1970. At present, moreover, there are many rural nonfarm families.

The county-based figures in table 6 document the dramatic decrease
in the number of farms since 1880 and the dramatic increase in farm
size over the same period. For both the change is over 50 percent.
These figures are a good approximation of what has happened in Mansfield school district since the village was first settled.

At a time when family farming was a dominant way of life in most
of the country, Ben Matthews came to Mansfield and purchased the
still published weekly *Mansfield Times*. He bought the newspaper in
the early 1890s and did not sell out until 1912. Matthews was a go-
getter in a solid, nonpejorative, old-fashioned sense. Though not a
Mansfield or area native, a fact which characterized the majority of
business persons in the past and still does today, he "pushed" (locally
pronounced "pooshed" and said with conviction) for Mansfield, wield-
ing his editorial opinions, as often found on the first page as on the
editorial page, like an old-time city boss delivering his favors, now
rewarding, now punishing, but ever vigilant to record his sentiments on
any matter of local consequence.

Never dispassionate or neutral, his outlook on the events of the day represent one dominant segment of public opinion in turn-of-the-century Mansfield. Progress! That's what Matthews desired. In an unprecedented gush of language, its like never again to be read in the *Mansfield Times*, he expressed this desire. In 1892, he recorded with satisfaction that more money had been spent "putting in improvements" in the past year than in the previous ten years. So much to the good. That there were public-spirited citizens did not mean there were no detractors, and in 1899 he detailed "five separate bunches" of "town killers:"

> First, those who go out of town to do their shopping; second, those who prefer a quiet town to one of push and business; third, those who oppose every movement that does not originate with themselves; fourth, those who oppose every movement that does not appear to benefit them; fifth, those who seek to injure the credit or reputation of individuals.

The town killers of 1899 are still recognizable types in the eyes of Mansfield's contemporary boosters. In fact, today's merchants still complain about residents who shop out of town. Matthews singled out teachers in 1900, reminding them that they take from the "public crib" and that merchants' taxes pay their salaries; he hoped his "hints" would help them learn a "lesson of patriotism and instill the same lesson in their little charges." Four years later he editorialized that all Mansfielders should "trade with their home merchants," although then as now the pages of the *Times* carried ads from larger nearby towns seeking the Mansfielder's trade. And then as now a sound economy was essential for a viable Mansfield.

But the rhetoric of reform is not meant to be read too closely. Its hyperbole both overstates and understates; what is consistent, however, is that the reformer wants change, often equates it with improvement, and whether he lashes out or lauds may simply reflect his mood at the time. For example, throughout Matthew's editorship, Mansfield changes: its population increases, waterworks are built, electric lights are introduced, a telephone system is established, and sidewalks, four miles of brick, stone, and concrete, are laid out. Notable accomplishments, indeed, and all this by 1900, notwithstanding his distress in June 1900 that with seven thousand feet of water mains available to property owners only three of them bought city water. The rest preferred to use their own wells. "Is it any wonder," he laments "that our town is in debt? Let's have a grand awakening of public spiritedness . . . a revival of patriotism." Only three months later, in October 1900, he felt much better. After detailing recent accomplishments he concludes, "Our splen-

didly progressive citizenship . . . is on the very crest of the waves of
success." Even if good times (translated as more money and more residents) lay ahead, Matthews's aquatic imagery never fully squared with
reality, though later residents would look back and see a golden past
that appeared enviable in contrast to their less well endowed present.

Over the years Matthews reacted to a variety of events and situations
in terms still honored today. For example, no Independence Day could
pass without an abundance of his superlatives:

> Mansfield's 4th of July celebration will be the biggest and best ever
> held in this part of the state. The cannons will boom louder, the
> screams of the Eagle will be heard farther and Old Glory will float
> higher and prouder than on any other occasion.

The day featured a sunrise salute of 120 guns, a grand parade of societies (including the Mutual Protective League, International Order of
Odd Fellows, Order of the Eastern Star, Knights of Pythias, Royal
Neighbors, Mystic Workers of the World, and the Mansfield Rebekah
Lodge), businessmen and Sunday school groups, plus a chorus of two
hundred. The political messages of the Fourth of July were immersed
in pageantry of a sort that was also unveiled for more secular occasions,
like the 1900 picnic of the Woodman's Fraternal Order, which began
at 9:00 A.M. with a reception of delegations, a cakewalk, and a Grand
Parade, and then continued all afternoon with a succession of patriotic
addresses and music, as well as bicycle, foot, sack, and three-legged
races, and greased-pole, pie-eating, and chopping contests.

With America's entry into World War I, by which time Matthews
had moved west,[3] the pageantry of patriotism expanded well beyond
holidays. War-related local news dominated the front page, general war
news was found inside, and even the sports pages extolled athletes,
mostly baseball players, who were engaged in war-related activities:
"Duffy Lewis of world series fame is now hitting 'em out for Uncle
Sam." When thirty local boys were drafted, the Saginaw Railroad carried an extra coach for the Mansfield faithful who wanted to accompany
the draftees to their disembarkation point. "About 100 members of the
miners local, the Mansfield band and a half hundred others made the
trip, many going in cars." Mansfield Township went "over the top" in
its Red Cross drives. Those unable to join the military services could
buy thrift stamps and liberty bonds, or they could serve through the
Township League, which sent food, books, and scarves to the boys in
uniform.

Since American small towns usually have enjoyed a robust religious
life, it is no surprise that a strong religious tradition has prevailed in
Mansfield. Religious activity and sentiment dominated Sundays, and

unorthodox expression of religious feeling was not tolerated. In Matthews's time, at least five churches served the community, and no particular feeling of brotherhood united them. Church members were true believers and defenders of the faith—their own. Members of other churches, while sharing the broader secular community, were heretics of a sort or, less harshly, persons who had missed the boat. While possibly still afloat, they had taken refuge on a lesser, shakier, more uncertain craft. (This feeling no longer exists.) Some religious groups could not be countenanced. The Church of Jesus Christ of Latter-Day Saints was one of these.

> Mormonism [Matthews editorialized in 1904] in all its hideousness, is being exposed . . . by the senatorial investigation now being held in Washington. It is sincerely hoped that public sentiment and official zeal will be aroused to a point that will result in the eradication, complete and everlasting, of this foul, festering and damnable sore on American honor.

With great pleasure Matthews noted the success of the Reverend C. P. Pledger, Billy Sunday's "right hand man." In one of several instances of the intersection of religion and schooling, Pledger addressed Mansfield's high school students. When he was done he asked all who wished to take a stand for Christ to come forward.

> For perhaps 2 or 3 minutes no one came. Miss Martha Brown, a pupil of the high school, was the first to come. With tears streaming down her cheeks she came forward. . . . In a moment they were coming from every part of the room. . . . The teachers went among and encouraged their pupils.

At other times, teachers were less cooperative. Several refused to teach against drink and tobacco or to begin each day with a Scripture reading. Samuel Archer, then president of the school board, cast the deciding vote to fire the teachers. "Perhaps," Matthews observed, "Mr. Archer will succeed in uprooting this atheism."

Religious orthodoxy also was associated with several other issues. Observing the Sabbath, for example, was rarely a newsworthy item because its sanctity was usually maintained. Times changed. By 1912, this particular sign of orthodoxy received diminishing support, as witnessed by Matthews's blast against Sunday baseball. On the occasion of the village board's discussion of an ordinance to ban this Sabbath violation, Matthews sought its passage, urging that "it is an open violation of the express command of our Lord when He commanded us 'to keep the sabbath holy,'" and, besides, Sunday baseball has become "a money-making scheme." A petition signed by 158 citizens of the village testified

to the size of the group which shared his view. However, not only did
the village board refuse to pass the ordinance, they also refused to
"appoint a board of censorship for amusements."

Temperance was a more troublesome issue. In the early decades of
this century a Women's Christian Temperance Union fountain stood
on a prominent corner of the town, strong testimony to the vigor of
opposition to saloons and drinking. Both Matthews and his successor
were staunch anti-saloonites who could divide people into scoundrels
or gentlemen on the basis of their stand on alcohol. Mansfield, voting
to go wet in 1935, now has two bars, their presence welcomed by today's city fathers for the sales tax they contribute to village coffers. Not
so in this earlier period when drinkers were incarnations of the devil
and Matthews applauded the 100-vote victory of the anti-license people
in a local election.

> The temperance people were on the ground all day keeping in touch
> with the sentiment of the voters. The 80 votes received by Kling
> and Gould represent the actual saloon strength in Mansfield and
> shows just how many fellows there are . . . who have no regard for
> law or morality.

The refusal to ban Sunday baseball may well have been rooted in the
Mansfielders' powerful interest in sports. The Mansfield Cardinals, a
proud baseball team of the past with a heavy schedule that extended
into October, at times played on five consecutive days against teams as
far away as fifty miles. Town baseball overlapped with high school football, which as a newer game enjoyed less support. The football team of
1912 had to solicit local businessmen and friends for funds to bring in
a college coach for a week or two of help. Matthews, ever the booster,
encouraged the team in September to think that only hard practice
stood between them and a move "into a faster class than the present
pace they are travelling," a conclusion based on the team's near "world
record" loss to Auburn by a score of 91 to 0. By November the team's
record almost pushed Matthews to straight reporting:

> The local team was lambasted to pieces down at Stanton Saturday.
> . . . The final score was 89–0. The last two quarters were shortened
> from 12 to 9 minutes. . . . A Stanton correspondent says that 4 new
> plays were used against Mansfield, which are destined to be world
> beaters. The new plays were: Gee Haw, Whoa Back, Flea Flicker,
> and Bizzy-izzy.

The *Mansfield Times* devoted significantly less space to racial matters
than to sports because nonwhites almost without exception did not then
live in Mansfield or in nearby towns. The exceptions were three blacks

—a maid, a groom who settled there for several years and was even buried in a local cemetery, and a barber who lived there for a short time with his family. Matthews's vituperations poured out, however, whenever an issue touched his racist nerves. In 1900:

> Mitchem, the "coon" barber who has been inflicting his odoriferous presence on this community this past year . . . wrote a letter to *The Republic*, a blackmailing sheet published in Auburn. Editor Hammond took the nigger to his arms. . . . When a white man associates himself with a nigger by publicly defending him against an outraged community, we draw a color line.

Later, in 1904, Matthews wrote of noticing in Brenton's newspaper that:

> Reverend Garner, a colored preacher ["colored" is still considered the polite way to refer to black Americans], tried to drink all the whiskey in that city and as a consequence got behind bars. Wonder if that's the same colored brother whose note is held by Mansfield parties for debts contracted during a "nigger revival" here a few years ago.

Finally, in the best scapegoat tradition, Matthews links race and riot in the state's capitol.

> The Bradlow riots [of 1908] were simply a combination of corrupt politics, too much Negro and bad politics. . . . Wide open saloons, unlimited booze and attendant debaucheries—natural results of the Bradlow brand of politics—together with the Bradlow negro brought about its only logical conclusion—riot.

The Heritage II

Blanche, Molly, and Agnes are old friends. Only Molly is not a native Mansfielder. She came to town fifty years ago, married, raised seven children, and feels no less rooted here than her companions who were born and raised on farms in Mansfield Township, went to one-room country schools and the town's high school, and have never lived anywhere else. All are "widow ladies," part of a large group of older persons who are both respected and regretted—regretted because each of them often occupies a whole house singly (thereby preventing larger families from settling in Mansfield) and none of them generate much revenue for village development. Nobody really objects to their presence, however; no architects of progress are so single-minded in purpose as to wish them ill. They are the Adopted Grannies to the girls in the Future Homemakers of America (see chap. 7).

When we take a break from recording the reminiscences that follow below, Blanche plays a hymn on her organ. Her friends soon join their harmonizing voices to her playing. To these religious women, hymns are popular songs. They also love talking about the past, their memories spanning most of this century. Though they speak about themselves, the events of their lives and their outlook are shared by many Mansfielders.

Blanche: Mother always told me that when I was born the weather was so bad, we had such a big snow storm and sleet storm, she said they skated from Mansfield to Neely [a distance of six miles] right over the fences.

Molly: That was the kind of weather we used to have.

Blanche: Well, I've gone to school sometimes when we had to walk over the fences.

Agnes: Do you remember the type of skates they used then? They were steel and they clamped onto the soles of your shoes. You had a skate key that you tied them on with. The lady's skates had straps in the back.

Molly: That's going back a long ways, isn't it?

Agnes: There was a pond up there north of town and we used to go and skate at night. All the young folks, the boys and girls, would go and skate.

Blanche: I just loved to go, you know. And I was so delicate and sick so much when I was little that my folks were afraid to let me get out and expose myself.

Agnes: They played whip cracker out on that ice.

Blanche: Yeah.

Agnes: We didn't have many fast trains then, did we?

Blanche: The children from Neely, when they got into high school, they came on the morning train and they went back on the afternoon. A passenger train ran east and west and back in the evening. And lots of freight trains.

Blanche: And do you remember when they had the first automobile?

Agnes: I can remember that Frank Lewis had the first one.

Blanche: He'd pick up people and take you for a ride. [She laughs.] And then there was Mr. Cook out here; he had the second one, I guess. He didn't know how to drive it, so to learn how he would take it out in the pasture and drive it around. His mom was standing out watching him, you know, and he got the thing going and he didn't know how to stop, so he said, "Take down the bars, mom, I'm a-comin'." [She laughs.] Instead of gates they had bars that they slide across, you know. I always laughed about that. "Take down the bars, mom, I'm a-comin'." Oh, we used to have fun.

Molly: I can remember when bread was five cents a loaf.

Agnes: Twenty cents a pound for butter.

Molly: Eggs three dozen for a quarter.

Blanche: Yeah, mom had hers spoke for from people out in the country and they brought them in every week on Saturday. I always carried lunch to my father and brothers at noon. And we'd buy a quarter's beef steak for our dinner and supper. Now it would take you three dollars or four to get it.

Agnes: My brother used to take the cows out to pasture in the morning. Those animals belonged to people in town. There really wasn't that much difference between people in town and people out in the country.

Blanche: No, no, no. Not at that time, and there isn't much difference now.

Molly: Very little difference.

Agnes: Saturday night, that was really a busy time. That was a big night.

Blanche: When the coal mine was in operation, you parked your car uptown in the afternoon because there was what we called a Kentucky reunion. Mansfield had so many Kentuckians here. Everybody would park in a good place so you'd have a good place to sit to hear the band.

Agnes: The young people would walk the streets.

Blanche: Why you could hardly walk. The girls and their boyfriends . . ."

Molly: People'd do their shopping.

Agnes: You had to be a Kentuckian to have a place to sit. [She laughs.] Tod Waring used to say, "Here come the Bowling Greeners from all around Kentucky."

Blanche: Of course, my husband, he had a barber shop and always worked so late on Saturday nights. I can remember they only got twenty-five or thirty-five cents for a haircut and fifteen cents for a shave. You had to go in and get a number. People would be lined up clear to where the bank is now. They'd go outside where it was cooler and they could visit. He came home many a Saturday night at 1:30.

Molly: Of course, the people didn't go to Stanton to shop, or Auburn, or all around.

Blanche: Not like they do now.

Agnes: But, you know, people sort of got to town because they wanted to visit, to visit with everybody.

Molly: Yeah, the stores had benches out on the streets to sit down and visit.

Blanche: One of the first things I remember was political rallies.

Molly: Oh, yes.

Blanche: My that was big doings.

Agnes: They'd have bands and bunting and decorations and speakers. Remember they'd have a big hay rack or a wagon and people would be there and talk, you know. Some candidates would come up in the square and make a big talk.

Blanche: Course the Republicans would have one and then the Democrats would have one. My folks were Democrats.

Molly: Mine were Republicans.

Blanche: I don't think there ever was a Democrat president until Wilson. I always felt so bad 'cause we always got beat.

Agnes: And William Jennings Bryant was always running. You remember how, come political time, the kids used to say, "Hooray for Bryant, he's the man, McKinley died in an oyster can." [She laughs.] Or they'd turn it the other way, you know.

Blanche: My mother's stepmother was a Republican and she took me down to the depot to hear McKinley. I was just a little girl. I remember I felt disloyal at a Republican rally.

Agnes: I guess a lot of people here were Democrats. They were Kentucky people. My grandfather was very bitter against the colored person. Well, of course, they had had slaves and his folks were pretty well-to-do.

Blanche: We had an old colored fellow here. He took care of other people's horses.

Agnes: That was Charlie Tanner. Old Charlie Tanner.

Blanche: And he would drive horses around town, exercise them. He had a little cart. All the youngsters would say, "Hello, Mr. Tanner," and we'd run out and wave at him. And he'd say, "Hello, little miss. Hello, little miss," and talk to us. I went out once and waved at him. And, oh, my grandfather called me back. He told my mother, "What do you mean by letting her go out and wave at him." Oh, he thought that was terrible. And if he saw him coming down the street, he'd get up and go in the house. I can show you Charlie Tanner's grave right down there at Langton's cemetery.

Agnes: He had a little cabin up there by that livery stable.

Blanche: Yeah, he never bothered anybody.

Agnes: We didn't have very many colored people in Mansfield.

Blanche: Well, no.

Agnes: We had a barber. And then Scrantons over there had a colored maid. But she was almost one of the family, wasn't she?

Blanche: Yeah, almost.

Agnes: The barber had a little girl, a little girl, and her name was Mitchem.

Blanche: Hazel Mitchem—and she was in first grade, I think. She was in our school anyway.

Agnes: They didn't stay here very long.

Blanche: When she first started, you see, she was the only little colored girl. We treated her right. She was sort of a novelty to us, you know. I always remember the time she went to the toilet outside and she lost her little red mitten in there and we just worried and worried with her to get that mitten. We went and told the teacher and she got the janitor, I think. And that's why I'll always remember Hazel Mitchem.

I don't know of any other colored family that really lived in Mansfield.

Agnes: We had a teacher once from Mississippi. Do you remember big Wilma Green?

Blanche: Oh, yes, Wilma Green. [She laughs.]

Agnes: She was just a cute little girl from Mississippi and she came up here to teach school. Of course, that's been a long time ago. I was in about the ninth grade. They were still fighting the Civil War.

Blanche: Long time ago.

Agnes: I mean, you know, it hadn't quieted down yet. There were two or three boys they soon found out they could aggravate her to death if they bring up the Civil War. It was just funny.

Blanche: She would get so mad.

Molly: The times are so different now. I think that kids can get so far from home in such a little time and they get with different environments, you know, then what we used to have.

Blanche: They can get out away from home and I think they have more enticement.

Molly: We were maybe too prudish in our beliefs.

Agnes: And now I think they're too promiscuous.

Molly: Too lenient, yes.

Agnes: I'll say another thing. When we went anywhere, anywhere, we took our whole family with us.

Molly: Yeah, and in an evening you visited your neighbors.

Agnes: Oh, yeah, that's what I mean, family style. And the country school was a big thing.

Blanche: When we lived those ten years out in the country we had one meeting a month, on Sunday, and everybody was in on it. All the families. I might say it this way, that parents used to have more time for their youngsters then they do nowadays.

Molly: 'Cause the mothers didn't go away from home to work, you know.

Agnes: And church life, I think it was more sacred than it is now, don't you?

Molly: They had a little more sacredness. And we had so many revival meetings. That was the good times, wasn't it?[4] Maybe last a couple weeks or more.

Blanche: I taught Sunday School since I was fourteen. Why I'd seat the children all up in front and let them sing all the songs. They loved them. And then we would go to class. We'd have cutout work, coloring, and things like that. But I always thought that it was important that a Bible story be told. I guess I'd pretty much stress the Bible. For example, this one day Mr. Blackford met me on the street and he said, "You must be a real thorough teacher. My son George came home and said, 'I'm going to be a shepherd.' " Today, I don't know. Now, they tell me—I haven't been in the primary department for a long time, but they tell me that much of it is put in on nature study and cutout work and things like that.

Molly: We were taught the real Bible stories. We had memory verses. Love thy neighbor as thyself. Honor thy father and thy mother. Be ye kind one to another. And we had a temperance lesson that taught it was wrong to drink strong drinks and on smoking and things like that.

Blanche: Our ministers used to take a text and preach from that, talk about sin, and on the way you should have been. The minister stayed with the text that he took and preached on it.

Agnes: Today, well, they preach more on general things. Psychology, or somethin' like that.

Molly: What do you guys think about this? I feel like, and I'm talking about myself also, that the majority of us don't want to hear hellfire and damnation like we used to hear.

Agnes: No, that's right.

Molly: But there is a hereafter and we will be punished. I think we need more of that.

Blanche: My mother preferred the Evangelical Church but my father was a Faith Memorial. So I've been sprinkled, poured, and immersed. [She laughs.]

Molly: You're really washed, I'll tell you.

Blanche: So I should be washed of my sins. I'm not saying I have, but I should be. [She laughs.]

Agnes: Did any of you belong to the Ku Klux Klan?

Molly: Oh, I belonged to that.

Agnes: Have you ever belonged to that, Blanche?

Blanche: Indeed, no, and my husband didn't either.

Agnes: Well, I did, though. Sam and I both did.

Blanche: My father and mother did, I think, but I'll tell you my husband didn't approve of it.

Agnes: It's nothing like it was in the South.

Molly: I think it was more between the Catholics and the Protestants.

Agnes: That's what it was.

Molly: I seen a lot of Mansfield people there.

Agnes: It seemed to sort of pick on the Catholics.

Blanche: My husband, he said he knew a lot of those Ku Klux Klan, he knew them real well, and they didn't have a right to tell anybody else what to do.

Agnes: There were more Catholics in town at that time.

Molly: Oh, yes.

Agnes: The Catholic neighborhood was over to the west.

Blanche: When the mine was in operation we had gobs of Catholics here in town.

Molly: I tell you, though, I think they did quite a bit of talking, but really this KKK didn't do anything. Oh, I remember one meeting we had they burnt a cross that night. But as far as really do anything against them, I don't think they'd do anything except talk.

Agnes: When we met we just had a good time.

Molly: One time we had a chicken fry and one time we had a wiener roast out in the timber. I know we had a good time.

Agnes: We had our robes and things.

Molly: Big long sleeves and a cap that fit on your head and a red tassle hanging off of it.

Agnes: Well, I'll tell you now, they was good people in that. They didn't do anything bad.

Blanche: I know that, too, but they don't have a good name, generally speaking.

Molly: I think they talked about how the nuns and the priests how they . . .

Blanche: Oh, they used to talk terrible about them.

Molly: How they thought that there were a lot of babies that were in that place that belonged to some of those. You know, because that's the stories that were spread. I didn't ever know, but they really made it very strong and there were lecturers who would come here and tell all those things.

Blanche: I told my husband, I said, well, you know America was started because people came here because they had freedom to worship and I said I don't think we should tell anybody what kind of religion they should have as long as it was a decent and good religion. And I have found out that if we were as faithful to our religion and beliefs as Catholics are, we would have better Christians.

Agnes: 'Cause they have certain rules that they have to follow, you know. Course they say some of 'em they can go to church and then go out and do what they please.

Molly: Well, that's in all churches, Agnes.

Blanche: Well, I was going to say, nowadays, used to be you didn't believe in washing and ironing on Sunday. Now women work so they wash on Sunday. You know, we used to think that was wrong.

Agnes: When we were growing up it was pretty strict.

Molly: I can remember we wouldn't hitch up to a wagon on Sundays.

Blanche: No, in fact you didn't do a lot of cooking on Sunday. I mean you had a big dinner, but you didn't cook all day.

Molly: Did a lot of visiting.

Agnes: We always had church at night and mornings too.

Blanche: Nowadays you can't get a crowd for Sunday night 'cause they're off in their cars going somewhere.

Agnes: Too much outside interference. Too much going on.

Molly: People used to have strong feelings then about their children marrying Catholics, but now it's different. Some of my best neighbors have been Catholics . . . some of my best friends . . .

Blanche: People used to be fussy about who their children married.

Agnes: Well, I couldn't say much about Kentuckians 'cause my grandfather Smith was a Kentuckian.

Blanche: They used to have what you'd call Blue Grass Kentuckians.
Agnes: Well, some of them that came here to work, they weren't as
  educated, you know. But I think the ones from Tennessee were the
  most uneducated, don't you?
Molly: But there was two kinds of Kentuckians. There was the Blue
  Grass and the Hills.
Blanche: And they were aristocratic, the Blue Grass.
Agnes: On Saturday nights, the women used to sit up there at Black's
  store, and we'd visit, you know. Of course, my husband worked late
  at the shop and we'd go in and get our groceries and sit and visit.
  We'd cut up. Some of these Kentucky ladies came in one time and
  left the door open. Well, it was kind of cold and the door just didn't
  latch, you know, and oh, I won't mention the lady's name but she
  said, "Who left the door open?" And someone said, "Well, I guess
  somebody raised in a barn, you know." Then somebody else said,
  "I'll bet you it's some of them Kentuckians." A Kentucky lady heard
  her and she said, "I'll bet you it wasn't. We got more sense of some
  of you Americans."

A Sense of Community I

Today the "hill" Kentuckians consider themselves American and the social distinctions created by being from Kentucky or Tennessee or being
a Catholic have diminished in importance. To be sure, social distinctions still exist, and parents do not consider just anyone's child to be a
proper match for their own. But these feelings are not a major source
of tension in Mansfield. A feeling of identity with and commitment to
Mansfield overrides distinctions of class, religion, and regional origin.

The impression that a sense of community existed derived from en-
counters with persons like Blanche, Molly, Agnes, and a host of others
interviewed over many months. At times it seemed a script had been
prepared for Mansfielders to follow; the strong community commitment
pervading their response to my questions was couched in general similar language and it sounded too pat to be true.

It was necessary, therefore, to go beyond my accumulating impressions to acquire more systematic data. To this end, I distributed by mail
a questionnaire to every other person listed in the Mansfield telephone
directory, taking care to get an equal distribution of males and females.
The return rate was approximately 50 percent (N = 239); two-thirds
of the respondents are females.[5] With regard to marital status, 74.8 percent (179) are married, 11.2 percent (27) are widows and widowers,
9.6 percent (23) are single, and 2.1 percent (5) are divorced. This distribution is quite similar to that of the entire community (see above).

The additional background facts in tables 7, 8, and 9 will help to characterize the questionnaire respondents, but they also suggest some demographic foundations to a sense of community. To begin with, as seen in table 7, 79.4 percent of the respondents considered themselves to be either local or native to Mansfield. Natives, of course, were born in the Mansfield school district. "Local" designates a person who feels sufficiently settled and accepted to have moved beyond a newcomer or transitional status, and, indeed, he may feel as fully attached to the community as a native. Transitionals, comprising 11.7 percent of the sample, are those who have lived in Mansfield too long to consider themselves as newcomers but not long enough to feel they belong as locals. Less than 5 percent placed themselves in the newcomer category, a percentage that probably underestimates the size of this group in the population if the views of natives and locals were the basis of judgment.

"You must remember," I would remind my interviewees, "that I'm a city boy and I depend on you to tell me what life is like in Mansfield." This query sometimes elicited a response which was at once a joke, a piece of advice, and a fact of consequence. "Well," I'd be told, "take care who you tell your insults to, because in Mansfield we're all related to each other." In fact, it does not take much genealogical probing to uncover vast kinship networks. Although many Mansfielders deny one must have family ties to feel at home in Mansfield, otherwise well-settled persons still admit to feeling left out because of the prominence of kinship in local social life. Younger residents report that their elders entertained themselves with genealogical games. "One of dad's favorite topics was who was whose cousin or aunt and how long they lived around here. He always seemed to know." There are many who still today play this game well.

Strong feelings may be generated for a place if one's family goes back several generations and one has many relatives still living there. Mansfield's current large families can easily recall times past when family reunions brought together fifty to ninety persons. A full 44 percent of the respondents (see table 8) go back three or more generations in the community, and 42 percent have, living locally, eleven or more relatives by birth or marriage, that is, persons *outside* their immediate family (see table 9). These facts establish the point of continuity between past and present generations and the stability of Mansfield's population referred to throughout the book.

In addition, there are other factors that contribute to social integration; they deserve mention but not elaboration in this study. Churches often are considered community-building institutions. If in the past they were divisive, today they seem to contribute to a broad, shared Christian sentiment. They also unite clusters of people who by virtue of their church's location identify with that location. The more aspects of a person's life that are situated in Mansfield, the more he is apt to feel attached to Mansfield. In this respect, clubs and service groups like the Women's Club and Kiwanis function like churches. And Ben Matthews certainly would want credit for his contribution to community development. In a 1912 editorial that mixed business and community interests he wrote:

> The family that lives among us, but never reads a home newspaper regularly gets few ties here. . . . It fails to find those common interests, those identical impulses of progress and improvements and common ambition, that ought to bind us all together. The home newspaper is thus a tie and an anchor which takes isolated units and binds them into a community.

The *Mansfield Times*, though not the newspaper it was in Matthews's day, is still read by most residents.

My assessment of an existing sense of community goes well beyond these facts. Through the questionnaire I also ascertained the amount of agreement about the type of place Mansfield is, views of contemporary issues, and identification with Mansfield. I reasoned that if, in addition to the evidence from the interviews, Mansfielders were also joined by an ideological web and a shared commitment to Mansfield, then I could indeed conclude that a sense of community prevailed there.

Drawing upon the characterization of Mansfield offered by many persons, statements were framed to solicit agreement or disagreement about Mansfield's schools and churches; its atmosphere for raising children; and other possible community attributes (see table 10). Agreement on the positive nature of these items is over 50 percent and often substantially higher. However, considerable respondent reaction is obscured in the response choice "neither agree nor disagree." Notwithstanding the indeterminacy of this response,[6] if we compare "agree" and "disagree" percentages, we see that on almost all items the level of agreement is twice that of disagreement, and in some instances, much more than that. For example, there is no doubt that most respondents believe Mansfield has good churches (66.1 percent) and schools (69.9 percent), is a safe place to live (91.6 percent), a good town compared with others its size (76.1 percent), a fine place to raise children (66.9 percent), and that its citizens can be counted on in times of misfortune (75.3 percent). Of all items on the questionnaire this last one (If you or your family had some misfortune, you could count on people in Mansfield to help out) points most directly to the existence of a sense of community. Although a shared outlook regarding schools, churches, and other aspects of the locality is important, an affective linkage must underpin community. This linkage exists in Mansfield; it is denied by only 9.2 percent of the respondents. Mansfielders are ambivalent (31 percent agree and 22.2 disagree) about wishing they had more privacy, sensing, perhaps, that a lack of privacy is both the basis for security and recognition and, to the contrary, the reason for feeling that one lives in a fishbowl. Contrast this ambivalence with the 56.9 percent who acclaim, paradoxically, that they enjoy life in Mansfield because "you know just about everybody and just about everybody knows you." And, finally, in the comparative terms that many Mansfielders like to use, 54 percent believe that relative to larger places people in Mansfield are friendlier and "better able to live the kind of life they prefer," though they stop short of believing Mansfielders are part of one big family. While this belief has its supporters (33.5 percent), it appears to overstate the actual degree of intimacy experienced by most persons.

In fact, one must take care not to overstate the uniqueness and the degree of intimacy of places that warrant the designation "community." Each of the five statements (items 2, 4, 7, 8, and 11 in table 10) that elicited a procommunity response of about 50 percent or less takes the case for community into uncertain territory. Persons otherwise positive about Mansfield may reject or be uncertain about the claims of small towns for superior living (item 2) or friendliness (item 8). And despite its acknowledged nurturance (item 6), Mansfield is not one big family. But, then, it need not be so considered to be identified as a community. Finally, no attribute may be more controversial than privacy; this is reflected in the 43.5 percent who selected an indeterminate response. However, when the question was not privacy (item 11) but the corollary one of being known by everyone (item 4), indeterminacy reduces to 23 percent and 56.9 agree they like being known by everyone. Each reader of these statistics may interpret them differently. I place them alongside my impressions and conclude that Mansfield is not just an aggregate of people, it is a community. The extent of, and commitment to, this community varies among Mansfielders, ranging from a hard core of 50 to 60 percent to a larger and less intent group of about 70 to 75 percent.[7]

Rural areas are considered outposts of traditional American values, places that hold fast to the old virtues of God, country, and self-reliance. Mansfielders, as table 11 attests, do hold common views on these and other matters which can promote social integration.

For example, despite their moderate church attendance, Mansfielders are avowedly Christian. Many secular organizations (the Kiwanis and the Women's Club) begin or end their meetings with a prayer. They seem to respect religious belief while not necessarily actively participating in its organized activities. This conclusion is verified by the 88.2 percent who thought it was important to believe in God. While the drift from orthodox religious expression has continued apace since the days of Editor Matthews, the central fact of belief in God and religion remains firm.

Not far behind God is country. To be sure, on national holidays the flag does not fly in the breeze outside every home, and summer outings no longer resound with speeches and patriotic music (though the Kiwanians sing "My Country, 'Tis of Thee" before each meeting). But the sentiment that sent great numbers of Mansfielders by train to see their boys off to war has not vanished. Not that they favor war—it is their country they favor. "The American way of life can't be beat anywhere in the world," say 74.1 percent, and 86.6 percent agree that "One thing that never should go out of style is good old-fashioned patriotism." Given the particular nature of their loyalty they dislike communism (53.6 percent), seeing it as the country's problem of highest priority, even when pitted against financial and energy problems at a time of double-digit inflation and long gas lines.[8] Their outlook, however, is not strictly isolationist—61.9 percent believe there is much to be excited about in what is happening around the world,[9] but they dislike (65.7 percent) the activist international role the United States played in the 1950–72 period.

Campaigning politicians strike a responsive chord in Mansfield when they despair of welfare. While sympathetic to their own nonwelfare needy and solicitous of their elderly, Mansfielders believe most welfare cases are not warranted (72.4 percent). Blacks are seen as welfare abusers and though there are no black Americans in Mansfield, Mansfielders think Stanton, with a recent history of black migration, is "not as pleasant a place to live as it used to be" (63.6 percent). And on an issue that vexes many Americans, 59.8 percent of the respondents rejected the abolition of capital punishment; about 20 percent were undecided.

I assume that the foregoing views are part of a conservative syndrome, with conservative defined as "one who adheres to traditional, time-tested, long-standing methods, procedures or views" (Webster). Although most of this syndrome appears to be corroborated, some portions are not fully verified. For instance, abortion was rejected to a lesser degree than I expected (42.3 percent), as were strong gun laws (37.7 percent) and women's liberation (41.4 percent).[10] Nonetheless, barring these three cases, there is a general shared thrust to Mansfielders' value orientations.

In a third area, affecting the case for Mansfield as a community in social psychological terms, the extent of Mansfielders' identification with Mansfield was probed. Many respondents, 52.7 percent (item 1 in table 12), indicated they felt more at home in Mansfield than they could anywhere else. This suggests a very strong community attachment, although the impact of mass society precludes such feelings of rootedness that would lead most Mansfielders to believe they could not live comfortably elsewhere. That this sentiment is not more widespread I attribute to the wording of the question, which attributes to Mansfield a singularity that transcends the affiliation of persons living in a modern, highly mobile society. In fact, I am impressed that the proportion reaches 52.7 percent. Only 25.1 percent (item 6) feel that they could live happily only in Mansfield. This group of at least sixty persons constitutes a decidedly stable community core; in fact, most communities may well lack so large a group of diehard loyalists. Moreover, while such a group may enhance a sense of community, it is extreme to think a majority of residents must feel they could be happy only in Mansfield for that sense to exist. Indeed, of all the items in table 12, perhaps only item 5—It is important to me what people in Mansfield think of me—refers to a feeling that is actually necessary for sustaining a sense of community. More than the other questions, this one inquires into a person's involvement in the web of community. To be indifferent or detached is to deny not the existence of community but, rather, one's immersion in it. Only 5 percent of the respondents rejected the salience of their fellow citizen's estimation of them; 81.6 percent affirmed it.

When questioned about moving preferences, 47.3 percent of all respondents said they would not leave Mansfield even if they could; only 11.7 percent wished they could leave right now. Interestingly, when asked where they would like to move, 33 percent preferred "somewhere in the countryside," thus suggesting that in previous questions about moving respondents were not thinking of Mansfield school district as the unit, which clearly includes countryside, but the village of Mansfield alone. This mistaken understanding may have reduced the percentage of pro-Mansfield responses in items 6 and 8. Another 23 per cent preferred to move to Auburn, the county seat, with under 5,000 population. Fewer than 15.0 percent were attracted to living in an urban area of 100,000 or more people. Student preferences for these locales matched adults' almost exactly.

Migration to and from the school district is not likely to undermine attachment to Mansfield. Definitive data on local migration patterns are not available, but the following picture emerges from telephone company information regarding new and canceled subscribers during six

different years between 1962 and 1971.[11] Approximately fifty persons
enter and fifty persons leave the community each year; they tend to be
either young people in their twenties or people over sixty. Families
enter and leave less frequently. And, most strikingly, slightly more than
50 percent of the newcomers have at least one relative already living
in Mansfield before they arrive and slightly fewer than 50 percent of
the newcomers have lived in Mansfield before. Such persons are therefore fairly readily assimilable into Mansfield life. Neither the coal miners who came in large numbers in the early 1900s and left when the
mine closed in 1924 nor the Kentuckians who came in the depression
period seeking work as farm laborers had sufficient numbers or influence to reorient Mansfield's social life.

Respondents provided several further clues to the extent of their
identification with their community. A sizable majority of them say
that they would get angry if they heard someone insult Mansfield, that
they would be bothered if the name of their town were changed, and
that they value community loyalty. It is this majority that Mrs. Brightwood, Jason Spoonover, and Tim Browne speak for (in what follows)
when they refer to the joys of Mansfield.

A Sense of Community II

Some Mansfield residents do not share in its sense of community; others,
while acknowledging its special qualities, recognize limitations that help
to place its benefits in perspective. For example, Guy Selman's ambivalence is clear:

> As a whole, Mansfield is an average small town, but maybe a bit be-
> hind in some of its attitudes. I feel concerned sometimes that the chil-
> dren aren't getting enough involved outside of their own little place.
> But then again it's a good feeling to be able to raise them where they
> learn what it's like to know and respect other people as a whole small
> village. Probably if we ever moved it would be to another place about
> the size of Mansfield. I get so mad sometimes when we are working
> to better Mansfield and everyone seems to be waiting for someone
> else to start the ball moving. But at least when it finally gets done
> you feel as if you had a part.

If Guy Selman is of two minds about his community, he still makes his
choice for Mansfield; he is not alienated.

Nancy Parker's ambivalence illustrates the costs of community, that
it both embraces and traps at the same time. She is a third-generation
native whose family has farmed since its nineteenth-century arrival in
Mansfield township.

I belong here as I would no place else. Because I belong, I am responsible to the community itself and to the people in it. Sometimes I resent this responsibility—at times it interferes with my responsibility to my own family and to myself. I dislike doing things because it's the thing to do rather than because it's what I want. My true feelings and real impulses are so often concealed that I wonder at times if I'm not some sort of product open for inspection.

Sally Harrod's experience is not at all ambivalent. She has arthritis and has been moderately disabled for several years. Nobody brings her dinner or rushes to get her mail, reports her friend Mrs. Langley, to whom Mansfield is a cold, cliquish place. When the big snow came this past winter, everyone shoveled a path from house to street. No one shoveled for Sally Harrod, who is not a native, has lived in Mansfield less than ten years, and does not attend a local church. "If you weren't born here," says Mrs. Langley, "you're an outsider. If you were, you're OK." Mrs. George is another outsider, a resident only five years, who feels you do not fit in if you have not lived in Mansfield all your life. After five years she hardly knows anyone's name. These women are not exceptions. They are joined by many others who believe that without relatives living in the community it is hard to feel you really belong, that your family name makes a difference how you are accepted, and that some Mansfield families get the breaks more than others do. These are the persons who share the space of Mansfield, but not its sense of community.

Persons no less newcomers than Mrs. George and Mrs. Langley, as measured by years of residence in Mansfield, have entered its charmed circle, where to be accepted is to be helped when you are ill, to be comforted when a relative has died, to be offered the use of a car by the observant woman across the street who notices you are still home at 4.00 P.M. when you should have left for work. "People said neighbor helping doesn't exist," commented Jason Spoonover, a native Mansfielder, who returned home to retire, "but it does."

Now take the field next door here. When the lad who farms it went on vacation, his friends combined his beans for him. And when I was cutting down that old tree, Baldwin came by to help and I didn't even know him at that time. He went home to get a saw and stayed with me till I finished.

And when the Nortons return from vacation they laugh at their daughters' teasing about the wild time they had in their parent's absence, certain that had anything out of the ordinary occurred they would have heard about it "twenty minutes after reaching home." The lack of privacy serves to reassure them. The Nortons, like many others, do not lock their front door at night and can safely leave the ignition keys in their car. The druggist's house has been robbed several times by persons in search of drugs, but otherwise there is little theft and no assaults. A general sense of security prevails in Mansfield.

The feelings of well-being and security operate within boundaries. I learned about the boundaries when I was trying to track down the graduates of Mansfield High School. I asked, among other things, if so and so had married a local person and if they lived locally. A frequent answer was, "Yes, she married Harold Spade, a local boy." or, "He lives locally." Though I had neglected to clarify what local meant, no one hesitated to respond to my question. After further questioning, "local" emerged as a region coterminous with the school district; its boundaries cut across several townships but encompass all of Mansfield village and Mansfield township. Save for those who live at the extremities of the district and adjacent to other towns, residence in the school district draws one toward Mansfield. It becomes a place for their concern, where they are prone to shop, seek medical attention, casually meet friends, and often retire, moving in from the surrounding countryside and even from more distant areas after a lifetime spent away from home. The school district thus establishes the psychological boundaries of community, the place invested with special meaning to school district residents. To marry someone from beyond these boundaries is to marry a nonlocal person.

The psychological boundaries of community encompass Mrs. Brightwood. Now in her eighties, she has been teacher, housewife, shopkeeper, and widow during a long life spent almost entirely in Mansfield. Living alone, still very alert and reasonably healthy, she welcomes visitors to her home, though they must be patient after ringing her doorbell because she walks slowly to receive her callers.

African violets adorn Mrs. Brightwood's small house just as she adorns her adopted community with affection. "What is it like to live in a small town?" I ask her. "It's nice for old people," she says, "because everything is so close and everyone is so helpful." To clarify her reaction further, she tells the story of her friend Adah, about her age, who lived in the city. Adah decided that while she was still of sound mind she would select a desirable nursing home and voluntarily admit herself. She did and was disappointed to find institutional life formal, structured, and cold; she missed the life she left behind and soon regretted her decision. Distressed by her friend's grief, Mrs. Brightwood declared that she would never have made such a decision, that she didn't need a nursing home. She is looked after. If she misses a Sunday school class, she can expect a telephone call as soon as services are over. Her groceries are delivered. The children next door, who call

her "Grandma," pick up her mail at the post office. Neighbors take out
her garbage when she is ill or the sidewalks are too icy. And she laughs
as she remembers the lady across the street who "keeps an eye on me.
One day she called up to ask after my health thinking I might not be
OK because I'd opened my drapes later than usual."

In pursuit of the generality of Mrs. Brightwood's experience, I heard
repeatedly about garbage being taken out, mail collected, groceries
delivered, and shades observed; I heard also about smoke watching.
"Something we do in winter before turning in for the night," many said.
"We look outside to be sure that smoke is rising from our neighbor's
chimney, because that means the furnace is working and they won't be
surprised in the middle of the night by a house turned frigid." Mrs.
Brightwood alerted me to Mansfield's nurturant network. It embraces her
so that despite her age she need not consider entering a nursing home.

Mrs. Brightwood laughs as she thinks about the neighbor watching
her drapes. Though too busy to bother about such things, she is privately pleased that while she lives alone in her home she knows that
otherwise she is not alone. This lack or seeming lack of privacy is an
essential part of life in Mansfield. From the viewpoint of youth, the
exposed, fishbowl life is oppressive; they yearn, so they say (see chap.
9), to escape to larger places where the details of one's life do not enter
the backyard gab circuit. Older persons note the same fact but see it
in a positive light. "Our neighbors," explained the Goulds, a married
couple in their late thirties, "were born and raised in Mansfield, so
they've known us all our lives." They went away for a weekend and
when they returned they learned their neighbors were angry.

> We didn't tell them we were going away, so they sat home all week-
> end and worried about where we were. People like them who never
> lived anywhere else don't really know what an invasion of privacy is.
> I don't think they're being nosy. It's sincere concern.

Mrs. Brightwood echoes these sentiments. Moreover, she feels she's part
of things. It's *her* church. *Her* Women's Club. "You're not a number,"
she concludes, using the same expression students use to clarify their
preference for a small school. To Mrs. Brightwood and to students it
connotes, "I am not just one more person. I am special and others
recognize and appreciate my specialness."

"Were you raised in a big town?" Tim Browne asks. "Well, you
don't understand." He explains:

> You should come over to the restaurant some day. It's just wonderful
> to be sitting there. All those men. I don't amount to a good damn
> here, but I bet you from 5:30 in the morning to 6:45 when I go
> home anywhere up to thirty-eight people will come by and say, "How

are you this morning, Tim. You're lookin' good." OK, you go to your bigger places and there's nobody to say, "How are you this morning?" They don't give a damn how you are.

Tim Browne, like Mrs. Brightwood, is an octagenarian. He's on welfare, a bit of a drinker, and always wears overalls. Old Tim also cusses, loafs all day, and never attends church, but like Mrs. Brightwood, the charmed circle also includes him.

The intimacy of the small community grows out of a simple, fundamental fact—knowing and being known. The school bus driver, Mansfield native Ted Randolph, drives along a country road and passes a farmer working in the field. He honks, gets the farmer's attention, and lifts his hand with his index finger raised to signal recognition. Randolph acknowledges and gets acknowledged in turn in a common ritualistic exchange that suggests both he and the farmer count in however small a way. Indeed, greeting at any time is a commonplace act. Your presence is taken account of; you do not go unobserved.

The elderly routinely observe the passing scene out their windows. As I talked to Velma Hodgkins in her home, she leaned over the edge of the couch and craned her neck to look out the window whenever she heard a car pass by. "Just a habit" she explains somewhat apologetically. With variations, it is a common one. She is not expecting anyone. Her habit is one of many acts that results in the monitoring of all that goes on publicly. This behavior, pursued within the context of Mansfield's social stability, high nurturance, and small physical scale, establishes a pattern of intimacy that perturbs adolescents and promotes a feeling of security for their parents.[12] In Mansfield one does not easily attain the anonymity of larger places; nor is the particular kind of loneliness associated with anonymity very prevalent there.

Some people stay in Mansfield because they do not have the psychological and financial means to leave. Many others stay because they pursue a life style that pleases them. "I don't know how to describe it," muses Ralph Tunnell. "It don't seem right not knowin' people. I grew up in a small town and I like to speak to people and be spoken to." His wife describes driving to Bradley for a movie and feeling frightened all the time she was there. There was something about the atmosphere that disturbed her. To her and the Brownes, Brightwoods, Nortons, and Spoonovers, the quality of life in Mansfield is powerfully appealing. They are accommodated to it. They eye city life with displeasure, not perceiving it as open, liberating, and uncloistered. Rather, they wonder, how can you tolerate so many people so close to you? "Is it safe? Do you know your neighbors?" they ask, perplexed that the persons living next door could be strangers. Mrs. Norton says maybe

Mansfield has the same problems as big places only on a smaller scale. She does not claim exclusive goodness for Mansfield. She reflects a moment and then concludes, "You couldn't get me to move. I'm just not a big-town person." Mrs. Spoonover agrees: "Well, I just feel comfortable. It's a secure feeling, you know. You try to explain it, but I'm glad I'm here. Really, that's about it."

To complete this picture, Mansfielders add that they benefit from good churches, a good school system, and good people. What more could there be? Of course, everyone complains about the lack of recreation, especially for children. Yet once past adolescence, Mansfielders adopt a routine of activities centering on school, church, organization, home, and the invariable drive to Auburn or Stanton for a movie or a special meal.

The dominant, readily evoked, positive image of Mansfield is held by the loyalists who get elected to the village board and the school board, hold lay leadership positions in the churches, and run the community's organizations, and also by many ordinary people who occupy no office at all. This view helps maintain a sense of community.

Nevertheless, still other factors contribute to this feeling. When Ted Randolph drives through town, the occasion can mean more than a chance to raise his index finger in greeting. Each day he passes the corner where his father, a country doctor, had an office. A nearby barn contained his father's horses, because doctors always had to be ready to travel. And across the street from the Evangelical Church he built the house where Ted was born and raised. Ted's daughter and her family live minutes away from him. Family roots hold him to Mansfield. Since Mansfield was the scene of most of the major events in his life, no other place can ever be of equal consequence.

High school memories invest Mansfield with special meaning for Nancy and Steve. Nancy recalls that she never dated a boy in her class. "No, they're like brothers. Didn't you feel that way about your class?" she asks her husband. "That you were such a small group that you were very, very close, like a little family?" "We'd get together and have parties," Steve recalls, "but no real dating." "Fun, strictly fun," Nancy affirms.

> On our senior class trip there were twenty-one of us and we all slept in the same room, but no hanky panky. I mean it was fine and dandy. We drank, and one morning I woke up and there was this fellow by the side of me. That didn't bother me because I knew him. He knew me. We'd known each other all our lives.

In addition to its memory-producing impact, the school experience, as Nancy's remarks suggest, cultivates an age-set sentiment. Thanks to family stability, at least half the members of each graduating class have been together since first grade; children from many different families literally grow up together. This has been true for many years. As a result, Mansfielders tend to date and marry persons from other classes and from out of town. After graduation the sentiment receives annual reinforcement from each Homecoming celebration, a fall football weekend that attracts alumni from all over the country. All persons with a known address from every graduation class receive an invitation and a self-addressed response envelope. "We'd be disappointed if we didn't see the folks for this chance to reminisce."[13]

The school is also important because it evokes considerable emotional response through its athletic program, and also because one's children are in Mansfield High School or one was himself a student there. How natural to be proud of what we possess—and the high school is considered "our own." Athletic events, the Christmas program, class plays, graduation exercises—all are community affairs. They attract more adults than those who happen to have children in school. In a small community like this, with few other organizations and institutions to boast of, the high school assumes a central place.

Of course, Mansfielders have more to reminisce about than their school experiences. Soup suppers, bake sales, Fourth of July celebrations, church ice cream socials, chicken fries, bazaars, ad infinitum, cram local calendars. For many residents these shared events put them into Mansfield's web and provide the occasion for countless "remember whens." One event stands out as having more than ordinary importance —Mansfield's centennial, celebrated several decades ago. Tim Browne smiles warmly at the memory.

You can't believe how people volunteered to work and if you told them to take a mop and bucket and mop the pavement, they did. They would have done anything. The ham and cornbread dinner— it was free. They had bean salad. They had slaw. Even sliced tomatoes till we ran out of 'em. We had some of the greatest free acts you ever saw. We had one about the Women's Christian Temperance Union raid on the saloons when they took an ax to the whiskey. I tried to grow whiskers but it got to breakin' out on my neck. Even the doctor said, "Tim, you better pay the dollar." If you couldn't grow a beard you had to buy a hat or a badge. I don't think there was a widow-woman in town who didn't make a guy some peculiar kind of uniform to wear. They had some kind of parade every day for a week. I never saw such cooperation in my life.

Present-day progress seekers often refer to that centennial spirit. They wish more of it were available to move Mansfielders toward new community development projects.

Marty Holmes, a native-born loyalist, likes almost everything about his birthplace, but he has some worries.

I see what's going on elsewhere and I don't think any of these towns have better schools. We've got good schools, churches, and people; we're a lot better off than other towns our size. But maybe people are too contented here. They're afraid to stir things up, to get involved. They'd rather stand on the side, afraid of what their neighbors will say. People don't want to expand. They're content with what they got. Some want growth but won't put forth the effort. They won't push.

Ben Matthews would have liked Marty Holmes, but if Matthews surveyed Mansfield today through his progress-obsessed eyes, he might find grist for a month of editorials. Despite the integrative factors that establish Mansfield as a community and the satisfaction many citizens experience in it, the viability of Mansfield's future is seriously questioned by more than Mr. Holmes.[14]

From Progress to Survival

Notwithstanding Matthews's often pessimistic outlook, Mansfield did once have days of progress that were not just the illusion of some aged person's imagination. There truly was a more dynamic past when the question of survival did not arise.

In 1880, when communication limitations necessitated a fair degree of self-sufficiency in smaller villages, Mansfield could boast of

four general merchandise stores, one dry goods store, three drug stores, three hardware stores, two grocery stores, four restaurants, one bakery, three shoe shops, one millinery, two implement stores, four grain dealers, two livery stables, one furniture store, two meat markets, three wagon and blacksmith shops, two lumber yards, five doctors, one dentist, one jewelry store, one music store, two barber shops, one undertaker, one photograph gallery, four hotels, four insurance agencies and three sewing machine agencies.

This beehive of activity contrasts with the comparatively somnolent picture presented currently by Mansfield's business section. Sharp-memoried natives, who may be no more than thirty-five, easily recall days of large, well-stocked stores, many service stations, a movie theater, and other means of recreation. The complaint nowadays is that you "can't even buy a pair of shoes in town."

A need for industry has always impressed some residents. Industry was the economic charm that would lift Mansfield out of the back forty of a small county and "put her on the map." And industries, so called, came and went over the years, as did dreams of industries. In 1892, Matthews argued that a cannery would be good for farmer, merchant, citizen, and investor. "Think about it," wrote Matthews, and that, apparently, is all that people did, for it never materialized. A cigar factory opened in a store in 1896; the Putnam Rotary Engine Plant considered locating in town and a curtain rod factory did open in 1904. Mansfield's "silk and satin" set raised $20,000 to finance this factory. It was expected to employ twenty-five workers and to "become one of the big enterprises of the west." It never did become a big enterprise, though in 1905 it was going "full blast with 20 employees . . . working a nine hour day."

Mingled with the hopes and realities of locating new businesses in Mansfield is the businessmen's association, first proposed by Matthews in 1904 to promote coal mining. In one form or another, the enthusiasm for such an association surfaces again and again during the next seventy years. In 1918, Mansfielders are urged to believe that since the "time is ripe and psychologically ready to exploit Mansfield's splendid industrial resources and inexhaustible coal and water," a businessmen's club should be organized. Almost thirty years later, Mansfield again is on the "brink of success." A company that makes staple articles and whose "work is respectable" is exploring local possibilities and the Chamber of Commerce is inquiring whether there are fifty women available to employ. But again nothing materializes, and the disappointed business association members of 1946 are soon replaced by more hopeful ones in a cycle that continues to this day. The costs of failure increase, however, because with urbanization, rural towns have become more and more fragile economically. One dramatic failure is Neely, a satellite of Mansfield several miles to the south, which today consists only of a church, a post office, and a grain elevator. No sign of its many stores remain to hint at the former activity of a town that is now dead, school and all.

The population figures (see table 5) for 1900 to 1930 record the rise and fall of Mansfield's great financial boom—its coal industry. Digging began in 1900 and revealed a three-foot vein of coal. Local interest was not sufficient to support exploitation, and the exclusive rights were bought in 1903 by an outsider. With his customary hyperbole, Matthews advised his readers to purchase stock certificates. In 1904, the Mansfield Coal Company began round-the-clock digging of a shaft. The first coal was hoisted four years later from a thirty-two-inch vein at 245 feet. By 1912, seventy-six men shared a $10,000 monthly payroll and more than a hundred carloads of coal were hauled away each month. The coal miners and their families arrived to create a new working class, a Catholic Church, and Mansfield's peak population. When the mine closed in 1924, victim of managerial strife and a severe underground water problem, the exodus began to other coal sites. The Catholic Church remains, as do a few former miners, their families long since having shifted to factory or farm work. North of town, visible from the road to Stanton, stands a large sculpture-like piece of concrete, all that remains of the air shaft that served this end of the mine. The large reserves of coal in the mine coupled with the energy crisis kindle dreams of a renaissance, but the mayor has been informed that the sulfur content of Mansfield's coal, by current standards, is too high for exploitation.

No more coal, no $10,000 payroll, no other industry. Only the dreams remain. Today Mansfield has a core of people who take pride in its past and are pleased with the present. They also fear for its survival—when asked to reflect on such matters.

The Survival of Mansfield

If, in decades past, village patriots were concerned with progress, today they speak more of survival. For Mansfield shares the often dismal prospects smaller communities face. If they do not grow, demographically and economically, they decline, and are possibly reduced to that skeletal entity that squats on so many crossroads of the American landscape: several gas stations, a bar and a small grocery store, a few short residential streets that dead-end in someone's corn or bean field, and perhaps the graying hulk of an aged grain elevator standing beside rusting railroad tracks.

The East Central Development Association, comprising Mansfield and other towns and villages from Cunningham and several other counties, was created to promote economic development. The association's manager wrote in a newsletter of the 1950s that

> communities without purpose, plan or drive either wither or die . . .
> There is no standing still very long. . . . Some people may like their
> town the way it is but they cannot keep it that way—standing still
> means slowly going down hill.

This prophecy is not without supporters in Mansfield.

What does survival mean when applied to a community like Mansfield? Older citizens may reflect nostalgically on a Mansfield that was more self-sufficient, more involved with itself, with local people more interdependent than they are today, so that the web of community encompassed one more firmly. Tim Browne, for example, recalls a Mansfield he liked better, though he still is pleased with what it has to offer. His sentiments are shared by other older persons.

Before World War II the town had spirit. I don't know, after the war was over everybody went crazy. They went home and stayed there. Only come out when they had to. Another thing, television come in. Last night it was, "Gotta go, 'Sonny and Cher' will be on at seven o'clock." The night before it was "Hawaii Five O." I've got to go home to see this and that. I want to be there for 'Dialing for Dollars.' "

To such people there is a Mansfield that did not survive; such anachronisms, moreover, seldom can. But that a sense of community existed in the past and still does today seems patently clear, however modified its manifestations—and such modifications are unavoidable.

The signs of survival are evident when a solid nucleus of people (who can estimate what the number must be?) act and feel as if they have a share in a community's present and future, possibly in its past. At the extreme negative pole, nonsurvival means the disappearance of residents, that is, nobody around to be called a Mansfielder. This has happened to small villages throughout the country. Or it means that migration changes the composition of the population so much that few persons remain who feel attached in the deep and general way the mainstream Mansfielder does.

Yet it takes more than the maintenance of the psychological indicators of community to survive; it takes economic well-being and competent leadership. Neither condition is common in villages and small towns, where generally the most educated and most talented seek opportunities not available at home. Tables 6 and 13 portray Mansfield's basic economic facts: on the one hand, the relatively stable, possibly growing wealth of the countryside, as measured by the average farm acreage and the value per farm; on the other, the stagnation of financial resources available to the town, as measured by sales tax receipts. Table 6, though covering all of Cunningham county, amply depicts the agricultural scene in Mansfield school district. The data show a steady decline in the number of farms after 1935; slight fluctuations in total farm acreage; and a steady increase in value per farm. After 1971 the value of farm land skyrocketed and, given increasing world dependence upon American agriculture, the value may continue to rise. Indeed, land is so high that farmers cannot afford to buy it; it is sold to banks, corporations, and doctors, all nonfarmers, all absentee landlords, so the pattern of external ownership and tenant farming becomes more and more pervasive. So far this trend has not led to nonlocal farmers taking up residence in the school district; if it did, community ties would be eroded.

The village's financial prospects are not very bright. Note the trends in table 13. Since sales tax receipts are figured in constant dollars, we can discount the effect of changes in the worth of the dollar. Mansfield collected more money in 1951 with receipts from only one type of tax than she collected in 1971 from three types of tax. After 1951, receipts decline and reach a low point in 1961, rise in 1966, and then decline again in 1971. Over this period, 1951–71, Mansfield has fewer sales-tax payers (40 in 1951 and 29 in 1971) and significantly less revenue to collect ($30,059 in 1951 and $22,157 in 1971). The impact of this decline has moderated in recent years by the availability of revenue-sharing money, but the downward trend is well established.

In short, the countryside is financially sound and the village, after a decline, is holding moderately steady in receipts but losing businesses to larger towns and cities. Several factors combined to erode the village's business district—Mansfield's limited market, high transportation costs to merchants, and easy consumer access to larger, convenient shopping centers. Apart from some needed and cosmetic alterations in the appearance of the village, as well as improvements in the water and sewer systems (these are vital maintenance measures, not growth developments), no fundamental changes have occurred in Mansfield since the coal mine closed in the early twenties. From Ben Matthews to Mansfield's present mayor, men have sought and failed to attract industry.

Residents often discuss their financial problem. They say Mansfield is landlocked because farmers refuse to sell land adjacent to the village. Thus new subdivisions are not feasible. In the recent period of urban exodus the village did not have the housing to accommodate substantial population growth. Village leaders are confident that if housing was available, families from Stanton would be attracted to their fresh air, good schools, and a community free of racial conflict.

What is the prognosis for the community? On this point, of 239 adult respondents, 38.4 percent agree, 20.8 disagree, and 36.8 percent neither agree nor disagree that Mansfield will have a good future. In addition, 41.7 percent believe Mansfield is "going downhill;" 32.1 percent disagree. And 63.9 percent feel that people talk, but nobody really does anything about Mansfield's future; 18.3 percent disagree.

Here are the views of major business leaders with a substantial stake in Mansfield's well-being. Their general impression is that the village's future is uncertain. Because they see no signs of growth, they fear that decline will occur and probably already is occurring at an imperceptible rate. Mansfield has the resources—water, sewer system, power potential—but it lacks the will to organize vigorously behind the idea of economic growth. Perhaps this is just another way of saying it lacks leadership and broad community commitment for what is decidedly difficult to do. Having failed to attract industry or build subdivisions under more favorable conditions in the past, when inflation was less flagrant and there was a pool of unused labor (basically women's), Mansfield may have missed its best opportunity. Nobody can explain this failure, but I often heard that some people are pleased by it. They fear that the influx of people who would follow the introduction of a new industry or a new subdivision would transform the village in undesirable ways. Although 74 percent of the respondents affirmed that Mansfield would be improved by the addition of at least one industry, only 50.5 percent agreed that Mansfield would be a better place if new people with new ideas came to live there. New industry, apparently, is attractive when seen in financial terms, but less so if its concomitants are new people and new ideas.

One businessman wonders why Mansfield has not grown. "The things are here to grow. Maybe everything but the desire on the part of the people." Another, active in banking for many years, recalls that

> we talked about industry for years, but it's hard to get one to move into town. They're afraid to take chances on a small town. It takes a lot of work. You need someone to give it full time and nobody is willing to do this. There should be new housing, but people are too conservative.

A relatively new and successful businessman says he tried and failed to stimulate growth. His ideas were rewarded with a classic village rejection: "We've lived here a long time and we think it's a pretty good town. You're a newcomer." This response may indicate both a sense of community and the insular quality that shelters villages from change. To be accepted, ideas must be attractive and articulated by the right advocate. This businessman concluded, "There's too many stagnant people here who don't want change, but they're getting it anyway—decline. It's so gradual people don't even feel it." And another Mansfield leader, a native, well-established merchant, sadly observed,

> In the forties I tried to put my thumb in the dike, but now I'm tired. I don't hear much talk about our future. People just like to push the matter aside and not talk about it. The mayor is anxious for an industry, but today I don't even think we could get the manpower for it.

Fears for Mansfield's future are well grounded, in the opinion of its leaders and citizens. The community's economic fragility makes Mansfield High School's community-maintenance functions even more critical.

3

Mansfield High School: "A Top-Notch School for This Community"

Approach Mansfield from any direction on any one of five Friday nights in fall and you will see, even while still a considerable distance away, a bright glow illuminating the dark sky. The closer you move toward Mansfield the sharper the glow appears until its source emerges—football lights. They stand like giants at attention guarding the school district's football field and the very small town adjacent to it. Football games are the focus of community concern on these five autumn evenings; they are played at night to accommodate the team's numerous fans. Many are college students who return home for the weekend to see these games, their presence a tribute to their loyalty to Mansfield and evidence of their preference for nearby postsecondary schools. People say Mansfield is a football town, and they are right. No other activity elicits the same degree of devotion and support. In two recent years, paid attendance for five games was 4,342 and 4,666: 1,876 adults and 2,466 students in 1971 and 1,810 adults and 2,856 students in 1972.[1] If we consider these figures beside the total school district population of approximately 2,100, and discount about 20 percent of the crowd as supporters of the visiting team, we are still left with more than 40 percent of all local persons standing and sitting under the Friday night lights, being seen, running with friends around the refreshment stand, strolling on the track that encircles the field, and even watching the game.

The football sideline is the most attractive place in town these Friday nights, its attraction enhanced if the team wins. More than just an athletic event, a football game is a significant social occasion, during which a variety of personal and communal needs and feelings are satisfied and reinforced. The football games provide unsurpassed opportunity for recreation and social interaction and for promoting and expressing community pride and loyalty. On these five nights, more than at any other time, the school can be seen as the heart of Mansfield.

The football field is part of several acres of baseball diamonds and playing fields that separate the high school from the elementary school. Because the vocational agriculture students rotate their crops, the entire education complex nestles against fields of corn one year and soybeans the next. It is bounded by Highway 71 on the south and Church Street on the north. In the parking lot next to the gym, the drivers park the five buses which daily transport more than half the students, most of them farm children (about 10 percent are from rural nonfarm families), scattered throughout the school district's seventy square miles. Bused high school students are dropped off at the main entrance on Church Street and enter a solid, chunky, reddish brown brick building built in 1901, with new wings added in 1919 and a new attached gymnasium built in 1955. Mansfielders think the building is too old, but there is no pressure for a new one. "We can't be sure," people say, "just when we'll be consolidated with Auburn and Oakfield, the other county schools. So why make a big investment, especially when it's more than likely we'd be allowed to keep only our grade school and have to send all the older students either to the county seat at Auburn or to a new school built somewhere out in the country."

Sentiment is generally anticonsolidation. Nevertheless, the need for supra-Mansfield affiliation is evident in already established cooperative linkages. For example, as Superintendent Tate wrote in one of his reports:

> In 1972 Mansfield School District became affiliated with the Western area of Special Education and maintains such membership with thirty-three other school districts in eight counties. During the 1962–63 school year Oakfield and Mansfield school districts began sharing the services of a speech correctionist, and Oakfield, Auburn, and Mansfield also began sharing services of a teacher for educable mentally handicapped pupils who previously could not be accommodated.

Ever since 1957, when the old grade school became overcrowded, the high school building also has housed the seventh and eighth (junior high school) grades. The old elementary school, now largely a pile of bricks in transition to becoming apartments, was replaced in 1969 by a new air-conditioned building, the envy of high school students and teachers who swelter during hot spells in their venerable but stuffy building. The bond issue which made possible the new elementary school is a good indicator of community support for education. A fuller view of school district finances will clarify the level of this support.

Through comparative statistics showing Mansfield within the context of the entire state and of Cunningham County (including the other two school districts with which she may one day be linked through consolidation), we obtain a picture of Mansfield's investment in schooling. Her effort rank, the most important measure in table 14, is 483 out of 1,084 school districts; it places her above average in a statewide population and better than Auburn though lower than Oakfield within the county.

Although critics of high school athletics point to undue amounts of money and student time devoted to sports, advocates counter that it is time and money well spent. Based on educational expenditures for a recent year (see table 15), athletic costs appear as a relatively small portion of the school budget, but more money is spent on either boys' football, basketball, or track than on any single school subject. However, it may not be possible to conduct both a safe and a cheap athletic program, and pride argues for uniforms and equipment that will not embarrass school or community. Thus, if the reduction of athletic expenditures is desired, a reduced commitment to athletics is required, and this would alter the character of the school experience at Mansfield.

On the face of things, modest sums are spent on instructional materials in the academic program. The subjects requiring equipment tend to show greater expenditures—music ($800.00), industrial arts ($500.00), and science ($699.00). Lesser amounts were spent on foreign languages ($75.00) and social studies ($75.00), although in a year that new textbooks are purchased the expenditure would rise appreciably. It is unconvincing to argue that the $100.00 spent on history was perhaps no more than the teacher felt needed to be spent, because teachers are socialized regarding what is a proper amount to request for expenditure. The $100.00 spent for history compared with the $380.00 spent for state music contests and awards reflects, on the one hand, the much larger number of students involved in music and, on the other, some sense of relative worth. And although it is possible to conduct an inexpensive history course, a band, like a football or a basketball team, has relatively high minimal costs for the purchase and maintenance of uniforms and instruments.

Finally, with regard to the financial side of the school, consider teacher remuneration. Rural small-town teachers are the poorest paid group of teachers in the country. Of course, in rural areas the comparatively low cost of rented and owned housing must be taken into account, but food and other locally sold items tend to cost somewhat more. By state standards (see table 16), Mansfield's salaries are below average; they are most competitive at the starting points—B.A. inexperienced—but become comparatively unattractive (about 10 percent less) at the maximum points. More than 80 percent of the teachers' families have a second, full-time, adult wage earner. The teachers do not seem attracted to collective bargaining; they belong to the National Education Association and see their membership in traditional, nonunion terms.

School board regulations embrace a view of the teacher role that is both traditional and disputed: "A teacher may be expected to assume responsibilities for a reasonable amount of extra class work and duties requiring time outside regular school hours." The frequency of after-

school meetings (see chap. 7) and occasional evening activities, especially those related to Homecoming and prom events, press hard on the
concept of "reasonable." In many districts the extra pay for extra work
principle is extended beyond athletics to include many extracurricular
activities. Not so in Mansfield.[2] The farmers who control the school
board know that they themselves do not count hours; they take pride
in their heavy labor and long hours at cultivation and harvest times.
When interviewing candidates for the superintendency, they were pleased
to hear one candidate announce that he did not keep hours, but worked
until a job was done—just as they did. This was the man they hired.

The stability of the school district staff is illustrated in table 17. Because it combines grade and high school teachers and administrators,
table 17 obscures the fact that until recently there has been a greater
turnover of personnel in the high school than in the grade school. The
latter was staffed by mature local women of rural origin, many without
university degrees, though it would have been difficult to distinguish
the teachers with degrees from those without. From 1964 to 1970, 60
percent of all teachers had taught for eleven or more years in Mansfield.
These figures clearly establish the basic stability of the school system.
Parents often can tell stories about their children's teachers because
they, too, were taught by them when they were children. This core of
old-timers contributes to a sense of continuity between past and present,
between young and old in Mansfield.

For 1972, the stability figures are available for high school teachers
alone (table 18). They are organized by a teacher's earned degree. Two
teachers—the chorus and auto mechanics teachers, do not have degrees,
but both of them are well-qualified for their work by experience and
talent. Half of the staff have been at Mansfield for six or more years.
The remaining half are the youngest teachers in the school and five of
them resigned between 1972 and 1975. They were replaced by other
young persons. At least one of them, Mr. Browne, (see his biography
in chapter 6), is the type who will stay in Mansfield and maintain its
stable core.

Among the virtues of small schools are low student-teacher ratios.
The average teacher-pupil ratio in Mansfield High School (MHS) during the years 1964–74 was 1 to 14 (see table 19).[3] The ratio has varied
with the decline in student enrollments and the fluctuation in number
of teachers due to the employment of part-time teachers.

Though there have been a few slight bulges in K–12 enrollment between 1964 and 1974 (see table 20), the basic trend is decisively downward. In this period, total enrollment dropped from 619 to 474 with no
indication that the trend will be reversed by demographic changes in
the school district. As noted above, land and housing are not available

to attract many new families, nor is there promise of economic growth to create new jobs. The downward enrollment trend has distressing implications for schools everywhere, but especially in smaller communities, where small enrollments can easily force the closing of advanced classes in math, science, and foreign languages. This reduces the richness of curricular offerings and contributes to the rationale for consolidation. While not a topic of daily conversation in Mansfield, consolidation will continue to be mentioned because it hangs over the school and community like a sword of Damocles, ready to lop off the high school from the school district.

Students at MHS not only have the opportunity to study in small classes, they also have a large choice of subjects from which to choose (see table 21). The larger enrollments in English I, II, and III (about 40), biology (about 45), and U.S. history (about 40) are spread over two sections; this cuts in half the enrollment in these required courses. Four years of physical education and one year of mathematics also are required. Until recently, when declining dollar allotments from the state created a period of financial stringency, classes containing as few as four students could be taught.

In past years, advanced courses like physics, modern math analysis, and Spanish III have attracted few students. Despite the administration's efforts to encourage students to take "book" subjects in their senior year rather than a program of industrial arts, home economics, business, art, and auto mechanics, many avoid classes they consider difficult. These practical courses are often soundly taught by qualified people, and so their attractiveness is genuine—not due merely to the lack of appeal of "book" courses. Auto mechanics has a limited enrollment because available facilities cannot accommodate more students; its appeal is far greater than the figures indicate. Enrollments in the other vocational subjects fluctuate in no discernible pattern. Home economics courses have enjoyed steadily increasing enrollments over the years. In fact, a major trend is the increasing enrollment in vocational subjects coupled with the declining enrollment in academic subjects.

Although most enrollment fluctuations during 1968–74, the period covered by table 21, can be explained by the decline in the number of students attending MHS, changes in personnel also had an impact. For example, the loss of an English teacher in 1973 eliminated a short story course and British literature, and the loss of a language teacher in 1973 eliminated Latin. The same English teacher had stimulated enrollments in English when she introduced courses in black literature, short story, creative writing, speech, and British literature. Enrollments in business education courses are unpredictable despite being taught by the same able teacher for over fifteen years. Civics and American government were offered for some years until their replacement by courses in current events and occupational information; the latter course boosted social studies enrollments. Most recently, the latter two have not been taught, and a course in minorities history was offered instead. After several years of low registration in physics, it no longer is offered; interested students (two in 1974) are bused to Auburn. Art currently enjoys a good student response attributable to a new, appealing, young teacher.

The breadth of courses available to students is well matched by the number and variety of extracurricular activities (see chap. 7). Table 22 contains the list of school organizations which stimulate these activities. The school newspaper and the yearbook are omitted from table 22 because they have no budget based on student-raised money. The classes of 1972–76 are included because they have such a budget and they, too, engage students during and after school in organized activities of a non-academic nature. Behind this list of classes and organizations lies enormous energy and time devoted to raising money. All the money listed in table 22 is a triumph of student volunteer activity; none of it came from school district taxation or state revenue sources.

An effort is made to spread the money-raising activities among freshman, sophomore, junior, and senior classes and organizations. Classes handle the concessions at football and basketball games. Only juniors engage in the annual magazine sale held the first two weeks of each school year; Mansfield residents wait for student salespersons to renew their subscriptions. Similarly, only freshmen sell subscriptions to the *Mansfield Times* in the campaign held each spring during a two-week period.

Money is needed for different purposes. For example, at Homecoming each class must build a float and decorate the windows of some shop in town. "We really go into it," says one educator. "If we let any class decide they didn't have to participate, then others wouldn't. Homecoming at Mansfield is as good as many colleges. You don't have the usual student-teacher separation when they're working on Homecoming. It puts them both on a closer plane." Each class also has minor expenses for funeral donations or flowers. Juniors begin saving as freshmen for the junior-senior prom. And the organizations take trips and plan parties which require money. It is rationalized that money-raising activities teach students how to interact with adults, and since they generally occur after school and on weekends there is no conflict with class time.[4] Though students are pressured to help with money-raising ventures, there is no penalty if they do not. Teachers are accustomed to the idea; they know of no alternate ways to raise the needed amounts of money.

The question of whether the activities noted above are beneficial or whether they demand a disproportionate amount of student time is not raised here. That these activities are an integral part of the school system in Mansfield, and that they contribute significantly to the character of a school, is beyond argument.

Maintaining this particular balance of curricular and extracurricular experiences depends not only on the response of local adults and educators, but also on external evaluations. Two such evaluations have impact in Mansfield, those from the North Central Association (NCA) and those from the state office of instruction. Based on the most recent NCA (1969) and state (1975) reports, these external agents clearly reinforce the type of schooling MHS already provides.

The following comments on English and science prepared by the visiting specialists suggest the flavor of the NCA report.

English

The teachers are well qualified and impress the observer with their interest and enthusiasm for their subject. . . . The one full-time teacher is very well prepared and the two part-time teachers have adequate preparation. . . . The appearance of the rooms is neat in spite of the fact that the building is old. Each room has available adequate visual material, numerous reference books, and magazines. Each teacher has prepared a definitely outlined course of study. . . . Writing is encouraged on all levels and there is good training in vocabulary and grammar fundamentals. . . . The point especially worth noting is the fine rapport that each teacher has with the students. . . . The size of the classes is ideal and the quality of the teachers is above average.

Recommendations

1. Since there is no speech course as such, perhaps more speech could be taught in the English classes. Debating could be effective on the senior level; this would encourage more research and individual work.
2. Efforts could be made to provide more for the slow learner. . . .

Science

The Science instructors . . . quickly impress the classroom visitors with their academic competencies and excellent rapport. The instructors . . . are all teaching in other subject areas. . . . It is quite obvious that the science facilities are being used rather effectively. The students as well as the teachers seem to take pride in the school and its equipment. . . .

Strengths

The course offerings are extensive for the size of the school. . . . The adoption of modern programs . . . indicate the school's desire to continually update and upgrade the science curriculum. The recognition by the school board and administration of the importance of science . . . has resulted in adequate materials for student use in most classes.

Recommendations

1. Developing a science committee to study the curriculum and to develop better articulation. . . .
2. Giving consideration to a program for the non-college-bound.
3. Reviewing the present policies regarding the order of offerings of the science courses—which would alleviate the problem of classes containing students with such varied backgrounds.
4. Encouraging more use of safety goggles in the laboratory.

The full NCA report indicates the visiting team reacted to numerous aspects of the school, finding fault with some and praising many others. Their measures of educational worth were not derived from the innovational frontiers of education as they existed in 1969. They reflected, rather, incontestable standards of safety—wear goggles in the workshop; quantitative views related to enrichment—offer more courses (electronics, metal working, music theory); and conventional wisdom—restrict enrollment in world history and sociology so ability variance is not so extreme, and "someone should coordinate the total physical education program." The point is not to judge the NCA team but to show that the impact of their criteria reinforces the traditional nature of education in Mansfield High School and thus allows it basically to continue doing what it has always done and still enjoy NCA legitimation.

While NCA affiliation is optional, each public high school in the state must be evaluated every three years by a state visiting committee. The state sends a team of teachers and administrators who descend on a school, walk the halls, visit the classrooms, attend meetings, and prepare a report. The visitors are themselves practicing educators who vacate their own classrooms and offices for the one-day evaluation. In preparation for this day, school personnel organize a special building clean-up, develop (possibly dust off) teaching plans, prepare bulletin board displays, and become nervous. The occasion may enable teachers to get out of a rut by encouraging them to reflect on what has become their routine. In 1975, the state visiting team's recommendations were no less reinforcing than those of the NCA. They advised that: (1) textbooks be updated, (2) no teacher have more than five preparations, (3) consumer economics be offered to meet state requirements, (4) more courses in business education be provided, and (5) a greater number of different courses be taught—40 is the minimum, 50 is recommended, and Mansfield has 44. The team's sixth recommendation, however, was that the school district consider reorganizing with other districts in the county, a recommendation which the North Central Association had also made. Thus, while supporting the details of educational life in MHS, both evaluations concluded with a suggestion contravening a most central role of Mansfield's high school—its contributions to the maintenance of Mansfield's community. Educators often overlook this critical noneducative function of schools. How ironical to place a stamp of approval on a school with one hand and to urge its disappearance with the other.

Within a month after the state visitation team had completed its report, Mansfield held a referendum to increase taxes for its education fund. The superintendent, in his regular newsletter to the school district, argued for these additional funds on the grounds that expenses could not be reduced further without jeopardizing state recognition, and that teachers' salaries already were the lowest of any school district in the area. Anticipating that some people might advocate consolidation as the solution to the district's financial problems, he presented the following case:

> (*a*) Consolidation is not the answer to all problems and we can't believe people in Mansfield want to give up their high school yet.
> (*b*) Consolidation does not reduce taxes or save money. [Whether consolidation does or does not save money is a raging controversy in consolidation battles.] The 1973 tax rates showed some consolidated schools to have higher tax rates than ours. . . . The point is clear; consolidation does not propose to save money.
> (*c*) Consolidation certainly takes something away from the local community. The farther away your school is located the less you know about it, and the less direct control you have over it.
> (*d*) The Chairman of the recent State Visit pointed out that *with the present rate and continued deficit spending, the district should be exploring possibilities of reorganization*; however your Board of Education, which you have elected to serve you, does not think you want that route.

In view of the antireorganization sentiment of school board members, teachers, and students (see chaps. 3, 5, and 9), the superintendent's appeal is well directed.[5]

Despite their approval of reorganization, neither the state report nor the NCA report question the capacity of MHS to serve its students. An important indicator of a school's effectiveness in individual terms is the success of its graduates in gaining access to further educational opportunities. Indicators of success in community terms may be drawn from data concerning where its students live after graduation.

Do Mansfield students continue their education after graduation? Yes, of course. In the 1947–65 period, we know that 35 percent of all graduates attended a four-year college, but with the limitations of the available data we do not know how many were enrolled in other types of postsecondary institutions (see table 23). In any case, because junior colleges are new in the vicinity (two were opened in 1967 and one in 1972), attendance at such schools would be a negligible factor before 1965. Also, of 64 students who graduated either in the top third (1947–56) or top half (1960–65) of their class, 38 or 59 percent went to college.

Of 233 MHS graduates in the period 1967–72, 47 percent attended either college, junior college, or a postsecondary training program (beautician, clerical, automotive), though most of this group pursued a junior college or college education (see table 24). Graduates who begin a postsecondary program complete it successfully, including those who go to four-year colleges. Thus I conclude, as did the NCA team in their 1969 report, that the quality of education at Mansfield High School prepares a reasonable proportion of its students both to enter and to complete a college education. An added fact is that with few exceptions, graduates attend universities in the state system and prefer its smaller branches, probably viewing the larger campuses of the state university system as formidable in size and often in qualitative expectations, as well. Students seldom enroll in out-of-state schools.

Rural youth have migrated to urban areas for decades; the modernization of agriculture and the increased size of farms (with a corresponding decline in the number of farms) has seriously limited their work opportunities at home. And if there is no local industry, village youth must seek work elsewhere. The data do not indicate a contrary trend in Mansfield, but they establish the home environs as a powerfully attractive place to a majority of graduates from at least as far back as 1947. The environs of Mansfield include towns in which Mansfield High School competes athletically, parents and students work, students date and cruise, and families shop and entertain themselves. Of course, students who attend college are more likely to move a greater distance to obtain the jobs associated with their type of education. Yet in the 1947–65 period, 46 percent of the college-goers remained in the Mansfield area, less than the 69 percent of the non-college-goers who remained there, but still a substantial number. More than 50 percent of *all* the high school graduates in this older, more settled group are living in the Mansfield area. In the 1967–72 period, 54 percent of all graduates resided in the Mansfield area and more than half of this group lived within the school district; the more recent the year of graduation,

the greater the number who lived in and around Mansfield. For graduates in the earlier period, contrary to expectations, the number of years
out of school does not predict the likelihood of their staying in the area.
The percentage fluctuates from year to year (the range is from 33 percent in 1962 to 72 percent in 1951) in seemingly random fashion.[6]

In the light of these figures, I conclude that the experience at MHS
both reinforces contentment with small-town life and constrains many
of its students from seeking, or seeking successfully, opportunities for
greater mobility. The nature of the school experience seems to support
a disposition to live in intimate surroundings. The impact of the particular educators Mansfield hires and the level of academic performance
the community expects (see chaps. 5 and 9) moderate the students'
occupational, educational, and geographical mobility, though this is not
an invariable consequence.

Finally, it is appropriate to discuss the goals MHS has articulated.
Prepared for different occasions, goals are part of the ocean of words
that engulfs every school system: goals to greet the visiting team of
educators from state office of instruction; district-wide goals incorporated into a school board code book; and course goals designed to establish scope and sequence among different subjects. When the words take
the form of policies governing specific recurring events, such as detention, the junior-senior prom, student use of automobiles, or corporal
punishment, we can expect them to have fairly regular use. When,
however, they are embedded in a document called "Goals for Tomorrow," their application is less clear.

In the school year 1972–73, the state's superintendent of public instruction requested each school system to prepare behavioral objectives.
During the 1960s and 1970s, the educational shores of the United
States were heaped high with behavioral objectives. Such objectives were
expected to improve teacher performance and, ultimately, student learning. While groups of Mansfield's teachers worked in their own subject
matter areas, the superintendent prepared the school system's general
"Goals for Tomorrow." They are included below under the heading
"Suggested Student Goals." As required, he then sent his list to all
school district residents inviting their reactions. Few residents responded.

Though the goals below do not have a predictable relationship with
classroom practice, they offer insight to the most recent thinking of the
school's leadership and, to a limited extent, of parents, students and
teachers.

A. *Instructional Program*

Provide for such quality education that should help every student
acquire to the fullest extent possible for his mastery of a good

basic education and to open further channels of study to him as
an adult. . . .

  B. *Suggested Student Goals* (Desired Learner Outcomes)

    1. Develop growth in their ability to think rationally, to express
their thoughts clearly, and to read and listen with understanding.

    2. Develop salable skills . . .

    3. Develop the ability and desire to understand the rights and
duties of a citizen of a democratic society, and . . . as members
of the community and citizens of the state, the nation and the
world.

    4. Acquire good health habits . . .

    5. Develop a better understanding of the methods of science and
man's environment, the influence of science on human life,
and the main scientific facts concerning the nature of the
world and of man.[7]

    6. Develop areas of concern that include responsibility, honesty,
self-respect, justice, courtesy and kindness, discrimination between
right and wrong, respect for individual differences, obedience
to parents and respect for authority and laws.[8]

    7. Provide opportunities to develop their capabilities to appreciate
beauty in literature, art, music and nature.

    8. To provide opportunities to learn to use leisure time well . . .

    9. To develop an understanding of the significance of the family
for the individual and society . . .

   10. To know how to purchase and use goods and services intelligently,
understanding both the values received by the consumer
and the economic consequences of their acts.

A comparison of Mansfield's "Goals for Tomorrow" with statements
prepared under the same state order by other school districts of approximately
the same size reveals many similarities.[9] A number of broad
categories dominate the goals of all the school districts: (1) basic skills,
(2) vocational skills, (3) consumerism, (4) leisure time, (5) democratic
citizenship, (6) health, (7) the arts, (8) thinking ability, (9)
family, and (10) personal qualities. In addition to these shared categories,
however, there are several others which Mansfield omits from
its list; they are either oversights or ideas to which the town is not
committed. For example, a number of schools, usually somewhat larger
ones, mentioned they planned to enable each student to "develop . . .
the ability to identify problems and to apply clear, critical, reflective,
and creative thinking . . . to reach their solution; . . . develop an awareness
of the history, influence and interrelationships of all cultures; . . .
develop an appreciation of the worth of himself and all other people;
. . . be . . . acquainted with his rights and responsibilities . . . as a

member of a pluralistic society; . . . develop intellectual curiosity and eagerness for lifelong learning." These goals are not rejected in Mansfield; they simply do not occupy the foreground of concern.

In contrast, the goal of providing "a good basic education" is of major concern. It is mentioned under "Instructional Program" above, and it is voiced frequently by Mansfield's school board members. It is one of three fundamental points that bear on the academic aspects of the school. The second is the development of "salable skills," listed under "Suggested Student Goals," and the third is the provision of courses that will enable students to attend postsecondary institutions.

The emphasis on the basics is not readily observable in the classroom. It is used more as a slogan, a conventional way of affirming that the board and administration do not concern themselves with lofty intellectual goals, that they do not have pretentions of sophistication, and that they mean to keep down the costs of schooling—for money spent on the basics is by definition money well spent. Mansfield's investment in the development of "salable skills" is evident in the variety of courses offered in home economics, business education, industrial arts, vocational agriculture, and auto mechanics. And the full range of courses listed in appendix B makes clear Mansfield's efforts to provide the prerequisites for higher education.

Several observations seem applicable to statements of goals such as those quoted above. First, they are useful for disclosing very general, possibly quite important, dispositions of a school system's educators. Second, from these dispositions one may often infer the values and priorities of the community that supports the school. Third, a school system may be known by the goals it ignores, as well as those it espouses. And, finally, the classroom behavior of teachers is significantly more important for inferring the nature of the goals which actually guide their behavior than is any formal list of goals.

4

Educational Guardians of Community: Mansfield's School Board

Superintendent Tate

Despite Superintendent Tate's death halfway through my fieldwork, this remains a study of Mansfield High School under his leadership. His replacement, chosen with the model of Mr. Tate in mind, did not intend to alter the school in his first year as superintendent. Throughout my contact with MHS, both during the first year, when he was alive, and during the second year, when the new superintendent took office, Mr. Tate's personality and views remained dominant.

School boards vary in the way they carry out their duties. Some are passive, deferring to the professional expertise of the school administrators. Others are activist, energetically trying themselves to run the schools under their jurisdiction. Mansfield's school board prefers a strong superintendent who can run their schools, but this preference rests on a critical condition—that the superintendent perform in a manner that fits Mansfield. For many years, they had such a man in Mr. Tate.

At the time of his death Mr. Tate had been superintendent for seventeen years. Before becoming an administrator, he had been associated with MHS as industrial arts teacher and as a coach of all sports—a successful coach, it should be added. His wife taught in the elementary school, they had no children, and he devoted his life to running the school system, coming early, working late, all week long, tirelessly dedicated. Outside the school he joined and took his turn as leader in the community's religious and organizational life. More than working long and hard, he worked well for the school, and his efforts earned him the respect of almost everyone in the school district and in neighboring towns as well. The school board had long ago learned that Mr. Tate was in charge and they didn't mind; he ran the school in a way that pleased them, though not necessarily *just* to please them. As a man of integrity, Mr. Tate did not shape his views to be acceptable to the board. It was a fine coincidence for Mansfield that he naturally suited them. As one board member said, "His feelings and ours were mutual, so we left well enough alone." He had lived and worked in the much larger town of Stanton and had received job offers from larger school systems, but he was clearly at home in Mansfield. Mansfielders were proud of him, and he had no desire to work elsewhere. While the school board wished he would reduce his work load by turning over more responsibility to the principal, who was certainly competent to take more, they resignedly accepted his continued unwillingness to do so.

Mr. Tate welcomed me and my project to MHS, promised and delivered his full cooperation, and made only one stipulation—that I not disturb the routine of the school. This condition stemmed from a matter of considerable concern to him and to the school board: they liked an orderly school. A substantial part of teacher esteem depends on their capacity to maintain good discipline. The school leadership was pleased to learn of the resignation of an "otherwise good teacher" who "couldn't cut the mustard with the kids" (keep them quiet). The prevailing view of Mr. Tate was described by one of his close associates:

> He was always helping people. Just the other day a kid came by to get him to cosign a loan for a trailer. And whenever boys went into the service he'd offer them money because he knew there's nothing worse than being broke when you're in the service. He didn't expect to get the money back. One night a man came to his house with a pot of dirty water. He wanted Mr. Tate to do something about it, but Tate's own water was just as dirty because the problem was in the town's pipes. People always thought he could solve any problem.

Characteristic of Mr. Tate's dominance of the school was his daily performance in the morning assembly.[1] Though students typically arrive at school well before classes begin and embark on a day-long series of informal social interactions, the first, formal organized experience of the day at MHS under Mr. Tate was the morning assembly. At the sound of the bell, students milled in from the many entrances to the gym and took their assigned seats in the stands. Female teachers sat in the first row below the students, while male teachers bunched together in several rows off to one side.

As the bell rang, Mr. Tate stood before the assembled school and looked up intently at the students until they were quiet and alert. While he spoke, the principal stood off to one side taking attendance. The assembly lasted five minutes and in this time the superintendent would praise the sophomore class for their well-organized, efficient handling of concessions at the football game, especially the cooperative clean-up effort; remind seniors that Archer's representative was coming to talk about taking their pictures; console the football team that though they lost they played a fine game and had no cause to be ashamed of their performance; and inform eighth-hour teachers that Future Farmers of

America students would leave at 2:30 for a field trip. Each morning Mr. Tate reminded, announced, praised, consoled, and mildly rebuked, leaving no doubt of his values, interests, and concerns. There was no public address system: he did not want one, preferring the directness, the greater intimacy, of the assembly.

In the months before Mr. Tate's death, the school board alternated between hope that he would live and continue to work and despair that he could never be replaced if he died or had to resign. To Mansfielders it was unthinkable that a man of such great strength and stature would ever die. Until Mr. Tate went to the hospital, he continued to work long hours, although not always very effectively. Unable to delegate responsibility, he struggled with next year's budget, hoping to the end that he would be strong enough to finish it. His death left the budget incomplete and the school board with the sad task of finding his successor.

School Board Members

Mansfield's school board is distinguished by the fact that since its origin board members have been natives, farmers, and, with one exception, men. The exception is a woman who for personal reasons chose to serve only for one term. Over the twenty years this board has existed,[2] the presidents and at least four of the other six members always have been Mansfield-born farmers, notwithstanding that most school district residents work in factories and live in town.

School board elections generally inspire a turnout of about two hundred of a possible seven hundred eligible voters, and the "right" candidates continue to get elected. The right candidates are those without the kind of axes to grind which might disrupt the status quo. Retiring members sometimes recruit suitable candidates as their own replacements. The best credentials of the newest board member were his status as a native and his well-known love for Mansfield and deep regard for its traditions. He defeated a six-year school board veteran of demonstrated skill who had lived in Mansfield only ten years.

Mansfield board members are not figureheads, merely rubber-stamping the decisions of the professional educators. Though their views are remarkably congruent with Mr. Tate's, they nevertheless are forthright, outspoken, questioning individuals, and the superintendent always knows the values to which he must be responsive. They take seriously their school board responsibilities, content that they have a reasonably satisfied teaching staff and a good school. These guardians of the school district like the school they are expected to oversee: most of them and their predecessors were students in the school; they are or have been parents of students in the school; and now they are its caretakers. They act as though they believe their work is important.

Listen to their tradition-oriented outlook. Board member George Robinson, one of three members portrayed below, refers approvingly to the time when teachers were expected to live in the school district that employed them. "If all the teachers lived here we'd have a better community," he says. "We knew every teacher in town in years gone by." Not that he consciously desires to control a teacher's life; he believes in personal freedom. Rather, he feels that a Mansfield teacher belongs in Mansfield, that the community is better served if teachers are part of the community, and that they would be known, in the way Mansfielders like to know one another, if teachers were local residents. Robinson would like teachers to walk by Mrs. Hodgkin's house on their way to school, giving her the chance to pop up out of her chair and monitor them as they pass by.

In language that we will hear again later from teachers and senior students, member Bert Holcomb observes that though greater academic and other opportunities are available in large schools, he is content with MHS. "As long as Mansfield can do an adequate job of education, I feel we don't need a consolidated school," Holcomb says. He emphasizes the advantages to residents of continuing their high school, but not of maximizing its scholastic output; if it does "an adequate job," he is content. His view does not imply that he would support a small school at any cost, but he does not indicate when the costs to scholastic standing would become too high. Only if a new high school building had to be built would he consider consolidation.

In general, the board members support a particularism that casts them as community defenders. Webster defines this quality as "based upon a particular situation or relationship rather than general principles . . . opposed to universalistic," and "exclusive or special devotion to something particular." In Mansfield the same quality would be explained as commitment to Mansfield: if we spend taxpayers' money, be sure that Mansfield benefits. Keep the money at home. Provide work for local people as long as they can do the job. What a person can do is important, but who he is is no less important.[3] Operate the schools so they suit who we are and what we like. Outside ideas and people should not interrupt our way of life. This characterization only slightly exaggerates the meaning of particularism in Mansfield.

Because decision making in particularistic terms suggests being unfair, Mansfielders seldom articulate this outlook. Board member David Gravely is an exception. Gravely said it was probably wrong to ignore seniority in the recent board decision about which cook to dismiss, but he is glad the home town cooks were not fired. He has known them all his life and it would hurt to see them go. Ordinarily, he does not feel this way about teachers because they are transients. However, he was glad Barton left and Kling got to stay, because even if Kling is not a better teacher, he has "been here so long that he seems to belong here." Gravely is a native son with a vast kin network living in the school district. He represents the point of view that dominates the mainstream Mansfielders. It contrasts with that of the "specialists"[4] (as the superintendent designated some visitors to school board meetings), whose outlook makes them first universalists and then (possibly) Mansfield loyalists. The Gravelys of Mansfield are almost invariably particularist and loyalist, even when they recognize that this may involve an element of unfairness.

George Robinson

"My family goes a long way back in farming around here. My dad and both my grandads farmed. After I left high school I worked in Stanton for a few years, then with my dad for three years before going out on my own. I think my son will farm. He doesn't like school, has a terrible time in class, but he lives and breathes farming. Otherwise I have one daughter and she's in college now.

"When I was growing up, farming was a way of life; everybody, all your neighbors, were satisfied with what they had. You could do anything you wanted on your own farm. Don't get me wrong. Oh, I complain about this and that, but I wouldn't do nothing different and I wouldn't go anywhere else. Farmers could do better and they could do a lot worse.

"I don't really have a philosophy of education. Hasn't been that much thought gone into it. Kids should know how to get out in life and get something done; I think this happens. What makes this country is there's nothing youth can't do if they want to do it. Few of our kids end up in jail. Basically we're doing a better job than other places.

"For a good rounded education athletics teaches a lot. It teaches you how to try hard and to win. That's another reason I got on the board —to improve athletics. I thought we could do better. Boys often don't learn to care and if they don't care they can't succeed anywhere.

"The concept today is not for the school to help the community, but to help the individual to make his way wherever he goes. If all the teachers lived here we'd have a better community. That's been one of the big changes since World War II. If the teacher taught here, he always lived here. Now it's slowly getting so that people hardly know the majority of teachers. We knew every teacher in town in years gone by. The old theory of the teacher was, they help in community activities and teach school. Today they don't feel a bit obligated to the community.

"The consensus now is that the school is properly run by administration, so there's little push by the board for other things than what the administration recommends. For hiring teachers they boil it down to three to five candidates and provide a file on each one. We never interview them; this suits me fine. We got many local persons now in the system because they came when it was hard to get outside applicants. They got tenure and stay forever. Local persons aren't given preference when we're hiring, only if they're better qualified.

"So far we're doing OK in our old building. I went through here and my kids too. It wouldn't be much trouble to build a new one if the right people got hold of it. Speaking of a new school, I don't see any gain in consolidation. For that we'd have to build a new school, too. We already have small classes. We should be able to spend more time on the basic three Rs. That's the heart of your life. Today, educated people go through a grocery store and can't even convert ounces to pounds."

Rex Borden

"Except for vacations and a short time at college, which I didn't like at all, I've never been anywhere but Mansfield. Small town life is something you feel; you can't always express it, we talk around our feelings, most of us can't express ourselves.

"The reason people come back here to live—there's a feeling they have they can't satisfy anywhere else. *This is home.* The whole thing about getting industry here is, when you get many industries you don't have a small town anymore. You start pulling people in. Even now we have many newcomers. Used to be that everybody was related to everybody else. My grandma says she don't know a third of the people in town anymore.

"I like to be independent. I've got a pond and can go fishing anytime I want. I got a swing and I can sit on it for hours and relax. There's no need to get away. They say a man needs a vacation; I prefer to stay home. Whenever I go away it feels so good to come back home. You can bet I'll encourage my son to be a farmer, though he should have four years of college so he'll have something to fall back on. Maybe when he goes away it'll look so good to come back that he will.

"Even if my kids grow up in the country, they're really part of an urban community. This is not an isolated rural place. Stanton is close to us; people work there. So our kids need the same training as anybody's. I guess people didn't think about such things when I was growing up. I went to a country school with one teacher and eight grades and all the kids in school were neighbors. The countryside was a unit. All the farmers got together for a hay ring, lots of visiting back and forth, lots of school programs. People would butcher together and hang paper together.

"Most of the work on the board is routine. We've had some building projects over the past two to five years that took a little time. Biggest part of a meeting is the bills. Once in a while there's some complaints. Next month, teacher's salaries come up; that's an annual matter. Sometimes teachers will get riled up. About two years ago they was wanting to be paid for ticket selling at ball games. But other than that, usually the board is generous toward teachers' salaries, so they really don't have much room to complain. Two years ago we agreed to pay for directing class plays and GAA [Girls' Athletic Association]. Other schools had begun to compensate teachers for extra duties, so we thought it only right to do the same.

"Bill Tate is great. We hardly have any work to do because he organizes everything. Still you got to really study and understand your superintendent's philosophy on teaching. If he can present a program to satisfy himself and members of the board, if he can sell that, it's not gonna be too far wrong. The important thing is, his feelings and ours is mutual, so we ought to leave well enough alone.

"It's getting to be more every year where the board and the administration have less all the time to do with running the school. It comes down from the state, maybe not directly, but if you don't meet certain standards, state reimbursement is cut out. If you get the dollars, you got to figure to be controlled. Our dress code was strict till a few years ago when some parents here objected and called the state. They learned it was illegal to force kids to wear any special clothes. So if you try to keep everybody decent looking, they'll just go to court and beat you. Just like your tenure law. I don't know who ever came up with that. All it does is protect your poorer teachers.

"Financially, we're doing OK. Other school districts are in trouble; not us. We never do anything to go in the red. So we don't have a need for consolidation. I'd hate to see that time. You know, the further away the school gets, the less you have to say about it. It's bigger and harder to control. Sure, there's the advantage of better facilities, but what else? People will lose interest. Not people with kids in school, maybe. They'd be interested though they might miss some games because of the greater distance to go to get to school. It would take dollars out of town. Our October payroll for all teachers was $33,486 and $2,059 for cooks, secretaries, and custodians. We also buy some of our lunch food in town. Parents would pick up their kids and do their shopping in town where the kids are, rather than in Mansfield. Teachers'd move away. I don't know how to say it—we'd have a deader town. Mansfield has a hard enough time now keeping on the map. If they moved the school, it'd be much harder. People go to things at school now even if they don't have kids in school. This is a football town and people know the kids. It wouldn't be the same saying rah, rah, rah for Auburn as for Mansfield. Really, I'd hate to see consolidation. I like things the way they are. I'm against change unless it can be proved the change is worthwhile. Maybe most people in small towns feel this way and that's why we don't have progress."

Rex Borden, like most board members, was an athlete; in fact most boys in schools the size of Mansfield High School participate in team sports. He seldom misses a home football game. Over the years, he has heard a profusion of rah, rah, rahs for Mansfield. The thought of directing those cheers toward Auburn is anathema. The games, the cheering, the ceremony, the devotion—all are focused on Mansfield. Borden and his fellow board members are steeped in loyalty; it entwines the community. To understand the relationship between school and community in Mansfield is to understand why Borden shudders at the thought of consolidation, even though it is not imminent. He acknowledges the better facilities that would accompany consolidation—they are too obvious to ignore, but his question "what else?" is followed by a string of particulars that lead him to reject some forms of progress whose impact would undermine the Mansfield he seeks to maintain.

Bert Holcomb

"I was born, raised, and educated in Mansfield and I've really never been away except during the Second World War. Back in the thirties I started working after school for $3.00 a week in a store in town. I'll bet I was the only kid with a job other than farming. My father was a farmer; I never was interested. After the war I came back here, got my old job again, and when the owner retired I was able to buy the business. Never thought of going to college myself, but I've got a kid at the university right now. This is a fine place to raise children. I've seen lots of places that look nice, but I never thought of staying there. I'd sooner be around people I know than people I don't know; I'm a lot happier, though I know it doesn't bother some people to be with strangers. There are a lot of freedoms in a small town. No way in the world in a big town can you turn your car around in the middle of the street. At the bank or the post office people cross the street catty whampus. You can't measure this freedom in dollars and cents. Another thing. I can walk across any farmer's farm. No farmer would turn down a friend, even if he don't like hunting. There's nothing can touch that as far as I know. One thing's taken away freedom is stop signs. Been too many of 'em put up in town.

"We lack a lot of things in Mansfield that you'd think we couldn't survive without. No clothing store, for example. And no dentist or lawyer. But I believe I've got as good a store as in larger places; same with the hardware and the drug store. Got a lot of good churches. Better than average schools. Maybe it looks like we shouldn't be operating, but we are.

"Now take this consolidation stuff. I've been hearing about it almost ever since my kids began school. Some day we may have a county high school. Maybe. There's a lot of disadvantages, like long bus rides. It's quite a way from the boondocks south of Oakfield to some central point where a new county school would be located. Kids get more attention in a small school. We'd lose some identity and we'd lose out in sports, too. It's something to be a football captain, but with just one team there's only one captain.

"It's the same with scholarship—it's a lot harder for kids to be tops. More kids means more competition, though this could be a good push to work harder. I guess the bigger the school, the better the facilities— automotive and industrial shops, a bandroom, no limit to the P.E. possibilities. But as long as we can do an adequate job of education, I feel we don't need a consolidated school. If our building can't be kept up and it would be cheaper to build than keep the old building, then OK. But as long as we can do the job, we should, though I don't know how to measure this.

"I'd like to see a change in parents' attitudes toward teachers. Parents seem to have swung toward the idea that kids are always right. Nowadays, a teacher's hands are so tied it'd drive me up the wall to handle a class. If kids need discipline . . . Why it's like when I was at school: if you were bad at school you'd get paddled both at school and at home. Respect for teachers is not there anymore.

"It bothers me that so much emphasis is placed on winning in class and winning athletics. Like the old saying goes, 'It's not important if you win or lose, but how you played the game.' You know, a young man gets so much out of sports besides winning. I still live by the rules I got out of sports. My coach said to us, 'Push yourself till it hurts and then push a little more.' This is true in more than physical aspects. Most of us took this seriously."

Holcomb, Robinson, and Borden share a common way of life as native Mansfielders and alumni of Mansfield High School; they have been shaped by the same powerful experiences. Faced with the task of maintaining the Mansfield school system, they respond in similar ways. Discord is absent from board meetings; few motions fail to get a unanimous vote. Though differentiated by age, temperament, and interests, board members clearly converge on matters involving school and community.

The School Board at Work

In one-to-one interviews like these, school board members may reveal something about their personal feelings, sensitivities, priorities, and values—as much as they are able and willing to show. But board members, like teachers, have a domain where they are on stage, where they most notably are expected to play the role of board member. That domain, of course, is the school board meeting. The person represented in an interview is clearly present at these meetings, but the presence of the other board members, and the superintendent and principals as well, shows the board member in interaction, with the press of the situation upon him. What follows shows three such occasions: a board meeting as manifest in official minutes; a board meeting as manifest in notes of an actual meeting devoted to discussing the curriculum; and a special occasion during which board members interviewed and selected a new superintendent.

Official Minutes of a School Board Meeting

Official minutes are inert statements. Their lifeless listing of events in chronological order records in skeletal form what occurred: that payment of the bills was approved, but not where doubts and questions regarding finances were expressed; that adult education courses were discussed, but not what was said and felt about adult education, the school's responsibility to such programs, and their contribution to the community; that board representatives will meet with teacher representatives to discuss salary matters, but without mention of the advice tendered, the concerns expressed, or a hint that the issue at stake goes to the heart of the school and its well-being. The most emotional and critical problems may be reduced to a terse "A discussion was held . . . " and "It was brought to our attention that . . . " We do learn, however, that something happened and, in addition, who voted for what motion. Posterity is served, though poorly, by such documents; more is not expected of them. Here is an example:

The Mansfield Community Unit District Board of Education met in regular session on Monday, February 12, at 7:30 P.M. in the Board room. Members present: Borden, Jones, Gravely, Engel, Farwell, Holcomb, Robinson. Also present: Mr. Tate, Mr. Knight, and Mr. Shepherd.

A motion was made by Jones and seconded by Engel to approve the minutes of the January 8 regular meeting. Borden, yea; Engle, yea; Farwell, yea; Holcomb, yea; Jones, yea; Gravely, yea; Robinson, yea. Motion carried.

A motion was made by Borden and seconded by Jones to accept the Revolving Fund Report as presented. Borden, yea; Engel, yea; Farwell, yea; Holcomb, yea; Jones, yea; Gravely, yea; Robinson, yea. Motion carried.

A motion was made by Gravely and seconded by Farwell to pay the January bills as presented. Borden, yea; Engel, yea; Farwell, yea; Holcomb, yea; Jones, yea; Gravely, yea; Robinson, yea. Motion carried.

The Transportation, Lunchroom and Athletic Reports were discussed by the Board and approved.

The January Receipts and Gross Monthly salaries were reviewed by the Board.

A discussion was held on the two Adult Education courses to be offered. Board representatives for the Salary Committee to meet with the teacher committee are: Jones, chairman; Farwell; and Gravely.

A discussion was held concerning the meeting attended by Mr. Tate, Holcomb, Borden, Mr. Knight, and Mr. Shepherd about the Stanton Community College. It was brought to our attention that all the High School Districts not included in a Junior College District have a timetable to follow in order to be in a Junior College District by January 1.

A motion was made by Gravely and seconded by Engel to accept the resignation of Betty Allen at the end of the school year. Borden, yea; Engel, yea; Farwell, yea; Holcomb, yea; Jones, yea; Gravely, yea; Robinson, yea. Motion carried.

A motion was made by Farwell and seconded by Gravely to re-employ Mr. Knight as Principal of the High School. Borden, yea; Engel, yea; Farwell, yea; Holcomb, yea; Jones, yea; Gravely, yea; Robinson, yea. Motion carried.

Meeting adjourned at 10:30 p.m.

Notes from a School Board Meeting

On the first Monday night of each month Borden, Holcomb, Robinson, and the other members of the school board meet in the high school teachers' room (in the preceding minutes called the "Board Room"). The seven members plus the superintendent and the high school and grade school principals sit around the large rectangular table that dominates the room. Board president Robinson sits at the head of the table, facing the door. The superintendent sits at his left and the elementary school principal at his right. Everyone always occupies the same seat. Visitors array themselves on chairs placed against the radiator and the bookshelves to the left of the door. A large plaster bust of Lincoln overlooks the entire room from atop built-in bookshelves. A small table to the right of the door accommodates the percolating coffee and refreshments that are served midway through the meeting. Several ashtrays are placed around the table; smoking is forbidden in the school at all other times. Board members and educators come freshly shaved and well dressed, the latter often in the jackets and ties they wore during the day. Meetings begin at 7:30 or 8:00 P.M., depending on the time of year, and seldom last less than three hours. These sessions are unhurried, notwithstanding the jokes members make about their length. President Robinson is low-keyed; he moves the meeting along deliberately, without pressure or manipulation, following parliamentary procedure, but not strictly. Since the superintendent acts as expert-in-residence, all heads frequently turn toward him for explanation; trusting him, they trust his explanations. Board meetings are open to the public, and parents with grievances or causes do come. One regular visitor is the local reporter for the *Cunningham County News*. She takes running notes during the meeting, occasionally offers an opinion, and writes up the meeting's highlights for her Mansfield page, which covers all community events.

Within the structure provided by the formal agenda, an aura of banter and joking, of easy informality, prevails. Interspersed among agenda items are references to the dominant force in their lives and in their community—agriculture. The rhythm of the farmer's life in spring and fall is dictated by planting and harvesting needs: arranging the annual inspection of the physical plant, for example, is complicated by their planting activities.

At no time do board members intervene directly in school affairs, that is, during the school day when students and educators are present and working. Of course, they are free to enter school at any time, and the president of the board may come to school to confer with the superintendent. While the public calls board members at home and approaches them with complaints anywhere in the community, it is at board meetings that the members are most influential. Their role is somewhat understated by the observation (made during Reynolds's interview—see below) that, "We expect the superintendent to be the actual leader, but we may make recommendations." In fact, board members continually establish boundaries within which the educators must act. They do this by the questions they ask—"What did we buy at the grade school that cost a thousand dollars or so?"; the decisions they make, such as eliminating class trips; the general mood they set— "I like things the way they are. I'm against change unless it can be proved the change is worthwhile"; and the specific priorities they articulate over time—respect for the basics, support for athletics, devotion to community, fiscal conservatism, and the like. That the adept superintendent can alter existing boundaries is evident, as when Mr. Tate persuaded the board that a male primary grade teacher could be effective. Generally, however, a superintendent ignores these boundaries at high cost.

The president brings the meeting to order, the roll is called, the previous meeting's minutes are approved, and then the meeting is underway.[5] Following the treasurer's report, the president asks if there are any questions. Automatic approval of the treasurer's report is not the practice, and disposing of financial matters occupies the early part of each meeting. The tone of the board's questions is friendly and information-seeking; yet their implication is, "We watch how the money is spent and will monitor amounts which are large and without self-evident explanation."

"This outstanding check for $1,115.00. Who is this?"

"There's a couple more for $800 in there."

"They're kickbacks."

"They didn't buy meat last week, so it's money left over."

"I don't see it here, offhand," the principal tries to explain, enjoying the members' joking.

"That's OK. It just seemed to be a pretty big check to be beholden."

"I see it now. That's for the life insurance company."

"That item for the junior college students. It was a jazz band, a real nice program. Music the kids could enjoy. Not long hair or hard rock either. It was nice to go in the gym and hear a pin drop. For payment they only asked for meals and they got what all the other students got." He laughs.

"What did you buy at the grade school that cost a $1,000 or so?"

"Chairs."

"Didn't we order 'em last year?"

"Yeah, but we just got the bill."

"Wish I got my bills that way."

"Any more questions?"

"Need a motion?" "Yeah." "So moved." "Second." The secretary reads the motion and there's an affirmative roll call vote.

"What's this annual spring visitation?"

"That's where you have to inspect the building."

"What time?"

"Next Saturday."

"Will you be in the field, George?"

"Could be."

"Make it this Saturday."

"No, we've got an art workshop going on."

"Why can't we do it some night?"

"You know the light bills already are over $1,000."

"Let's do it while the ground is still wet [and the farmers are unable to work in their fields]."

"OK. Now let's try for Friday evening. Over at the grade school unless you're notified different. Got that? We'll check out the gym roof and gutter repair."

"Any correspondence?"

"There's been some applications for the janitorial position." Members study a dittoed sheet of brief résumés the superintendent passes around.

"Who is Jones?"

"His woman called to volunteer him. Said her man needs a job." They laugh.

"Age is a factor. I don't mean to knock older people at all, but we got some complicated mechanical equipment over there [he points toward the grade school] and it'll take a few years to learn. I'm not knocking them. We'll all be old sometime."

"We got three from our own community and they're well qualified. My opinion is we better work with these three."

They continue to discuss applicants and their qualifications, finally selecting one local man whom they then call to verify his willingness to work at the available salary. They naturally make the decision that favors a local person.

"We got any reoccuring problems that have come out?"

"Don't think too hard or we'll have another meeting next week."

"I've missed two 'Gunsmokes' already."

"OK. We've got one smaller thing we ought to talk about before we look into the school program. Students and teachers have asked questions about the senior trip. What we're going to say about it. What do you think?"

"They're useless. They take seniors away from school."

"What if we postpone the trip until after graduation?"

"Nothing changes. We're still responsible if we authorize the trip."

"It's a big responsibility because we run into student defiance on the trip. The responsibility is very heavy."

"That's why we got a request from the teachers for a board member to be present on the trip. How many of us want to assume such responsibility?"

"How would it be if a student got pregnant and the courts have to decide what the cost would be for the damage done to this girl over the years?"

For several minutes more they continue this discussion. The tone is decidedly negative; from whatever angle they consider this once bright addition to their school program, they find no justification to keep it. A motion is made to eliminate class trips. All vote yes. Sensitive to the American public's increasing recourse to the courts, they vote to remove the school system from one possible source of legal suits.

In the remainder of the evening the board explores the high school curriculum, discussing each subject area, questioning the principal and superintendent, but not making any decisions, even when questions have policy implications. Basically, this was a time for elucidation, not for decision. The superintendent does not check to see if there is need for reconsideration following board members' observations. To the contrary, he responds no more than is necessary before moving the discussion to the next subject. Meanwhile black literature and new math are disparaged, opportunity for advanced mathematics is assured, the teachers of auto mechanics and art are lauded, the importance of business education for girls is recognized (as well as home economics for boys), and, occasionally, the traditional counterargument of "the way we did it" is advanced.

The high school principal hands out a list of all courses taught in the high school.

"I had a talk with Sally Robson, I think she's in her second year at college, and she recommends improving the math program, including calculus. She also said we ought to assign compositions and grade them like they do in college."

"How many years of English are required?"

"Three."

"How can speech [a mini course] be taught in nine weeks? We had it in English IV [which lasted a year when he was a student]."

"I'll bet you didn't have black lit."

"No. I didn't want it either."

"It's popular in suburban areas and in black areas. There they can really preach. Rhetoric courses are taught in some schools. It's writing and research designed for those going to college. Smaller schools don't have enough students for it."

They continue to discuss the teaching of English, wondering about the advisability of offering a course in composition. As interest in this topic wanes, they move to the mathematics program.

"Next year we'll be teaching math on an individual basis. We're sending Mr. Shipley to look at a program where they do this. Seven students are signed up for algebra II. We hope to individualize the program for them. We'll help them go as far as they can go, even up to calculus, if they can get there."

"What do you do for the freshmen?"

"There's general math and algebra I."

"Wouldn't it be better to offer algebra I and II, geometry, and trig [the mathematics sequence when he went to high school], rather than general math?"

"General math has a purpose. We can help out the kids who aren't ready for algebra."

"And never will be."

"I can tell you one thing they have in the sixth grade is fractions." Everyone laughs because they know his son is in sixth grade.

"Is modern math still taught?"

"A little. If Dr. Beberman only knew how many people he caused headaches. He's the father of new math. He wrote the SMSG program."

"What's that?"

"Some math, some garbage. . . ."

"Do we have enough students in physics to teach it?"

"No. Only one signed up this year."

"It used to be a big class."

"This is happening across the state."

"Why?"

"Students aren't interested in higher sciences. We put physics on such a high plane we scared the kids away."

"What do you do with the student who wants physics? Are ten to twelve needed for a class?"

"No. We'll offer it to five or six, if they're interested."

"What do you think of a math course for seniors who took general math? You know, interest rates and this sort of thing?"

"Is there a textbook for such a course?"

"Yes, pitched for seniors."

"Why couldn't that be included in a home economics course so at the same time kids can learn to sew up a pants leg or fry an egg?"

"I strongly favor having the boys introduced to home economics."

"So do I."

"Do you just look sideways if a boy signs up for home economics?"

"No. Not any more. We would have a few years ago."

"Let's take a look at the language program. I hate to say it but I see language on its way out."

"What's the benefit in it? Of necessity, is there anything there?"

"No necessity, but some pretty good jobs, like translators. It also helps you in language development."

"Will Spanish do that?"

"No, really only Latin. In some years there's been good size classes."

"How's enrollment next year?"

"Not too high."

"Today there's more people speaking English throughout the world. They want the Yankee dollah."

"We've got an ag 1 and 2 course. Ag 1 will be an intro course. Then they begin specializing—seeds, fertilizer, soils, mechanics, followed by the advanced phases of power machinery. Our introductory industrial course looks at four areas in nine weeks—drawing, woodworking, electricity, and metalwork. They have introductory welding and machine design and repair. Then advanced welding and advanced machine shop operation. Vocational auto mechanics has an A-1 rating. It's our best vocational course. I wish you could see Butch work with those boys. You'll never see a better organized course with more interested students. He never dresses down a boy."

"The boys know Butch won't put up with nonsense."

"They know he knows what he's talking about. This has something to do with it. There's also a heavy demand for the art program."

"You've seen the pictures out in the case?"

"That one picture is Keller's. This class has made a new boy out of him. His teachers wonder what's happening."

"He's not very good with book work, but teachers can see he's able to do well. Some individuals don't work well with their minds but can with their hands. I've really been interested in what Roy Smith's doing down there. Students who aren't working in other classrooms, by gosh, he keeps them busy."

"Here's how the business courses line up for next year: 24 in book-keeping; 18 in office practice; 6 in shorthand; 48 in typing; and 21 in general business. Thompson teaches six periods with no study hall."

"Looks like there's pretty good interest."

"The girls' found out that no matter what they're interested in, it doesn't hurt to get this training."

"Are the college bound guided into shorthand so they'll be able to write out everything they hear in lecture?"

"Shorthand's disappearing because of the new equipment."

"I talked to a man who said he wouldn't hire a girl without it."

"I still think it's good. Maybe you'll never use it, but it's there."

"Well, are there any more questions?" asks the president, trying to terminate a very long meeting. It is nearly midnight and the members have been bleary-eyed and yawning for some time.

"Just one more thing. Let me see if I got this straight. There's one year of math, one year of science, three years of English, one year of history, and four years of P.E. Is this what we got for requirements?"

He is answered in the affirmative. The president gets a motion to adjourn and the group breaks up.

The Board Selects a Superintendent

Superintendent Tate's death forced the school board to take action it had not taken for seventeen years—selecting a new superintendent. Only one of the current board members was on the board when Mr. Tate was selected, but to their benefit, they are secure individuals, sure of themselves and of their community. Out of this background they probe the candidates and reach a decision. The Cunningham County superintendent of schools facilitates their task by identifying candidates, collecting their credentials, and choosing the five applicants to be interviewed. This procedure saved the board considerable time and effort; it also excluded them from the screening process. Certain that the decisions of the county superintendent (he is an Auburn native from a well-known family) would truly reflect their best interests, they did not ask to see the credentials of any but the final five candidates. Their interviews and deliberations took place over three hot days late in August; they hoped the man of their choice—not a single woman was considered—would take office as early as possible in the upcoming school year.

Because of the first candidate's interest in nongraded classrooms (his interview and one other are not included here), the board sounded out all subsequent candidates on the same subject. Unhappy with several tenured "poor" teachers now on their payroll, the board sought assurance that a candidate had the will to dismiss a teacher and the knowhow to prepare a legally sound case for dismissal. The board also tried to identify a candidate's position on discipline. In addition to the questions implied by the above points, the board asked other questions which showed the candidates to be wary of teacher unions, fond of sports, church members, active in community affairs, critical of the unpatriotic orientation of college life, and hard working. These traits are favored by the school board. They are summed up in the self-description of one candidate:

> I am a Lutheran, belong to the Kiwanis, and active in Little League. I'm not a big joiner but I get around and see people. I like people. My kids aren't great brains: my girl's a good musician, my son's a normal boy—he doesn't like school. My wife's a country girl.

He did not get the job, though he surely thought he had the proper credentials.

Interview with Candidate Hagedorn[6]

Board member: What do you look for in teachers?

Hagedorn: Their grades in their teaching subject, good relations with students, if he commands respect from students as far as discipline goes, and if he has the personality that you can say, "I kind of like that person; he fits into our community."

Board member: Do you look in credentials for all As?

Hagedorn: Makes me feel kind of bad if a person has all As. This is the bookworm. We look for the all-round person, but no Ds in his teaching specialty.

Board member: How do you keep teachers away from the coaches' throats? The athletic program can get all it needs and the teachers may need microscopes. What would you give priority if you were superintendent?

Hagedorn: I'd take into consideration all the facts. Community pressure has a priority. Microscopes can't be sacrificed all the time for athletics; eventually science needs to have its share of the pie. The athletic department shouldn't be the controlling factor, though it is in many communities. What's your philosophy on P.E.? [he asks the school board].

Board member: The first concern in small schools is athletics, but teachers often go without equipment. I believe in education first. Seems like we don't hire anyone who's not a coach, anymore. We're coach poor.

Board member: Bert, I'm on your side. Education is first, then sports and music. But, then, I'm not sports-minded. I do think music and sports are stressed more.

Board member: I think we got a pretty well-balanced program.

Hagedorn: Most communities emphasize the athletic line. Even the suburbs. They used to be academic.

Board member: Can you delegate authority?

Hagedorn: Yes. Maybe even too much. My secretary has lots of work. What's your philosophy on curriculum?

Principal: The new teachers in the high school have developed new methods. We always try to keep aware of new methods and the possibility of change. We go slow, though, because this has been a traditional school for years. If the teachers can handle it, we don't mind introducing a change. Right now it's more an open philosophy.

Principal: In grade school we consider the basics—reading and math. We're traditional on the whole. Individual teachers have the freedom to try different things and see how they work. If they're comfortable with certain things, I don't believe I should push them to new things. Rather than press new math ideas, we should develop the basics first.

Interview with Candidate Rogers

Board member: How do you feel about stepping into Tate's shoes?

Rogers: There's got to be some change. For a year or two it'd be enough for me to hold my own. I'd need support from the staff.

Board member: Tate was a leader and that's what we're looking for.

Rogers: Good. You're to be commended. You want a leader and you'll support him. I understand that Mr. Tate ran the show. That's not my philosophy. If you keep a tight rein on people, they don't grow.

Principal: Tate was both superintendent and principal and he was used to the final say. We let him do things the way he wanted. I didn't begrudge him the way he ran things. If that's the way he wanted it, I went along. What do you think about tenure?

Rogers: My hope is that before they go on tenure you do something about the teacher because it's almost too late after that. Teachers are learning rebelliousness in college—that Washington was a bum and a drunk, that Columbus didn't discover America. This isn't good. I believe in my country and God. I'm a hard liner. By the way, what's your philosophy on discipline?

Principal: Whatever's needed to solve the problem—from detention to corporal punishment as the last resort.

Rogers: What do you teach besides the three R's? [he asks the educators].

Principal: Citizenship.

Rogers: Do you really work at it?

Principal: Yes, I'm an old school man.

Rogers: Good. You need to take a stand. The media are tearing things down. We need to thrill kids that the country is great.

Interview with Candidate Reynolds

Board member: What is your philosophy of education?

Reynolds: The superintendent's job is to work with, within, and be part of the community. The school should take a kid and prepare him to the best of our ability in the community for a vocation so he can earn a living and be a productive citizen or go to college. We should prepare him for recreational activities he'll take part in.

Board member: How do you feel about nongraded schools?

Reynolds: Lots of people have tried it. It's good in philosophy but is very difficult to organize and administer. We should worry about moving kids and materials where they should be and not worry about nongraded business.

Board member: What do you look for when you hire teachers?

Reynolds: A person to do the specific job for which he's hired. I look for success in college, work experience, experience with kids, and balanced preparation.

Board member: Do you require teachers to have lesson plans?

Reynolds: Yes, but I'd leave this to the principal if I were superintendent.

Board member: What do you look for in coaches?

Reynolds: The same as for teachers.

Board member: What's your philosophy of discipline?

Reynolds: Pretty rough. A teacher needs control of the classroom; that's first and a must. There should be respect for the teacher. Order is necessary for learning to take place.

Board member: Would you fight a teacher on tenure?

Reynolds: Yes. You need to organize a file on him and follow the state code. With proper planning it can be done.

Board member: As superintendent would you feel it necessary now and then to visit classrooms?

Reynolds: I ask my superintendent now to come in to rooms so I can see his view in relation to mine as principal.

Board member: How's your relation to the board?

Reynolds: Not perfect, but it's good.

Board member: But you always manage to agree with the board in the end?

Reynolds: Yes, basically.

Board member: Can you live with decisions by the board that you disagree with?

Reynolds: Yes. That's their job to make policy. If I can't live with it, it's my duty to leave.

Board member: What's your thinking on dress codes and long hair?

Reynolds: What I prefer is not what we can demand. I think you act the way you look.

Board member: How do you feel about teacher's unions?

Reynolds: I've worked with them. I think they have a place. However, I don't feel that sincere professionals require a union. We should be part of the community enough to do without them.

Board member: What's your religious affiliation?

Reynolds: Methodist.

Board member: Would you work as we do, like farmers, from dawn to dusk to get the job done?

Reynolds: I worked all but three days this past summer even though I wasn't paid.

Board member: To what extent should the school help other organizations in the community?

Reynolds: It's OK within reason. The school should be a total part of the community, but you need supervision and you need a Board policy. I'd like to ask a question here. Do you expect the superintendent to be a leading administrator who makes professional recommendations for your consideration or should the board do the leading?

Board member: We expect the superintendent to be the actual leader, but we may make recommendations. We're hoping the superintendent has 100 percent backing from the board.

Even before the third and final night of interviews was complete, the board members were fatigued. Determined but without great enthusiasm they began their deliberations. The president asked for a straw vote on the five candidates "just to feel out the board." But as one member commented wearily, his feelings shared by the others, "Wouldn't it be nice if we decided right now?" They voted and the results pointed clearly to one man: yet as soon as they finished tallying their rankings they agreed that they must discuss the candidates, that they had taken no more than a straw vote. The seven board members, the two principals, and the county superintendent were present for the final discussion.

The School Board Decides

Board member: Should we talk about Hagedorn to see why we don't want him?

Board member: Yes, let's get the feeling of the board on him. I believe we have better men. Not quality wise, though. He could handle the job and the P. R. I just don't think he's the type we're looking for.

Board member: I hate to say it, but his physical appearance is against him. You need to call a spade a spade.

Board member: He's not stable like some of the others.

Board member: I'm afraid he'd be the brunt of behind-the-back jokes.

Board member: He's carrying far too much weight. That's a strain on the heart.

Board member: He's soft. He didn't have arms and shoulders, but the longer he talked, the better he got.

Board member: He was tired. A man that size gets physically tired. We shouldn't kid ourselves. Image is very important. That size is against him.

Board member: The next one is Dargan.

Board member: I was impressed, but I feel he's too big for our town and school. His ideas are for the city, for bigger schools. We're not ready for all that.

Board member: I felt he would probably be anxious to start a lot of things I don't know if we're ready for. He's definitely for a nongraded system. He said he'd start slow, but he wanted it pretty bad. Knocking down walls scares you just a bit.

Board member: I was impressed, but then we had more fellows in. We learned more about this nongraded idea. He would be a pusher, I'm sure.

Board member: Other fellows spoke of the nongraded idea but . . .

Board member: He had too many ideas to start off with. You need to see what a school has before jumping in.

Board member: I thought he might be a little slow with discipline problems. Before our meeting in the afternoon he was a little slow answering some questions. But he thought them out. His wife always carried the lead in discussion. He is a smart man, though.

Board member: I'd like to meet all their wives.

County supt.: They're an impressive couple. His wife would be an asset to the community. I'd give him a high score, but I wouldn't want to discredit the feelings of others on the board about him. I don't feel I have enough information on any of them.

Board member: He seemed to come on awful strong. I saw dollar signs clicking around in my head when he talked. He may be too intelligent for this community; he may talk over the heads of the community.

Board member: Another thing. He was emphatic about four weeks vacation.

Board member: Salary wise he asked for the most.

Board member: Well, this Dargan, he said he wanted to come to a small community. I think he may want to bring too many ideas from the city with him. He may be more than we want.

County supt.: You need to understand the environment of someone who has been in the city. He may bring fresh ideas with him. If he could adjust to our slow pace, it's to the good.

Board member: That's something it would take a year to find out.

County supt.: You know, you'd rather have a man with lots of ideas and you guys can hold him down.

Board member: That's true.

Board member: He might have strong feelings of going ahead and if the board tries to hold him down, you know what'll happen then.

Board member: What did you like about Morgan? These next three are a hard pick.

Board member: He gave a nice impression here of, I believe, of getting along with the public and the kids. This impressed me more than anything.

Board member: To me he talked generalities.

Board member: He had a tremendous speaking voice. He's young.

Board member: His voice got very nasal at the end when he got relaxed.

Board member: He wouldn't stay.

Board member: He's on his way up.

Board member: I believe he'd be a forceful individual.

Board member: I didn't get the impression he was forceful.

Board member: If the man had a problem, he'd act individually, cope with it, solve it himself without interference. That's the approach I got.

Board member: Take this other man, Rogers. I had a feeling about him. He said, "If you hired me and I accepted it." I don't think he's too anxious for the job.

Board member: I can see why he was offered a job selling real estate. He's got the voice. He'd have your name on the line. I'm inclined to believe he'd talk himself out of most situations. Getting down to brass tacks—he spoke in generalities and he admitted he didn't know too much about new things in education. We need more specific answers.

Board member: More or less this leaves us with Reynolds.

Board member: He's the man to put on top.

County supt.: I'd hate to pick any one of the top three over the others.

Board member: Both Reynolds and Rogers said that they have no hours. They work by the job. Reynolds worked his way through college.

Board member: He was on ground floor as far as salary goes.

Board member: And he's country.

Board member: Rogers, I'm not sure he wants the job.

Board member: I like him, but I don't think we'd keep him more'n two-three years.

Board member: He'd throw things back at you. Ask your opinion on things. We had a good discussion with him.

Board member: Reynolds, he'd be pretty strict.

Board member: What's your wish? Should we eliminate some of these?

Board member: Let's vote again and vote for two so we have a choice.

They vote again and since Reynolds wins, as he did in the straw vote, they feel confident he has the necessary support. Brief attention is given to the details of contacting their chosen candidate and ascertaining when he can move to Mansfield and begin work. One member remarks ruefully, though not as a point for discussion, that perhaps the most outstanding man for the job could not apply because he lacked the credentials the state requires for the superintendency. This man happens to be a Mansfield native employed elsewhere in the state.

After rejecting candidates for adverse physical appearance and for holding city and big school ideas, the board selects Reynolds, who worked hard (like a farmer), would settle for a "reasonable" salary, and was "country," a designation that had not before been mentioned as a criterion for selecting their new superintendent. Indeed, in a year of close contact with Mansfield I had never heard this legitimating label attached to anyone or anything. Perhaps it should have been self-evident that no one could be chosen superintendent of schools in Mansfield who was not "country," the board's shorthand term for a person who would suit their rural-dominated, tradition-oriented school district.

A recapitulation of board member comments shows the values that underpinned their selection process:

"His ideas are for the city, for bigger schools. We're not ready for that." Suitable ideas are for the country, for smaller schools.

"He had too many ideas to start off with." They are not opposed to ideas but they consider themselves traditional and expect to move slowly and deliberately toward change.

"I thought he might be a little slow with discipline problems." The board and other Mansfield adults are distressed about the decline of discipline in American society and thus cannot support a candidate who would not be firm. "He'd be pretty strict," is the language used to compliment Reynolds.

"I saw dollar signs clicking around in my head when he talked." Fiscal conservatism is their ideal. They spend the school district's money as cautiously as though it were their own.

"He may be too intelligent for this community." Intelligence is not rejected, but one can be intelligent in ways that mark one as unsuitable for Mansfield—by speaking over the heads of people, for example.

"He spoke in generalities." Mansfielders are down-to-earth; they speak plainly. Accordingly, they are uneasy with someone who is vague or beats around the bush.

"They have no hours." This is high praise. Farmers believe they work without regard to hours. Anyone who works like they do works well.

From these comments a picture emerges of the type of person the board members feel would do a good job *for Mansfield*. They are emphatically not interested in some abstract "best" person; what is best must be defined for a particular setting—Mansfield school district. Compelled to select a new superintendent, the board members, then, through their interviews and discussions, articulate their values about education and educational leadership.

"I wouldn't do nothing different and I wouldn't go anywhere else," says board president George Robinson. His colleague Rex Borden observes, "I've never been anywhere but Mansfield. Small town life is something you feel; you can't always express it." And Bert Holcomb agrees, "I've seen lots of places but I never thought of staying there." These are the underlying sentiments that selected Mansfield's new superintendent. To be sure, board members did not seek out their alter ego. Nonetheless, after hearing their deliberations, who could doubt that they sought a person who would administer the school system in their spirit, true to the prevailing outlook? "He's country," they agreed and thereby reassured themselves. Neither in questions to the candidates nor in their deliberations afterward did they focus on a candidate's capacity to lead Mansfield to academic grandeur. They inquired, instead, about a candidate's fit with their orthodoxy and then eliminated one man after another until they discovered they felt most right about Reynolds.

5

Giving the Community What It Wants: Mansfield's Teachers

To learn what values guide a teacher's behavior with students, that teacher's classroom must be visited. He must be seen lecturing, discussing, counseling, testing, laughing, and anguishing with students—in short, engaged in the multitude of things teachers do in their classrooms. Nonetheless, though the classroom is a significant setting for inferring teacher priorities and value orientations, there are other means for learning about teachers. Two are presented here: the first consists of teacher biographies and the second of data from a survey questionnaire.

Mansfield High School's teachers are distinguished by their origins: they overwhelmingly come from small towns and villages. Each of the seventeen teachers has spent the greater part of his life within fifty miles of Mansfield. Ten were born and raised in or near towns of under 2,000, three in towns of 2,000 to 4,500, three in towns of 4,500 to 15,000, and one in a city of over 500,000. The one teacher with a big-city background has spent most of her life in Mansfield and is one of five teachers married to a Mansfield native. Four teachers are Mansfield natives, five graduated from Mansfield High School, and five others were born and raised outside the school district but within ten miles of it. Unlike the school board members, agriculture is not the dominant family occupation among teachers; only five of seventeen teachers had fathers who farmed. Not only do the teachers grow up in small towns, they also attend the smallest of the state universities, Central State University,[1] and after graduation they get teaching jobs in places very much like their home town. From all indications they are at home in Mansfield; when asked about their ideal place to live, 75 percent preferred towns of 4,500 or less.

School board members admit to no preference for hiring teachers with a local or area background but, just as the board did not articulate any criteria that would fix their prospective superintendent as "country," neither do they consciously select small-town teachers. One board member indicates simply that local persons happened to be available in a period when teachers were in short supply. Mr. Browne, a teacher, explains that "Mr. Tate always tries to hire home-town people. I suppose he thinks he could never go wrong then." Despite the lack of any fixed criteria, however, board member preference is clearly reflected in their choices—small-town teachers occupy Mansfield's classrooms. Given the nature of the school board I doubt that they could have hired any other type of person.

Teachers and board members share a respect for order and discipline; they also share a feeling of dismay that in recent years children have changed and not necessarily for the better. This feeling extends to parents who will not join teachers in reinforcing good behavior. Actually, poor discipline is not a serious problem at MHS. Teachers and board members are reacting more to changing standards than to actual difficulties at school. They are uncomfortable with long hair, profanity, drugs, and the apparent flaunting of cigarettes and alcohol. Although the abandonment of the district's dress code no longer is an active issue, they refer to its loss as indicative of declining standards. Even Mr. Browne, one of the youngest and newest teachers, regrets the changes in student behavior that have occurred since his own student days. Granted that changes have occurred, does it follow that the traditional relationship between school and community in Mansfield will be altered? Discussions with high school seniors (see chap. 9) provide the basis for speculating about an answer to this question. Meanwhile, teachers and board members hold a generally common view about the role of order in school and share disappointment over changing times.

They part company, however, on the attractiveness of the small community's social control, which quietly pressures male and female teachers to avoid drinking in public places, females to avoid public smoking, and both to resist subscribing to *Playboy*. The image of teacher as saint annoys Mansfield's teachers. Yet all but two of the teachers live in the school district; one of these two lives five miles away in a village one-third the size of Mansfield and the other commutes forty miles from a town of 13,000. For a few teachers, living in Mansfield may have received some impetus from the board's and Mr. Tate's clear preference for Mansfield residence. Even so, most teachers, especially the older ones, have accommodated to the constraints of their small town's face-to-face social life. They enjoy its security and the intimacy which simultaneously comforts and controls. Their physical and psychological past and present are virtually identical; in Mansfield, they remain close to their origins.[2]

Teacher Biographies

How different a teacher sounds in different settings! In those important, unguarded moments during the school day, teachers may berate students and gain relief from the tensions of teaching: "They can get the work done on the Homecoming floats or whatever. And if they don't, OK. I've had it up to here with soup suppers." "Why are Billie and Pat allowed to wander through the halls? I don't trust them, especially Pat, one of the worst possible persons to wander." They also may show their identification with the antiblack strain revealed in the reference to black literature during the board meeting devoted to curriculum. One teacher teases a secretary that a black family is moving to town:

"Really, that can't be true."
"I'd sell my house to one for $50,000."
"What difference does it make who moves in?"
"Anyway, anyone who could afford that much money would be OK."
"I couldn't do it. I'd feel too bad about my neighbors. Did you hear about those five black players who quit the Stanton High team?"
"Yes, and the team won without them."
"Don't forget, it's only one game they won."
"Wasn't it a racial thing?"
"Yes, they were angry because there wasn't a single black girl who was a candidate for the Homecoming court and last year a black girl was queen."
"You know what? Give 'em an inch and they want a mile."

The same berating teacher, back in role, addresses students in the teacher's timeless prose:

You just can't waste your time and fool around in high school. Even if you don't like a subject you should work on it because it will help you in the future. And don't play the game of taking easy subjects or ones you won't be required to work in. You're the one who will suffer.

And, after school, he despairs over a particular class:

Look at these grades. Did you ever see so many Fs and Ds? In all my years I've never had to be so tough. I tried to be fair, though, and gave them many assignments and tests. I don't know what's happened to them. God made them that way. He just made the whole group in the same way and I don't think they will ever get it.

In what follows teachers step out of their school roles for brief biographical interviews focused on the teachers' past lives and their response to teaching, youth, Mansfield High School, parents, and the like. The setting is evocative, albeit lacking the spontaneity of classroom or corridor commentary.

Mrs. Adams—Physical Education and English Teacher

"Mansfield is my home now and it always has been my home; we'll be here when we die, I'm sure. Our roots go very deep. Charlie has a sister in Michigan and I've got one living near Gary, but the rest of our family is right in this area. We've never really considered living anywhere else. My dad started as a tenant farmer and ended up as a landowner. My brother still farms the family land.

"I'd never gone to school anywhere else until college. I went to a one-room country school and had the same teacher from third to eighth grade; it was Mrs. Wood. She's still teaching over at our grade school. After high school, I went to the university to major in physical education. My minor was English.

"Since graduating in 1945 I've taught off and on in different places, but I've been right here in Mansfield since 1958. I love to teach. The trouble today is that teachers aren't committed; they don't have any enthusiasm. When I teach phys ed I run around as much as the girls do, and the day I can't keep up with them is the day that I'll quit. You know, even if I can be accused of a thousand things—and God knows that's the truth—I can't be accused of conducting a listless class.

"I feel that a teacher should be an example, someone worthy of respect. Certainly there are restrictions, to the point that where the local pub sells very good food and I wouldn't go in myself to buy fried chicken. However, in Forest or Auburn I'd go anywhere. Ten years ago I probably would have been embarrassed to be seen in any bar in the area. Not now. But in Mansfield the children would see me and that wouldn't be right. I smoked for fifteen years and never in public. No parent or kid ever saw me smoke; only my family and close friends. I've quit now.

"You know, teachers like to think they can make a difference in the lives of their students. However, teachers don't really inspire kids to great things. They may take a special interest in certain children, maybe one or two. I think that sometimes a teacher can straighten kids out. They may have more influence with a problem child than with one who has no problems. Some kids have to fight their family environment. If a kid is trying to improve himself, but his family reputation keeps getting in the way, the only solution may be for him to leave town. If you come from a poor white trash family (there are no really poor families here), it's hard to get away and change. Boys can get away better than girls because boys are accepted out of their class better than girls."

By some standards, Mansfield's poor are better off than, say, urban poor in terms of housing, social service support, and the promise of employment. But that Mansfield has few welfare cases cannot mask the existence of many comparatively poorer, isolated, nonparticipant, nonmainstream families, whose children are readily identified in school. Mrs. Adams appropriately acknowledges their situation in school; she may understate the magnitude of their problem in the community. The poor are not well off anywhere. Their plight may have an added dimension in a small rural town because they may not constitute a visible subgroup that must be taken account of, nor one that even has a distinctive neighborhood life of its own.

"There was a time when this community had a lot of farm hands, and they weren't too well off. Mechanization has just about taken all their jobs. This is certainly still a farm area, but in a sense farming is going by the wayside. Agriculture probably should be dropped from the curriculum; there's no need for the boys to take it. Farms are getting bigger and we need fewer farmers. All the farm kids we have in school now, well, we should educate them for adjustment anywhere in the world. If they're capable of living anywhere, then they'll always be able to manage in Mansfield easiest of all."

Mrs. Adams is right about farming: opportunities to farm continually decline and the child who can follow his parents into farming is indeed fortunate. The implications of this fact are clear—modify the vocational agriculture curriculum so it relates to the existing opportunities in agribusiness. Her second point—educate farm kids "for adjustment anywhere in the world"—is debatable, both as a desirable and as a possible outcome of education for Mansfield. The high proportion of MHS graduates who live in Mansfield and environs results from a socializing experience that leaves many of Mansfield's youth with neither the competency nor the will to live just anywhere. Rather, their parochial experience serves to maintain the community's stability and continuity. To be sure, if these Mansfielders are compelled to live in an urban setting, they can do so. Urban living, however, is not their choice, and it would be a strain to make the adjustment. In all probability, a high school curriculum somehow designed to have a universal outlook could not counterbalance the full experience of growing up in Mansfield, which includes the modeling of those seventeen small town-oriented teachers. Even now, other than its agriculture program, MHS does not have a rural curriculum; there is no rural science, math, or social studies. Do such subjects even exist? Instead, because of Mansfield's rural location, rural examples are offered in class by both students and teachers. The issue of adjustment that Mrs. Adams raises relates more significantly to the total impact of school and community than it ever can to the specifics of what is taught.

"I sometimes wonder if we're as strict as we should be with our students. Seems we're more lenient because we're familiar with them and their families, not as strict academically as maybe we should be. Our closeness to the kids makes us inclined to be more lenient, but I really don't know. When you look at our exceptional students, those that have gone to college, they seem to have done OK under this system.

"Kids not going on for further schooling need the basic tools to earn a living—English, math, reading. School hopefully adds to their moral concepts, to their patriotism. You know, these things seem to be more important in a small town. I think they die out harder in the Midwest. Education should prepare girls as well as boys because both will need the same basic tools. Lots of women are going back to work now after their children are grown, but they're not going to work here in town. Oh, there's a handful of jobs in the bank, a few of the stores, and as cook here at the school. Really, jobs are scarce here and that's why I say it's too limiting for the school to be geared to serve just this little community. The school should be seen as part of the bigger society. What will happen to Mansfield? Well, I don't see why more people don't move to little towns like this from out of places like Stanton. They have so many problems there, ones your own kids could run into."

Mr. Browne—Shop Teacher

"I've never really gone very far from Mansfield, at least not for very long. Of course, I went all through grade and high school here and when I was going to Sheridan College in Stanton I lived at home, commuting back and forth daily. It wasn't bad. Stanton's filled with small-town people. I'd already visited state universities, and the size of the big ones made me shudder. I wouldn't have gone to school if I'd had to go to such big places. At Sheridan the atmosphere was like being in a small town even though it's located in Stanton. I mean it, the people talked to one another.

"I'm new here, but I really have the equivalent of three years' experience. When I graduated, this job wasn't available and Mr. Tate helped me get another one. He knew me from high school and was always very encouraging. When the opening here came I quickly applied and was accepted. Mr. Tate always tries to hire home-town people. I suppose he thinks he could never go wrong then.

"Things have changed since I was a high school student. Freshman and sophomores smoke now; in my day we'd have been thrown out of school for carrying cigarettes in our shirt pockets the way kids do now. There are more liquor arrests also, though perhaps this is a result of better police methods. I think there's more of an I-don't-care feeling and much less respect for teachers. The things students have said to me would only've been whispered among students when I was in school. A lot of the things we did was with great sneakiness so we wouldn't get caught. If students went out drinking, nothing was said till two or three years later. You know, they'd say, "Remember the time we went out and got plastered." We were much more hidden about it. We didn't have any alcoholics, but there were some who might go out once every week. To be truthful, I'd rather see drink than I would the dope problem. I think people can cope in their minds with alcohol better than with dope.

"The thing that hasn't changed is football. Football was and is king. Everything was scheduled around it and I've still got to go with that old philosophy. If it wasn't for the football team, this school would've been consolidated with somebody else a long time ago. This is a football town, so the loyalty to the football team is pretty good. Our new scoreboard we got through the efforts of the town people. That's why people are against consolidation—if they consolidate they'll lose their football team and the people just can't lose their football team."

Mr. Browne goes "with that old philosophy"—it's football in Mansfield, basketball or both elsewhere. Often surfeited with soup suppers and the seemingly endless preparations for Homecoming, and dismayed by the virtual loss of a day's academic pursuits on the eve of a big game, Mansfield's teachers are nonetheless more than passive participants in their school's athletic program. Of course, they are required to take tickets (without compensation), but the chorus teacher pridefully sings the national anthem before each football game and Mrs. Adams never misses one. No sideline gossiping for her and the other women with their new Friday night hairdos; she sits in the one small span of bleachers and yells with gusto. Mr. Browne never misses a game either; he brings his little son, stands along the sideline railing and agonizes over each play. Thus do Browne and Adams show their commitment.

"To me, living in Mansfield is great. You know those slogans, Love is . . . Well, to me, love is living in a small town and being able to drive down every street in five minutes. That's what we used to do in high school. We used to cruise the streets, driving around town. We'd do that after supper two to three hours at a time.

"In a small town it's just nice. I guess you know everybody, I don't really, but I mean you recognize the face. Oh yeah, she lives down there at the north end of town. And you don't have to worry about making new friends. You're in an established place and you feel secure in your own being. You know the routines and you can help out the newcomer. Like Wednesday night, that's church night, you can ask the new people to come to church with you. You feel secure because you know what's happening. I don't know, maybe it's an inbred characteristic. I was born here and I would never feel comfortable in a large town.

"The kids talk about going away. They say, 'This town is dead. I'd like to get away quick and I'll never come back.' Some go away; not as many as you'd think. I think they want to come back. Maybe it's nostalgia, you know, trying to relive your childhood. Like teaching here. Seeing some of these things happen reminds me of what happened when

I was in school. It makes me kind of reminisce, and I feel bad in a way because I know I'll never get it back, but in a sense I'm getting to do it all over again.

"Teachers do have it pretty good here. Of course, it's easy for me. I guess there is some pressure to be different because you're a teacher. There's no verbal or written restrictions, though everyone knows that in a small town you can't go around loud-mouthing or stirring up trouble. People probably notice more what teachers say. They're expected to go to church just because they're teachers. I don't; I've backslid a little. Teachers used to be expected to help in community fund drives, etc., but they've pretty much put their foot down on that sort of thing. The only thing that could make it difficult here is if I had colored students in my class. I don't know what I'd do because I don't think I could teach them. There aren't any in town and never have been. There's a little bit of long hair and some beards. At one time this would have been looked at as some form of rebellion. Now they're pretty much overlooked and accepted. I guess the older generations are becoming more tolerant."

Browne's feelings about Mansfield epitomize the special place it is for natives. Recognition, old friends, security—in a word, attachment. Momentarily, he toys with the notion that it is nostalgia that impels a person to remain in or return to Mansfield. He concludes that only the presence of "colored students in my class" would make it difficult to work at MHS. Browne and other Mansfield adult natives can mix the joys of nostalgic past with pleasurable present. It is this enjoyment that Browne reinforces for the youth in his class; the model of the moving American does not get equal time.

"As for the kids and their education, I guess they should be prepared for outside Mansfield, for the faster pace, for more independence. The school should provide movies and social studies about city life because there's a difference. School is just a step along the way; it gets kids ready for the next step, though preparation won't do much good if they aren't ready."

Browne and Adams, native Mansfielders, MHS alumni, are stalwarts in the organization of community adults who invest hours each year in arranging the Homecoming celebration. Both are sensitive to the school as an agent to prepare students for life beyond Mansfield, while both rhapsodize about the community of their birth and choice. Listening to Browne trace his life history, I wonder if he had a choice. In any event, junior staff member Browne joins his senior colleague in a job that is more than just a job. Like the board members, they bring a commitment to their work that derives from their rootedness in Mansfield. This commitment does not insure that they are more artful teachers than their nonnative associates; it does incline them to a greater concern and dedication to student and school. They may feel like the Mansfield person who said about his neighbors: "I can't explain it, but somehow you feel different about a person when you know the name of his grandmother's pet canary."

Fortunately for the students and the school, one need not be a native to be deeply committed. Listen to Shipley and Norwood, both Mansfield move-ins, Shipley, near to retirement and Norwood on her first job and about to begin a family.

Mr. Shipley—Mathematics Teacher

"I know that my mom's father was a farmer, but I can hardly remember my other grandfather. By the time I got to know him, he was just an old man, a Civil War veteran who'd fought for the Confederates since he was living in North Carolina at the time. Somewhere along the line he moved north, because my father was born here.

"We lived in the same small town all the time I was in grade school and high school. Then I went away to Central State University when it had under seven hundred students and most classes were held in Old Main. By 1928 I'd finished the two years I needed for a teaching diploma. In fact, I never got a bachelor's degree until 1953 and then nine years later, thanks to Sputnik and the money it provided for training math teachers, I got a master's degree.

"I came to Mansfield for the first time in 1946 and stayed until 1951. My starting salary was $200 per month, which wasn't at all bad for those days. I returned in 1956 and was glad to be back. I like the community and I love teaching. Having grown up in a place about the same size, I feel right at home here. I can't imagine living anywhere else. This is my home.

"Teachers aren't like other people in town. They're supposed to be better than anyone else, to be saints, and not fight with their wife or beat the kids. Also, we're pressured to live here. This doesn't bother me, though I know it does some of the younger teachers. The only thing my wife has found cheaper to buy in town is hamburger. You'd be a fool to shop here if you could go twenty minutes away and get better prices for the same quality.

"When you come to think about it, Mansfield's schools are just about what the people want; they do what they are expected to do. There aren't enough people in the community interested enough to have some of the cultural activities some of us think it could. Parents send their kids to school to graduate; what they learn is besides the point. Few kids who go to college ever come back. There are few educated people besides teachers and ministers and some farmers. Not too much you can do about it.

Shipley does not resonate with Mansfield as do Browne and Adams. Convinced resident, he nevertheless betrays that last full measure of devotion Editor Matthews would exact from all Mansfielders (especially teachers, since they feed at the "public crib")—shopping in local stores. Few are so dedicated. Browne and Adams know well this ethic; it is recited regularly. In this instance, the pocketbook transcends community loyalty.

With a touch of noblesse oblige Shipley bestows his label of success on the local school system: "The schools are just about what the people want." He implies that he and his colleagues, able to provide a more substantial measure of success, provide what the traffic will bear. He may be right.

"The language I hear in the halls and even in some classes is disgusting. We used to read in the newspapers about the problems in the ghettos, and we thought those kinds of things could never happen here. Then we read about the same kinds of things happening in cities that were closer to us, like Stanton. And all of a sudden we found our own students acting the same way. We thought it would never get here, but all you have to do is step out in the hall during the change of classes to realize that it is. We teachers must accept the challenge and instill respect; we have to counter the permissive atmosphere that the students find everywhere else and get back to the basic truths."

Thirty-five years make a difference. Browne and Shipley agree that student behavior has changed. The younger Browne, a car nut himself, finds common ground with today's bolder adolescents. Shipley sees students parading under a banner of permissiveness.

Mrs. Norwood—Social Studies and English Teacher

"My first school was a two-room country school near Lowell. There was lots of individual attention and, on the average, kids from our school did very well when we went to junior high in town. The transition wasn't too hard, only in town I wasn't the smartest anymore. I liked going to school, and when I went to the university I majored in history, I guess, because my favorite teacher taught history. I like teaching and will always come back to it whatever else I do. Somewhere I heard or read that 89 percent of all teachers don't enjoy teaching; I'm one of the 11 percent.

"I guess I'd say we're settled now. At first I thought Mansfield was just another little town and we'd be here temporarily. After fixing the house up we couldn't think of moving, we put so much work into it. Even the school system seems better to me. I thought I wouldn't want to raise my kids in this school. Now I think the school's OK and I'm getting more and more rooted, though I'm not sure I want to die here.

And it's convenient because we're close to my parents and close to Stanton. We do everything there—shop, go to the movies. If you drive through Mansfield as a stranger you might think you're seeing a dumpy little town; that's not the real picture. There's a lot of friendliness and kindness here."

After several years of residence in Mansfield, Mrs. Norwood occupies the position of "local person." She is past the newcomer stage and, of course, she can never be a native. Like Mr. Shipley, she can say about Mansfield, "This is my home." Join, participate, don't push, don't take over, don't criticize—this is advice for newcomers desirous of acceptance. Mrs. Norwood implicitly grasps these commandments. Her own background and good sense prepared her for an easy transition to becoming local. It is an achieved status. Yet, as she clarifies in her following comments, she is comfortable with the prospect of a consolidated school and troubled by some prevailing community norms. Her Mansfield love song contains a verse endorsing change; she provides counterpoint to the loyalists who seem bent almost exclusively on stability.

"In general, I think that the attitude in Mansfield toward teachers is not good. Most teachers are considered outsiders; we're not like those who've lived here all their lives. People are leery of us; the feeling borders on antiteacher. Even if you join the Women's Club it doesn't change their attitude. Teachers are seen as teachers, not as persons. In a small town, teachers aren't just outsiders, they're outsiders without relatives who've come just because of a job.

"This whole matter of what the school should offer its students might well be solved for us if we go to a county high school. There's hardly enough students in Spanish and Latin classes, for example, to justify the cost. This school just can't offer to students all that it should. Some people would complain about losing their football team if we consolidated; I wouldn't be sorry to see such a move. It's not the end of the world, you know. People say we'd lose that close relationship with students. Well, I found my teachers in high school and at college still cared for me. Right now some of the kids' interest areas are never even touched and if they don't go on to college then that's it."

Mrs. Hartline—Foreign Language Teacher

"French and Latin were my major subjects at the university, though I'm teaching Spanish right now. I taught a bit before I was married, then stopped to raise my children. I've been teaching foreign languages here since 1956, except for one year when I taught in Germany. In fact, other than when I travel I've never lived very far from here. I've always liked the idea of a small town—the friendliness, people not being right up close to you, yet the advantages of a city are within a short drive. There's a feeling of security here.

"I have different ideas than a lot of local people, so I just keep my mouth shut. The talk in the teacher's room about orientals and negroes—I don't have those same opinions. When I went away to college, my ideas changed a lot. I was surprised when I first came here that there weren't even facilities for smoking. It's because Mr. Tate doesn't like it. Teachers wearing pants was a big thing, too. We didn't wear them at all last year because Mr. Tate didn't care for them. But this year we decided to start and at first everyone wore them on the same day—Tuesday."

Mr. Tate's impact as standard bearer emerges clearly here—one smokes or dresses in keeping with his preferences. He would be distressed by Mrs. Hartline's heresy; she does not display it at school. "I have different ideas than a lot of local people," she says. The aberrant Hartline is absent from her interactions with students and teachers. She knows the boundaries and while on the job stays within them.

"I think this is a top-notch school for this community. Maybe we could do more than we do; however, I'm not sure I really think so."

Mr. Cahill—Physical Education Teacher

"When I left for college my mother told me, 'Don't be ashamed of your father.' He was a farmer in Oakfield and he only finished high school; my mom was a housewife and she'd gone to college for a year. I was just a green kid when I started at the university in 1942; I studied agriculture for two years until I went into the navy. This was a real change. I became a sonar man on a subchaser in the Pacific. Boy, when I looked at a map did I feel far away from home. Back then kids had a different philosophy. They thought something was wrong with you if you didn't go; now they think you're queer if you join the service.

"We've lived in Mansfield ever since we've been married. I just couldn't enjoy myself teaching in a city. It's those discipline problems. The kids here won't pull a knife on you. I've got a cousin teaching in a suburb and she says they've taken guns away from kids. We thought of living in Stanton but couldn't take the closeness of all the people and all the noise and traffic; so we moved here. I'm really a small-town person. I've had opportunities to travel or take a job in a bigger school, but I like this way of life. I've been to cities in the East and to Chicago, Saint Louis, and Indianapolis. I think country people are friendlier, but in the city you're like a number. People there put so much store in what kinds of clothes you wear, your house, and whether you go to college. Not what you do with it. Whenever we have visitors from Stanton, they always run around locking the door; we have to keep things locked so they'll feel at home. Here there's no security problem.

"Years ago teachers were looked up to as smarter than others. Now they're just people doing a job like a factory worker or a storekeeper or a housewife. Sure, teachers have pressures you wouldn't find in a larger town, like against drinking and smoking. I don't buy *Playboy* here or even subscribe to it; I get it out of town. They like you to spend your money here and go to church, but there's no real pressure. And if you're single you better not bring a boyfriend or girlfriend to your house. I guess you have a tendency to think people watch your actions, even including like what time you come home. I think the superintendent and the board expect us to attend school social events. I'd probably go anyways."

No one is more explicit than Mr. Cahill about the implicit structures that govern the life of teachers and other residents in a small community. No teacher who in Mansfield's terms belongs there would need to be told about these constraints, these boundaries of appropriate behavior. The anti-city liturgy—you're a number, you need to lock your doors, and so on—trips readily off the tongues of Cahill and compatriots; it bolsters the pluses they attribute to their little mecca. How aptly he conveys the meaning of a small community's face-to-face relationships: "I guess you have a tendency to think people watch your actions." Cahill, in the end, voluntarily submits to this control; to do otherwise would indicate his unsuitability for Mansfield.

"It seems to me parents are behind the school; almost all of them will support what we do here. If a student is in trouble with his courses, his parents will usually agree with what we suggest. Of course, getting the child to agree isn't quite so easy. Parents almost never call on the phone. Most of them I talk to see me outside school, uptown, or at a football game. Often there's a fairly close relationship between students, parents, and teacher, so I'm not always so objective about kids and grades. There have been times we passed kids for other than the right reasons. Children, you know, more or less adjust to their environment.

"All things considered, the school's doing a pretty good job in giving the community what it wants. As far as costs are concerned, the school is run very conservatively. Most people are concerned with a little music and the band gives them that; they're concerned with sports and the football team gives them that. In fact, I think the high school does a better than average job socializing the students for this community. For the future, I can see that the high school will be consolidated into a county network. I hope this doesn't happen even though it would mean better vocational training and a greater variety of subjects offered. Even sports would benefit."

Browne, Shipley, Hartline, and the rest of Mansfield High School's teachers do not speak eloquently about education. They are not accustomed to viewing education in broad, general terms. Ask them to discuss a particular lesson or a unit—Julius Caesar or the Civil War—and they will be explicit about their goals. But nothing in their training equips them to expound on the relationship between schooling and different aspects of society—national and local, urban and rural. Aware, though, that MHS graduates must work outside Mansfield and often will live in larger towns, teachers generally frame goals that support a student's capacity to live anywhere, to adjust to the larger world, to "make it" outside of Mansfield. That these are realistic preferences cannot be doubted. Yet they are curious ones in light of all that happens in the school to insure it remains a fitting agency for life in the community.

Some teachers are modest about what the school can accomplish, hoping they can reach at least one or two students in a serious way; none are basically critical about their own and their colleagues' ability to do something of value. Like Mansfield parents, teachers view the school favorably; one teacher admits that now after teaching at MHS, she can even see her own child attending the local schools, and another observes that the school gives the community what it wants and does a better than average job in the process.

In the absence of a formal survey that would ascertain what residents want their school to accomplish and whether they believe they get what they want, I must depend on several sources of information which indicate only indirectly whether community adults are satisfied with schooling in Mansfield. Data from 239 adults, representing perhaps one-third of the families in the school district, show 69 percent agree that one of the things they like best about Mansfield is its school system (7 percent disagreed, and 23 percent neither agreed or disagreed). This fairly high figure,[3] combined with the minimal complaints presented at school board meetings and to administrators, the dearth of adult responses to the superintendent's invitation to react to the new "Goals for Tomorrow" sent to every boxholder in the school district, and the disbanding of the PTA, suggests that the community is essentially satisfied with its school. These facts do not indicate adult apathy so much as a lack of issues to arouse them. They clearly are interested in education. In 1969, they voted to build a new grade school; in 1975, they approved an increase in their tax levy at a time when such successes were rare events; and throughout each year they demonstrate their affection for the high school by attending its many activities. Thus when a teacher observes that the school gives the community what it wants, her judgment appears to be verified.

Mr. Cahill refers to a teacher's close relationship with students and parents, the outcome of relative teacher and community stability within the intimacy of a small rural area. "Children more or less adjust to their environment," says Cahill, and the environment they adjust to is one in which teachers admit to being less than objective because of their close relationships with Mansfielders. They are also "more lenient because we're familiar with them [students] and their families," that is, "not as strict academically as maybe we should be." Mr. Shipley's observation that "schools do what they are expected to do," and Mr. Cahill's that "the high school does a better than average job socializing the students for this community," are warranted. While adults might be unhappy with a particular teacher, a poor football season, or a specific incident, they are basically content with what they perceive the school to be doing to its youth—with the shape, though not necessarily with every detail, of their children's education.

Perhaps part of teacher acceptance of Mansfield's academic status quo, of their rationalization for providing a comparatively limited academic experience, results from their assessment of what the community will tolerate, their making peace with their own present level of occupational success, and their comfort with a system similar to one they were educated in. But for some teachers (recall Mr. Browne's observations on consolidation), the school, because it is linked to a highly valued community, may be not only accepted but inviolable. For them, if the school is changed, the community is changed.

The teachers' comfort with the education they provide may also be attributed to their own upbringing in communities much like Mansfield and their contentment with small-town life. The reasons for their contentment strikingly resemble those offered by Mansfield's nonteaching adults and students—the security, lack of anonymity, open doors, friendliness, and uncrowded feeling of life in a slower-paced atmosphere. "We'll be here when we die, I'm sure," says Mrs. Adams, a native Mansfielder, and "I can't imagine living anywhere else," concludes Mr. Shipley, an adopted Mansfielder.

Given the teachers' small-town orientation, they understandably reject school consolidation. They are not so attached to academic opportunity as to override their commitment to a small school. Clearly, academic good is a highly contextual, relative concept. Mrs. Norwood alone disagrees with her colleagues, though her more cosmopolitan perspective is not so controlling that she is unhappy with Mansfield ("I'm getting more and more rooted, though I'm not sure I want to die here."). She sees limitations in the local school system which would be overcome by the organization of a countywide school. But her argument that "this school just can't offer to students all that it should. . . . Right now some of the kids' interest areas are never even touched" would not persuade the consolidation antagonists, who would view each gain from a larger school system as more than offset by the likely losses which teacher and board member readily detail.

Teacher Values: Results from the Questionnaire

The questionnaire referred to in chapter 2, from which data were used to establish the existence of a sense of community among Mansfield adults, was also administered to all teachers and administrators in the school district. Twenty of the thirty-two educators in the entire school system and two of three administrators responded. Their answers indicate that educators and community adults mostly share a common set of values. This congruence suggests the effectiveness of the process of teacher selection and teacher self-selection in creating a faculty able to reinforce the community's out-of-school socialization impact.

Educators' perceptions of the nature of Mansfield generally square with those held by Mansfield adults on almost every item (see table 25 compared with table 10). Though the strength of their agreement regarding a positive picture of Mansfield is less than that of the other adult residents, they are even more positive on the critical item of being able to count on Mansfield people in time of need, as well as on their view of schools and the safety of life in Mansfield. Educators are less convinced about the superiority of small towns as places where people can best live the lives they prefer, about how good it is that everyone knows you in Mansfield, and that Mansfielders are friendlier than people in larger places. In general, on this set of items they chose the neither-agree-nor-disagree category less than the community adults, though they were about equally indeterminate on items 4 and 11, which deal with that double-edged issue of privacy.

On the contemporary issues scale (see table 26), educators reveal a conservative orientation, as do nonteaching Mansfield adults, with one notable exception: they favor the legalization of abortion. This belief, however, is *not* reflected in a more positive view of women's liberation. And teachers see communism as a less major issue. Otherwise, the two groups share a common outlook on patriotism, the American way of life, belief in God, and the like. The classroom performance of teachers (see chap. 6) supports this outlook.

Notwithstanding the teachers' preference for small-town life, they present a mixed picture so far as their identification with Mansfield is concerned (see table 27). In general, they identify with Mansfield to a lesser degree than do other Mansfield adults (see table 12); this is not surprising. Teachers do not like to hear somebody insult Mansfield; they would be bothered if the village's name was changed; they believe in community loyalty, though less than other Mansfield adults, and like them they could leave Mansfield, though nearly one-third would prefer to stay even if given the chance to move. Also, teachers, even more than other Mansfield adults, reflecting probably their sensitivity to the relationship between community opinion and their occupational well-being, believe that what people in Mansfield think of them is important. Thus what betokens a sense of community for nonteaching Mansfield adults betokens this as well as some other sentiment for the teachers. On the question most indicative of Mansfield identity—"I probably feel more at home in Mansfield than I ever could someplace outside of Mansfield community"—teachers, compared to nonteacher adults, are twice as ambivalent (36.3 to 18.8 percent) and much less in agreement (22.7 to 52.7 percent).

The point, of course, is not to verify an identity of perceptions and value orientations between Mansfield High School's support community and its educators. Such a view does not fit the facts. Moreover, a detailed, probing comparison would reveal differences other than those suggested by the brief comments made above; it would probably indicate, for instance, that educators' views are more sophisticated, reflecting their generally greater education and disposition to be well-informed, than those of the support community. Nonetheless, except on the identification with Mansfield scale, the substantial congruence of views between the two groups underscores the harmony that is one signal attribute of the school-community relationship in Mansfield. On the face of things, the school board had good reason to accept Superintendent Tate's choice of teachers. Whether or not this congruence is evident where it counts most—in the classroom—remains to be explored.

6

God and Country:
The Classroom Experience

A Sampling of Classrooms

The measure of a school, though not the only one, is in the classroom. More than this, the measure of many communities is in the classrooms of their schools, and this is certainly true of Mansfield. Notwithstanding uniformities resulting from the influence of textbooks and common teacher-training programs, and variations resulting from teachers' idiosyncracies, what happens in classrooms is generally established by what is acceptable to the school's support community; these people set forth the constants and the degrees of freedom. In Mansfield, this process is passive, haphazard, and successful.

Transcripts of five classes are presented below—U.S. history, taken by all students either in the eleventh or twelfth grade; tenth-grade English; biology, a required, typically ninth-grade course; chorus, a popular option open to all students; and current events, a social studies option chosen mostly by twelfth-graders.[1] The class transcripts are often followed by student reactions to the class. These reactions provide a useful picture of the impact of a particular teacher or lesson. Several teacher-made tests, which aptly confirm teachers' priorities, are included in appendix B.

U.S. History

As though to reconfirm daily the existence of the world beyond Mansfield and Cunningham County, Mrs. Norwood begins each U.S. history class with a brief review of current events. She accepts tales of local incidents as current events ("Last night Sally Peters missed the bad curve north of town and ran off the road—her car rolled over once and she only skinned her knee"), but prefers more serious national or international items. The review format encourages a televisionlike recitation of the facts, though there is some analysis. As the reporting of news items slows down, Mrs. Norwood moves the class to the day's assignment, which in the present example is a dialogue between two girls who take the role of slaves; one belongs to a harsh master and the other to a kindly master. The ensuing discussion provides an opportunity for several boys to express their strong antagonism toward blacks, possibly voiced more strongly than they feel in order to irritate the girls who disagree with them.

Mansfield's children grow up with opinions of blacks shaped by the same influences as their parents—a consciousness of the black American's increasing presence in American society, their growing prominence in athletics, affirmative action in schools and industry, and fear of blacks. These feelings and perceptions surface in Mrs. Norwood's class. The students' negative views of blacks are also closely linked to their negative views of persons on welfare. In light of the mixture of error and opinion in their discussion, it is uncertain that they will grow up any less antiblack than their parents. Faced by their strongly expressed, stereotypic thinking, Mrs. Norwood does not so much set straight her students' views as sound a note of moderation, acclaiming a middle-of-the-road ideal that recognizes discrimination on both sides.

Given Mansfield's antipathy toward black Americans, it is surprising that the high school offers a course on black lit. It is a nine-week long minicourse (recall the school board discussion), one of a series offered to juniors and seniors under the heading of English, taught by a young, fairly new, popular teacher. She is an Auburn native married to a third-generation Mansfield native. Were she an outsider with indeterminate personal credentials, perhaps she would not have been allowed to teach the course. So far, she reports, no parents have called to protest the course in general or any part of it. The course introduces black literature, poetry, and music, and students prepare a research paper on some aspect of black American life. One black lit class surveyed feelings toward blacks. The results, though based on a small convenience sample, reasonably approximate the community's racial feelings as expressed in the general survey (see chap. 2). The results of one question—"Do you feel Mansfield is at a gain or loss for not having Negroes in town?"—are shown in table 28. While a negative view dominates—of sixty-seven persons, forty-four said it was a gain, eighteen a loss, and five neither loss nor gain—proportionately more high school students and teachers, compared to farmers, businessmen, and factory workers, feel that Mansfield is the loser for not having Negroes in their community.

U.S. History tests, like the one prepared for the biology class (see appendix B), require students to respond with small packages of facts —list five provisions, name two stipulations, and state three principles. Yet, through her assignments and classroom work, Mrs. Norwood regularly provides the occasion for more expansive intellectual experiences to which a grade is not so neatly attached. Contemporary historical interest in Mansfield centers on genealogy and local history; neither topic

gets significant attention in school. Mrs. Norwood, however, did begin
the year's study of U.S. history with an assignment requiring students
to report on the national origins of their families.

A U.S. History Lesson

Teacher: OK, current events. Glenn?
Student: Pablo Casals, the well-known cellist, died at ninety-six.
Teacher: OK. Shush! Jim?
Student: The war over in the Middle East is still going on.
Teacher: Is it going on in the same way? Frank?
Student: Egypt asked for Syria to intervene. They want a security meeting or a quick meeting of the U.N. Security Council.
Teacher: OK, for what reason? Do you know? Anyone know why Egypt has called a meeting of the Security Council of the U.N.? What has the Security Council just initiated?
Student: A cease-fire.
Teacher: A cease-fire. So what's Egypt claiming?
Student: Israel violated . . .
Teacher: Israel violated the cease-fire. And what's Israel claiming?
Student: Egypt violated the cease-fire.
Teacher: That Egypt violated the cease-fire. But Egypt has put in a request to get the Security Council to work on it. Both countries have claimed . . . I forget how many violations of the cease-fire.
Student: Yeah, but it's slowed down a lot.
Teacher: Yeah, at least it's a violation of a cease-fire instead of a war. You know, it's a different category, I think. OK, any others? Jill?
Student: Something about the president firing the special investigator. I'm not sure I understand it all.
Teacher: What is it that a lot of them are saying? As long as President Nixon appoints the special investigator, he can fire the special investigator. What are they recommending that should be done? Joe, do you know? Nick?
Student: The investigator ought to be under the control of Congress.
Teacher: Yeah, that either Congress or the court should now get together and appoint a special investigator. So far neither of these could be done. OK, now, let's go on with the lesson. Amy, I think you were going to go first.

Mrs. Norwood quickly redirects the class from discussing a Watergate issue, the so-called Saturday night massacre, to listening to the two girls who have prepared a dialogue for today's lesson. Each girl has notes in hand, but they are used infrequently.

Delia: For our discussion today you're going to have to put yourself back to January 5, 1862. This was four days after Abe Lincoln had freed the slaves with the Emancipation Proclamation. We're going to

be thirty-year-old slaves, one from the North and one from the South.
And we want you to pay attention because at the end we're going to
have kind of a discussion whether you believe like the North, what I
believe, or if you believe the Southern side.

Harriet: OK, first for our background. Now don't laugh at us [she adds
as she hears snickers from the back of the room].

Teacher: OK, let's get to work.

Harriet: My name is Harriet Griswald and I'm thirty years old and I've
been a slave ever since I was twelve years old. I was raised in northern Virginia right on the other side of Richmond and she was raised
on the Southern side. And we worked out there and I was sold and
part of my family went with me. My slave master, we called him
Master James, he was real strict with us and everything.

Delia: Well, my name is Delia and I'm a thirty-year-old slave from
Richmond. I had a very nice master and his name was Jeremy. He
was a very sweet guy and our mistress was very nice and everything.
I can pick so many pounds of cotton a day. You had to know this
stuff when you went to a slave auction and you had to be able to tell
your background and everything and that's about all of the background that I know.

Harriet: I squint a lot because I have a vision impairment and my masters didn't like any of us that much. Like if we were sick or something we still had to go out into the field. He didn't want to do anything for our well-being like getting glasses or anything that could
help us see better or help us work better.

Delia: Oh, Jeremy was very nice to us. You know, it was good to be
sick 'cause our master didn't make us do anything. And like with
older people, when they would get sick or anything, they wouldn't
have to go out in the fields. Heck no. He'd send his wife down, we
called her Miss, and she'd take care of us and feed us, give us all the
hot food they had, you know. She'd come down everyday and she'd
pray for you or tell you stories to keep your morale up.

Harriet: Maybe your master came down, but our master wouldn't even
be seen in the kind of houses we lived in. We cooked outside and
when it rained, well, we had leaks. And every morning when we
woke up we could see that beautiful white house up there with trees
and bushes and flowers and everything around it. That was our biggest envy. Why couldn't we live in a place like that, instead of the
shack that we lived in? The only person that would come out to us
was the overseer. He'd come with his little whip and he could make
it so we'd work. We was up at sunrise and went back at sunset. If one
of us would die or get sick, master would just make sure he'd get
another one to replace us.

The students, as Harriet and Delia, continue their characterization of
contrasting slave lives: they refer to Father Abraham, Union soldiers,

General Sherman burning Atlanta, and the Emancipation Proclamation. Finishing, Harriet makes transitional remarks to get the class to evaluate the two views. "And now we'd like to ask you guys to comment." Mrs. Norwood helps her. "Which do you think gave the most factual account, Harriet or Delia?" For a short time, the class does assess their cases. Then the murmuring undercurrent erupts—"They still ought to do what I said and ship them all back to Africa"—and current events takes over again.

Teacher: OK, anything else?
Student: Remember, the whites are getting segregated now.
Student: Well, it's true. Down in the South now in some places Negroes are being hired and whites are better qualified. In Florida there's a guy who's got a court case on. He says he's discriminated because he's white.
Teacher: And what's your opinion on that?
Student: Well, that just shows that government's giving the black man too much.
Student: That's right, because they've got that law that you have to have so many coloreds and so many whites and so many this and so many that working at a lot of factories. So when they passed that law they had to fire a bunch of whites just to get the colored in.[2]
Teacher: Are you sure they fired 'em?
Student: Yeah, they fired 'em, they laid 'em off, that's just the same as firing.
Teacher: OK, I do know at Vulcan's in Stanton they have this because they have government contracts, but there they aren't supposed to be fired. Everytime a position comes open, then they have to hire, you know, a certain percentage of minorities in the office. It's not just discrimination against blacks, but it's discrimination anytime you don't let a woman on the football team.
Student: Doesn't bother me. If they're good enough, why don't they get to play?
Student: Yeah.
Student: Yeah, if they're going to play football they have to take a shower, too. [Everyone laughs.]
Teacher: I don't think those fellows in the back are listening to these other people talking.
Student: We're mad.
Teacher: If you want to say something, fine, but you listen to what other people are saying, too.
Student: She said the blacks have been segregated a long time and nobody cared then.
Student: No, I didn't say that.
Student: Well, that's approximately what you said.

Student: I said the whites haven't been discriminated against half as long as the blacks have and they were treated even worse than we are.

Student: Them poor things.

Student: OK, let's say it comes down to a war. Which side are you going to be on, the whites or the blacks? You're not going to go with somebody that's a different race; you go with your own creed.

Student: It depends on what you're fighting about. Like you wouldn't really have to choose sides; I think people can feel both ways. There were people in the Civil War that felt both ways.

Teacher: OK, this idea of the pendulum swinging back and forth that we were talking about yesterday at the end of the hour. Think about this just a little bit. No matter what we're talking about, it could be anything, campus riots or whatever, usually it's like a pendulum. Things are usually far off to one end, then they swing far off to the other end, before they eventually get back to the middle. Now I'm not saying that everything is exactly fair that happens to blacks today, but think about that pendulum. One time it was way over there—unfair; today maybe it's over here—being a little bit unfair the other way. Maybe tomorrow it will be back here—in the middle.

Student: I doubt it.

Teacher: And that's what we're really trying to get at. It's not over here or not over there that we want. It's like, you know, in the middle that we're wanting to get at. It may take a long, long time, but eventually if it gets back to the middle, that's what we want.

After-Class Student Discussion

After listening to such a vituperative exchange, one may question whether the boys who taunted the girls with "ship them all back to Africa" were really playing it straight. According to the following student reaction, some were and some were not.

"It's been like that the whole year. Any assignment or anything like that, we did it from the North's view or the South's view."

"Well, today we were giving our true point of view, I think."

"Yeah, everybody got kind of rash, though."

"We weren't role playing."

"Oh, no."

"Jimmy was and I was getting mad at him, 'cause his point was going against mine."

"I think we ought to give 'em a fair chance. Jimmy kept saying, 'No, no! We shouldn't give them the money; we give them too many breaks,' and stuff like that."

"Brian, he always says, 'Ship 'em back.' "

"That wouldn't solve anything. They wouldn't go back now; maybe then they would have. It would just cause more problems; it would just cause a bigger revolt. They'd just want to rebel more."

"I'm afraid of that."

"Yeah."

"Like the riots and stuff becoming like another civil war except it would be whites against the blacks. Like you've got to consider in the cities they have rival gangs, the Puerto Ricans against the Negroes against the Italians. Pretty soon it will spread on out; it's not going to be held to the city. It could get out across the country."

"My grandmother's afraid of 'em 'cause they're always in those riots and things and you always hear more about the black people in fights. And she's just always afraid of 'em and she doesn't like 'em. But my mom does; she just treats 'em fair."

"A lot of times older people will just kind of close out what they hear bad about the white people."

"And the black news centers in on their mind and that's what stays."

Student reactions after class indicate they took seriously their discussion in Mrs. Norwood's class. Some were angry at the racist remarks of their peers. Others revealed the fear which may underpin the feelings of many—that blacks will extend their rioting beyond the cities. "It could get out across the country," one girl said. This fear was not expressed in class; perhaps it is a subject not easily explored in the circumstances of a school setting. In any case, it is thus that teachers unwittingly reinforce an ideological status quo.

Sophomore English

Far beyond anything he might have imagined, Shakespeare is honored in American high schools. *Julius Caesar* appropriate for fifteen-year-old sophomores? Of course, that is the way of things, with *Hamlet* and *Romeo and Juliet* designated for other grades. And in the tenth grade at Mansfield High School Mrs. Adams has taught *Julius Caesar* in her English class for many years. One mid-October day she introduces the play. She looks for and finds parallels between her subject and the world beyond the school, hoping to clarify for students that the implications of past events can illuminate contemporary life. "So you see," she says, "he [Julius Caesar] has touched our lives. Don't think he hasn't." Leaving nothing to chance, she energetically swings from the play to the present and back again to the play. One need not guess what the connection is or what values move Mrs. Adams.

Mrs. Adams and the sophomore class study *Julius Caesar* for three weeks. They explore its facts in great detail, embellished by the teacher's flair and by her love of the play, as well as her tangential excursions. She reflects, for example, on the possible marriage between Cleopatra and Cleopatra's brother, refusing to condemn them even though "we can't today in our Christianity, understand how these people could do this." As she begins to expand her thoughts on Christianity she interrupts herself: "Well, let's go on . . . You people can get me off the subject." On another occasion she uses the dilemma of Brutus, who must choose between friend or country, Caesar or Rome, to comment on American patriotism, pained by the recent past, when to be patriotic was to be dismissed as a square. Toward the end of the unit on *Julius Caesar*, Mrs. Adams invites the class to see a connection between Brutus's deed and Watergate. "Boy," she remarks, "we're having social studies now . . . ," but when she prepares her tests there is no doubt she is teaching English (see appendix B); clearly, Mrs. Adams expects her students to master the play's details.

Sophomore English Lessons

October 16

Teacher: There are many reasons why we study *Julius Caesar* in American school systems. It has a parallelism to our government, to our desire to show the importance of individual freedom, and to show what may happen if internal jealousies and suspicions and hate become too well-planned. Suppose we have an internal jealousy in the Republican party right here in this state or a multitude of people that are not getting from the state government those services they think they should get. What do you think will happen to our governor if either of these things happen here? [Long pause.] Do you think he would dare run for reelection, Kurt? Do you think he would have any hope of aspiring to a higher office? No, if you are politically ambitious you have to learn to please certain people. Well, Julius Caesar was that kind of man. And then you say he has an affair with Cleopatra. All right, Cleopatra was queen of Egypt, but she really beat him at his own game. OK, anything else about Julius Caesar? We've already talked about him being politically ambitious.
Student: He introduced the calendar.
Teacher: Debbie?
Student: He adopted currency reform.
Teacher: Yes, what would you say that meant?
Student: Some kind of money.
Student: Wasn't he kind of short or something?
Teacher: Very short in stature. He was less than five-five, a stocky man, not a fine-featured man. A man that possessed a profile that displayed a Roman nose.
Student: Is he the first Caesarian section?
Teacher: Yes.
Student: Is that how he got his name?

Teacher: No, that's not how he got his name, that's how the name came to be called the Caesarian section. So you see, he has touched our lives; don't think he hasn't. So why shouldn't we read about him? We will find more and more ways he has touched our lives.

October 19

Student: There's something I want to ask. How come if Caesar . . .
Teacher: Not "how come."
Student: Why?
Teacher: Why.
Student: Why, OK, if Caesar killed this girl's dad and two brothers, why would she marry him?
Teacher: I don't know. I really don't.
Student: That worries me.
Teacher: We will find a very touching scene in this play when Portia openly pleaded with her husband Brutus to tell her what is wrong. What is mentally disturbing you? Can't you share your problems with me, your wife? Now what is that telling you about the husband-wife relationship?
Student: The lady is usually kept out of things.
Student: She [the woman who was to marry Caesar] didn't want to marry, but she had to marry him anyway. Is that the way it was?
Teacher: If it was going to be a politically advantageous state for the family, yes. All right, I think I told you, this is clear off the subject, but I told you about being in the audience listening to a talk the other night about life in Tunisia. Well, this young woman was telling us about the marriage situation. The bride nor the bridegroom in Tunisia never see each other; they don't even know who it is until the day of the wedding.
Student: Oh.
Teacher: Don't say "oh." This is a country custom. So how do we know that this marriage of Caesar's wasn't a type of prearranged thing for political power, for political solidity, see, in Rome. From where we're talking, here's Rome, and right down here is Tunisia. We're talking about a country that is not native black. We're not talking about African natives; we're talking about a civilized nation. And it isn't African yet, but it's in northern Africa right next to the Mediterranean Sea. And the bride nor the bridegroom never see each other till the day of the widding. They haven't the faintest notion who or what they look like.
Student: I looked up all of last night about Cleopatra.
Teacher: She's a real doll, isn't she, that Cleopatra?
Student: She poisoned her brother.
Student: How come she was supposed to marry her brother?
Teacher: To solidify the kingdom so that she wouldn't have any outsiders. We still don't understand, we can't today in our Christianity

understand, how these people could do this. But what did I tell you yesterday? I don't condemn them for their barbaric attitude, for their unchristianlike acts. I condemn you for not living Christianity when you have a chance to do so. I think it is more dangerous for us in our nation, than it was for them. Well, let's go on. Now we're down to question six. . . .

October 23

Student: Does Brutus really want to kill Caesar?

Teacher: Well, he's terribly mentally confused about this. It goes back to that first question, "How did he feel about Caesar the man?" It was known in Rome that probably the very best governmental approver that Caesar had was Brutus. When Caesar was out in the Gallic wars and there were those back in the Senate who perhaps could criticize the way he'd been fighting, who do you think would have said good things about Caesar? It would have been Brutus; that's the kind of relationship they had.

Student: Then really he didn't like him as a leader, but he didn't want to kill him 'cause he liked him as a man.

Student: I'd hate to be in his spot.

Teacher: True. We have to have some compassion for the mental torment that Brutus is going through. It is difficult for us to honestly feel and understand what Brutus is going through. All of us are without any comfort at all unless we have friends. And Brutus has been asked to destroy the greatest and the fondest and the dearest friend he has because Caesar is overambitious, overzealous for himself, not for Rome. And this is where the conflict comes. How many of us daily, daily, every day of your living life, would ever question giving up a friend if it meant doing something for your country. See, this is the thing that we don't understand, this is a thing that we are just now getting turned back to, class: to the fact that about three to five years ago you were a square, and I mean a square, if you at any time showed any signs of patriotism or loyalty to your country.

Student: Since they were such good friends, why didn't Brutus just try and talk Caesar out of being so overambitious?

Teacher: 'Cause we wouldn't have a nice play [she laughs], an entertaining five acts.

October 25

Student: The first question, is that supposed to be scene 3?

Teacher: No, it's scene 1 of act 3.

Student: Oh, all right.

Teacher: [She laughs.] Those overalls are weighting your mind down, honey. Those shoulder straps are just pulling right down on your neck. Today is the ides of March; Caesar is to meet with the senators. We know that. Artemidorus and the soothsayer come on the stage

from the left. They are among a crowd of people gathering to honor Caesar upon his arrival at the capitol. The crowd bursts into cheers. Caesar enters from the right, followed by Antony, Popilius, Publius, and then the conspirators. Caesar advances till he faces the soothsayer and he speaks directly to him, very defiantly. Can't you just see this? Caesar says, "The ides of March are come," like, "OK, buddy, remember what you told me about a month ago? See, here I am. It's the fifteenth of March." And look what the soothsayer says, "Aye, Caesar; but not gone." Then Artemidorus says, "Hail Caesar! Read this schedule." A schedule there means like a petition; Artemidorus prepared that little petition. Now several people had prepared petitions but Artemidorus says, "O Caesar, read mine first." And this is the mistake he made if he really wanted Caesar to pay attention to his petition. "Read mine first; for mine's a suit that touches Caesar nearer. Read it, great Caesar." It was a terrible mistake for Artemidorus to have said that phrase 'cause look what Caesar said: "What touches us ourself shall be last served." So here's all these petitions, but where is this one going to get?
Student: Last.

Through the effective combination of vernacular and quotation Mrs. Adams sets the scene for the assassination of Caesar, establishes Brutus's role in the killing, and then leaps across time with her next question.

Teacher: I think we see a direct tie here, class, of what is going on in our own nation right now. What is it?
Student: Watergate.
Teacher: Why certainly. Not just Watergate, but what in the last couple days is so parallel to this thing right here? Kirk?
Student: Watergate tapes.
Teacher: What about it?
Student: Well Nixon doesn't want to hand them over.
Teacher: Why?
Student: Because he was afraid there was something on 'em.
Teacher: He says that it was to protect the office of the president in years to come. Now, according to the laws of our land, what was he told?
Student: That he's got to give them up.
Teacher: That's right. According to the laws of the land, the court said he has to release them. His first decision was what?
Student: Not to.
Teacher: He was defying the law of the land and said, "What I do because I am president, I can do; what you do because you are just a citizen, you must abide by the laws of the land." Now you see what Caesar declared he could do because he was number one is really very much the same as what President Nixon said he could

do because he was number one. He wasn't thinking what impact this was going to have on just plain old citizen man, citizen woman, citizen young voter, citizen old voter, citizen teen-ager. I say this, kids, and I say this very sincerely, be open-minded adults. I am tired of one political person trying to feather his nest with hearsays, not with facts. Until all the facts are in, we are in a very precarious position in this nation. We are without a vice-president as of the very hour that Spiro Agnew resigned.

Student: Do you think he should have done that?

Teacher: With the philosophy that I have I cannot believe that Spiro Agnew is anything but guilty regardless of what he said.

Student: I think he is, too.

Teacher: I'll tell you this: unless you people start standing up when you are guilty of something, take your quinine medicine, stomach it, and puke it back up . . . unless you learn that you are responsible for that which you do, we are going to be in trouble in this nation.

Student: Isn't that what the Russians are wanting to happen, for us to destroy ourself?

Teacher: Why, I think this has to be true. That's right; I honestly believe it. If they can just keep things stirred up and get us suspicious and keep using everybody as a scapegoat and a fall guy, then we are just playing into their hands. They are just going to show the world that the capitalistic world cannot rule itself.

Current Events

The subject matter of the current events course ranges broadly over contemporary affairs; it follows the topics in *Senior Scholastic*, a publication designed for students. The brief article "What Kind of Family When You're the Boss?" stimulates discussion with two scenarios. One pictures the American family "on its way out" and the other "sees the family alive and well in 2001." Students are given class time to read the piece before they launch into discussion, and they are easily launched, venting their irritation at a future characterized by government takeover of traditional family prerogatives.

Students, like their parents, are easily provoked by threats to those freedoms they are aware of enjoying, in this case the freedom to decide the number of children they can have and how to rear them. More abstract freedoms enjoy less support. These children of the cold war easily associate the restriction of freedom with communism. If you have to get approval to be married, a student says, "it ruins the whole meaning of a free country." "We'll be communism then," adds another. The teacher asks, "How about religion?" This question picks up the communist thread again and develops a full-blown discussion of religion in which the students are ready participants.

Mention of God comes easily to Mansfield teachers without objections heard from students or parents. ("I condemn you for not living Christianity when you have a chance to do so," said Mrs. Adams.) Nor do parents complain about the school's policy to avoid scheduling any events on Wednesday night during the school year. Wednesday night is church night in town and the school honors this occasion. As a Christian community, Mansfield accepts naturally the signs of Christmas and Easter in school. No value question, as the final section of this chapter demonstrates, received higher agreement than the one relating to belief in God.

Mr. Blount's current events class interlaces communism and religion; apocalyptic feelings surface. Fear of communism mixes with anxiety about nuclear cataclysm to produce the cold war syndrome and its companion, fear of the end of the world. Mrs. Adams also refers to Russian machinations: "They are just going to show the world that the capitalistic world cannot rule itself."

To culminate the period Mr. Blount asks his students about their church attendance and soliloquizes about his own belief in God and the outcome of a recent junior varsity basketball game. The discussion stimulates a variety of invited after-class responses.

We might well ask, "Is this a good lesson? Is it pedagogically sound?" and then stand back to collect the criticisms. Indeed, some Mansfielders may believe Mr. Blount exceeded the limits of good judgment in asking personal questions about a sensitive subject and in stating his own views. But I think that the general acceptance by the class of traditional views of family, the dangers of communism, and belief in God would find a solid, supportive community audience.

A Current Events Lesson

Teacher: I've given you five minutes to read the article. The family and our families of the future—that's the question we want to discuss now. Are families of the future not going to be?

Student: Not going to be what?

Teacher: Not going to be here.

Student: We were reading that you have to take a test to get married and to have children. Well, if you have to take these tests and you don't pass them, you aren't going to have any, you know. I don't think that's right.

Student: I think we'll have families or there ain't going to be no people.

Student: Only the smart ones would have kids then, wouldn't they?

Teacher: That's true. Good point, Mike.

Student: No matter what, I mean, somebody makes a mistake now and then.

Student: Isn't this where the ones that have the kids will be put into the nursery where they have people trained to take care of 'em. They'll have 3-D televisions and everything by then. And that's how everything's going to be.

Student: That's what communism does.

Teacher: All right, are they going to stop you from having kids? Art?

Student: I think that if the government is going to take over, then you're going to just be a number after you get so many people.

Teacher: All right, this is a question that's going to come up.

Student: I think the nursery will be a family in itself because they'll be there from kindergarten through college. They won't even know who their parents are.

Student: It won't matter because we won't be around then.

Student: Well, in twenty more years, the way things are going, somebody's going to explode an atomic bomb over there and blow us all up.

Teacher: Stuart?

Student: Well, you know, if it happens that you have to take a test to get married, a test to have children, and all this, it ruins the whole meaning of a free country.

Student: We'll be communism then.

Within a short time after the class begins there are two student references to communism and its impact. Mr. Blount does not respond to either comment, but a moment later he refers to communists waiting for the wrong persons to get into government and then "they'd just go bananas." He shares the students' view of communism as a bogeyman, as a lurking menace. All forms of "undesirable" control are labeled "communism." Student ambivalence regarding the scope of the problem is clear in their answer to the question about whether it is the number-one problem facing the United States: 31.8 percent neither agreed nor disagreed, 39.4 percent agreed, and 27.9 percent disagreed. Comparable figures for teachers are 13.6, 45.3, and 40.8 and for community adults are 9.6, 53.6, and 36.0. From students to adults, ambiguity declines and fear of communism increases. However, the question obscures the extent to which Mansfielders are generally fearful about communism because it pits it against financial and energy problems (see tables 11, 26, and 30).

Teacher: If you don't want to have children, you either have to practice the birth control methods or . . . like who is going to be in power or who can say how many you can have will be the question of the future in 2001?

Student: I think that after a while the government is going to try to control everything, the way things are going today. And it's going to be very hard to have a family.

Student: I don't act like it all the time, but I'm religious. I think the people that go to church, after a while they're going to tell them to not go to church and stuff like that. And that's what is keeping our family good.

Teacher: All right. You think the key to the future would be the church organization?

Student: See, a lot of countries, their religion is one of the main parts of their government, like say in England in their cabinet. But here in the United States it doesn't mean anything.

Teacher: All right, Joe?

Student: Well, I like the format of our government now. It's just the people that's running it, they are crooked and all this, so I think we should put in different people.

Teacher: What you are saying is the government is good but we have chosen the wrong people. If we take them out, we have to have maybe better people or the communists would want in. They're just waiting for the right moment and they'd just go bananas.

Student: I can't believe that we'll be here in twenty years.

Student: Are you talking about the earth or just us?

Teacher: The whole thing; the whole thing.

Student: Do you go to church every Sunday?

Student: You don't even go.

Student: You can't tell today when the world is going to end.

Student: But what's he trying to tell . . .

Teacher: Now wait a minute. Would you please be quiet?

Student: He could destroy the world anytime and he didn't want to; it's up to him. It says in the Bible it's inevitable. It's going to happen.

Student: Oh, Satan . . .

Student: It could have happened twenty years ago.

Student: We have some false witnesses . . .

After the class has gotten very agitated and the future of the American family has been set aside, Mr. Blount reestablishes order by asking a series of questions about student religious belief and practice. They seem to respond honestly and readily. Students raise their hands to indicate that the majority believe in God (as do 82.7 percent of all students at Mansfield High School), only six of nineteen go to church, and half would like to go.

Student: Oh, I'm afraid that when the world ends, I'll die in hell.

Teacher: All right, Barb?

Student: That's what I mean; that's why I go.

Student: I got in the habit of going and I just don't feel right if I don't go.

Student: I figure if Christ died on the cross for us, I can get up on Sunday and go to church.

Teacher: I'm the first one to admit that I don't always practice what I preach, but I'll be the first one to say that on Sundays that's where I'm at. I know that somebody's up above, I know that if I'm bad I get penalized, and I know if I'm there on Sunday and trying to help the youth of America that I'm usually rewarded. I don't have to tell you guys that are in the locker room that before each game we say a little prayer. And we do it when we come back in. If they don't get nothing else out of these twenty-nine games, at least they get a little religion. Here's the last thing I want to make a point on. Last night in our JV game at Forest we should have buried this team; there should have been no contest. And we got beat by four points. Now at the free throw line we were seventeen for twenty-seven.

Student: Owwww!

Teacher: This is a perfect example of where I think the guy up above is telling me and the rest of the team, "Listen, dummy, you've not been watching your free throws, you haven't been shooting as many free throws as you should have been, you haven't been doing the right coaching." So there's a perfect example. The guy up above says, "Wait a minute, dumbhead," and maybe we'll win some games later on.

After-Class Written Comments by Students

"I liked this class. Maybe he'll talk about God again. That was one of the best classes because he sounded so honest. He kind of sounded like a preacher."

"I really am scared about this world. I am afraid that in a few years I'm not going to be here. Our country is really in an uproar now. Watergate has made everyone not trust the government they have trusted for so long. A lot of the kids are on dope now and don't seem to care about our country. There is one thing that really scares me. I'm afraid that communists are going to take over our country."

"The family as an institution is on the way out for a number of reasons. First and most important is that most families just don't get along. They fight too much about everything. Another reason is TV. There are so many different shows that nobody agrees and there's a big fight. The third reason is that the house we live in is no longer home. It is just a place to eat, sleep, pay bills, and fight. I think unless something happens soon to bring families together the word might become obsolete."

"In order for the world to exist and prosper, the family must also exist. People were made and meant to have families. This is God's will in my eyes."

Chorus

Chorus attracts about forty students, only one-third of whom are males. They take this elective subject in the period just before lunch. In fact, when the dismissal bell rings, it is almost worth your life to be caught on the narrow stairway leading from the chorus room to the hall which goes downstairs to the lunchroom.

Mrs. Taylor's singers master songs of a seasonal nature; in the lesson below she prepares for the chorus's fairly extensive Christmas activities, which culminate in a well-attended community program held the Sunday before Christmas. Each Christmas a few of her best singers perform before various community groups, including the Masonic home in Auburn. At the end of the school year, of course, they learn songs appropriate for graduation exercises.

Mansfield's students regularly entertain at the Senior Citizens' potluck. This dinner is held the second Tuesday of each month and brings together thirty or more persons, mostly women, the mayor, and one or two local ministers for eating, singing (always hymns), and entertainment provided by the members and by outside groups. Mrs. Taylor prepares her singers for their potluck performance: "Remember, they're mostly older people and they think you're wonderful." Such performances before the Senior Citizens, the work of the Future Homemakers of America with "adopted grannies," the athletic program, and a myriad of other activities constitute a critical connection between school and community. Service to community comes naturally to many Mansfielders. Mansfield High School reinforces this disposition.

Mrs. Taylor, vivacious and attractive, leads her chorus through many songs. She is businesslike, hard-working, and expects her singers to meet her standards: "Be lively." "You can't sing with mumbles." "Pay attention." "Sing this with more energy." She chides them to perform so she can be proud of them now, at Christmas time, and on the other ceremonial occasions in which her chorus participates.

A Chorus Lesson

"OK, class, may I have your attention please? Chewing gum out of your mouth please. [Several students go to the wastebasket and throw away their gum.] Now, when I stand up here like this I want you to look at me and not talk to your neighbors. [The class grows quiet.] I want you to sight-read this music. Sarah [the pianist], would you play the tenor part please? Now the bass. Oh, before I forget it, mixed ensemble, you did an excellent job last night. You do this every time. You worry me terribly and then come through great in the end. The older people just think it's great that you take the time to do something well. Tomorrow, you know, we perform again. If people come up and want to talk to you, give them the time of day. It sounds hard, but it's really very easy. We'll leave walking through the audience singing 'White Christmas.' Remember, they're mostly older people and they think you're wonderful. Now, girls, tomorrow you'll have to wear a dress. I'm sorry, these are older people, we have to conform a little bit.

They discuss the calendar of special forthcoming performances. The ensemble schedule is: December 7, 12:30 P.M.—Evangelical Church; December 7, 6:30 P.M.—Kiwanis Building; December 12, 12:30 P.M. —Senior Citizens; December 19, 7:00 P.M.—Women's Club.

"OK, let's sing. One and a two and a three . . . [They sing "Jesus Christ Superstar."] Let's practice 'Snows a Comin' ' with pep. Be lively. OK, let's go. No, no, no, don't shift keys, and you can't sing with mumbles. Ready, OK, a one, and a two . . . [They sing.]
"Oh, that's terrible. If you don't get it, ask questions. C'mon now, get your part right, stop talking, pay attention. OK, mouth the words if you can't sing. I know you're tired and hungry but you have to sing this with more energy. OK, one more time. [They sing "White Christmas."]
"OK, good. Take the bass back down. And let's sing 'Day by Day' with feeling. Get with it fellows. [They sing.]
"Who needs music for 'Requiem'? [She passes out some music.] OK, let's go. [They sing "Snow's a Comin'."] Let's try again one more time; the words aren't distinct enough. All right, try to do it without the music if possible. [They sing "Godspell."] We're getting you know what?"
"Flat."
"And what else?"
"Sloppy."
"That's the trouble in a popular song. You hear it all and think you know it. Listen, we've got a lot of work to do. Pass your folders to the end person."

The pianist and Mrs. Taylor stand at the piano talking for the last few moments until the bell rings and the whole chorus charges down the stairs to lunch.

Biology

Although Mansfield High School offers botany, zoology, chemistry, and physics, it requires only one year of biology for graduation. Science is not a popular subject at MHS; course enrollment in all sciences save biology is small. The school's laboratory is attached to the science classroom by a connecting storeroom. The sessions presented here took place in the science classroom.[3]

Mr. Riggs, the biology teacher, is a graduate of Mansfield High School and has lived in Mansfield most of his life. He is an enthusiastic, confident teacher, one of the school district's senior faculty members, and memorable to former students:

> Biology was something that none of us kids really wanted to do. We always wanted to go outside and catch butterflies. In order to motivate us he'd say, "If everybody gets an A on this quiz, I'll stand on my head." We did and he did. He got up on top of his desk and stood on his head. When I was an undergraduate I came home one weekend and called him up to tell him what a great teacher he'd been.

Mr. Riggs stands comfortably before his class explaining ionic charges, mitosis, DNA, and fossils, at ease with student jokes that are encouraged by his own sense of humor. On the eve of a test, students bombard him with questions, knowing, because he has told them, what ground the test will cover. He answers their questions the same way he lectures, without the use of notes; for him this is old material. He discusses fertilization in straightforward fashion, with no attempt to bootleg sex education which, by name, is not taught at Mansfield High School. Neither the school board nor the community would sanction formal instruction in this area. However, classroom references to sex seem to be made with the frankness that has become typical of American society in the last ten years.

In response to community criticism of the science objective in "Goals for Tomorrow" Mr. Riggs said, "I teach evolution like anything else. Those people in the community wrote negative reactions, but no one has ever talked with me." If they had talked with Mr. Riggs, an unnecessary act for many parents who themselves studied biology with him, or, better yet, if they had sat in his classroom, they would have learned that he has no intention to unsettle his student's religious beliefs. To the contrary, he and his wife are regular churchgoers and he volunteers his time and labor for a variety of church activities.

Early in the discussion of evolution that follows in the transcripts below, Mr. Riggs offers his own perspective, careful not to be misunderstood. As students volunteer their mostly incorrect answers to his question about what the earth was like at the beginning of time, he states, "Now you can put any slant on it [the question of origins] that you want. It's your privilege," though this is not a position he takes toward what he regards as biology's factual matters. After explaining how life *may* have resulted under naturalistic conditions, he adds that this explanation "doesn't take away the possibility that this was under the guidance of some superbeing." Last century's conflict between science and religion gets no support here as Mr. Riggs concludes that "evolution is not necessarily contradictory to religion of any kind," and that the notion that the earth was formed five billion years ago is just a theory, albeit one "respected by a lot of scientists." This perspective goes unquestioned by the students as they listen to one technical point after another, unaware that they have skirted past one of the great controversies of the Western world.

Biology Lessons

December 12

Teacher: At the beginning of time on earth, what do you suppose conditions would have been like?

Student: The earth would have been barren.

Teacher: Just a plain old piece of dirt here, is that it? [Students laugh.]

Student: From the very beginning, the very, very beginning? Do you want to go back to the beginning?

Teacher: Yes.

Student: Just water.

Student: Not one thing, not even the earth would be here.

Student: Volcanoes.

Student: Grocery stores. [Everyone laughs.]

Student: I don't think there would be any life, just plants and water.

Teacher: Well, aren't plants life?

Student: No human life or animals.

Student: Like the Bible says, the beginning was Adam.

Teacher: I'm talking about the beginning of time, on the earth itself. Now you can put any slant on it that you want; it's your privilege. Could we all agree that perhaps at this time—regardless of who in your mind and according to your own morals brought about the formation of the earth, or what brought about the formation of the earth and the beginning of life—we could all picture the earth in this manner with no life on it. Then this is where the differences perhaps begin to take place: we have to arrive on earth or develop through conditions in which we have those things necessary for the formation of living organisms, whether the formation of that living organism came strictly by happenso or under the guidance of some superbeing.

At that time on Earth, maybe tied up in compounds in the form of minerals and gases, we had carbon, hydrogen, oxygen, nitrogen, phosphorous, and potassium. All the natural elements on the earth were supposedly here at the formation of the earth. Now, if these were all present and conditions became exactly right, we could say some form of energy, perhaps lightning or a spark from a volcano or something or other, brought about the beginning of the formation of compounds that resulted in life.

Now by this theory this is what we had to contend with in the beginning of life: that we had all of the time and we had all of the elements necessary. The earth had progressed to the point where conditions were possible for life.

A few years ago some scientists simulated the conditions at the time of the beginning or what might have been present at the time that life began on earth. And you know what? They did discover a new organism capable of living under those conditions. This organism hadn't been identified before, but this still doesn't take away the possibility that this was under the guidance of some superbeing.

The thing that we don't know is, was the earth always spinning at the same rate that it is today? Was it always spinning around on its axis every twenty-four hours day and night? Or was there a time when it took one year or a thousand to go around? The Bible talks about the earth being made or the world being made in what? Seven days. What was the length of the days back then in the Bible? I don't know, I don't think the Bible ever says. Maybe fossil remains were sent over on rocket ships. Could you believe the theory that life originated here on earth by coming over on a space ship? What are you grinning at? Would you believe me?

Student: No.

Student: Yeah.

Teacher: Some say "Yeah," some say "No." Why couldn't you believe me?

Student: Because there's not any spaceships come back to earth, so I wouldn't believe that.

Teacher: We talk about the beginning of life on earth and we think that it probably started in a simple form and through the process of someone's guidance or through the process of evolution, and evolution is not necessarily contradictory to religion of any kind, it's gone from a simple organism to a complex organism. The length of time is a factor that we are not aware of or know about.

December 13

Teacher: By the way, what is a fossil? The other day somebody walking behind me said, "There goes the old fossil." Now what was he talking about? [All students laugh.] The remains of plants and animals? OK, now, let's say that this is a fossil fish. Is this actually the remains of the fish? [Students offer various guesses, that a fossil is an imprint, a rock, bones, gills, eggs, scales. Mr. Riggs finally explains.] All right, think of it this way: here we have a cell, it's a living cell, and it contains about 85 percent water, except the little cells don't contain that much. This cell is about 85 to 90 percent water. Now this fish was in the water here and covered up. He fell down to the bottom; the minerals and clay particles and things began to filter in. What happened to this perpetually permeable membrane when that fish died? It no longer was perpetually permeable, right? So these materials filtered and fussed their way in, in liquid form. They began to get more and more concentrated and pretty soon they are solid like a what?

Student: Rock.

Teacher: Solid like a rock. And what do we have left then? What do we call this thing?

Student: Fossil.

Teacher: If we find a fossil remain and if we have U-238 which has a half life of 4,500,000 years, then we can determine the age of the fossil with a certain degree of accuracy by measuring the age of uranium-238 that has disintegrated into lead.

Now, if we can tell the age of the fossil remains, what are we learning? We are learning what the earth might have been like hundreds or thousands or millions or billions of years ago and we can perhaps determine the pattern of development. That may not be of great consequence to us at the present time because we're dealing only with life that will amount to a hundred years or so, but as long as man's curiosity is such that he wants to find out about these things . . . Let's take a look, then, at the picture on page 196 and 197. According to this synopsis of the earth's history, and this is just one or two or three people's theory, although it is respected by a lot of scientists, the earth may have formed five billion years ago. . . .

And so Mr. Riggs closes several days of generally guarded and cautious discussion. Yet he probably acknowledges more than the students absorb when he refers to "man's curiosity" in a sentence that trails off to incompletion, its invitation to intellectual exploration not underscored. His words would not fully reassure the minister who equated the teaching of science with an endorsement of evolution. Nor would the minister be comforted by Mr. Riggs's final statement that respected scientists believe, contrary to the biblical account of Genesis, that the earth may have been formed five billion years ago. In the end, who Mr. Riggs is has greater consequence than what he says. A community stalwart, his views are not perceived as dangerous.

These five classes do not begin to capture the depth and breadth of the classroom experience in Mansfield High School; however, they do show several recurring features. Though teachers in these classes encourage student responses, their own presentations clearly dominate class time. A question-answer format prevails, but more open discussion allowing considerable student opinion develops readily once the lesson shifts to somewhat tangential topics. Issues involving matters of value emerge unplanned in discussion. When subject matter happens to elicit value-oriented interactions, students willingly engage in them without expecting that their effort will be legitimated on their factually oriented unit tests.

Adolescent fashion may dictate negative student comment on teachers and classes. Yet there are high spots in the MHS student's academic experience when he is aroused and concerned, alive to what is happening. The transcripts contain many such moments. In U.S. history, for example, the slave dialogue opens up a lively discussion that continues to animate students after class. Similarly, in current events prosaic questions and answers on the family develop into an impassioned discussion of religious behavior. The discussion was not planned by the teacher; it was allowed to happen. Students at MHS, as elsewhere, take joy in the lesson that departs from plan and leads to an often formless debate of a topic that interests them. Some students habitually make this happen. The current events session is likely to be memorable to students long after better planned ones are forgotten.

The lessons on *Julius Caesar* inspire references to contemporary events as Mrs. Adams strives to make the play come alive. She is less concerned with the play's literary qualities than she is with its relationship to matters of possible concern to her students, ranging from Watergate to Spiro Agnew's resignation to Soviet communism. Her neglect of the play's literary qualities does not necessarily reflect her appreciation of the play so much as it does what her students will tolerate.

We see several instances of teachers taking a middle view of controversy, one that is least likely to antagonize the parental public; in fairness to the teachers, however, a middle view may represent their own ideological position rather than an intent to placate community adults. Over several weeks, the biology teacher outlined a sophisticated picture of proteins, cells, fossils, and conditions on earth before life began. When he came to evolution, he clarified that it was one of several theories explaining the origins of human life. He did not indicate that he favored any one theory over another. And the U.S. history teacher, after an animated venting of student claims that blacks were given undeserved privileges in sports and jobs, summarizes the session with a moderate view that may not have pleased either side of the controversy.

If one observes carefully and long enough, one may identify many different patterns in the content of classroom instruction offered during a school year, and these patterns may support a range of conclusions about what teachers value and what world views students are exposed to. Moreover, one can question conclusions based on edited excerpts from much longer transcripts, the transcripts themselves representing a limited number of the total number of lessons presented by all teachers in a school. Nonetheless, the teaching portrayed here is indicative of a pattern of conservative orientation to political and social issues.

To be sure, MHS teachers do not coordinate the ideological or value orientation of their instruction; they do attempt to coordinate subjects which have a sequential basis—English, for example. But there is no party line, no *conscious* effort to endorse a particular view of religion, politics, patriotism, or community. No such efforts are necessary if there is stable leadership to insure that when teachers and administrators pass successfully through the selection process, they have thereby established their orthodoxy. Though there are differences in the degree to which teachers hold their beliefs, the evidence from their classrooms shows that one version of traditional American values gets reinforced in Mansfield High School.

The Student's Outlook: Results from the Questionnaire

One of the most difficult educational questions to answer is "What outcomes can be attributed to a student's school experience?" I cannot answer such a complex question for Mansfield High School. After extensive observations of the classroom experience, I can only suggest some likely possibilities. The classroom data definitely reveal that Mansfield's teachers are in basic accord with the ideological cast of the community. Even though no calculated effort is made to establish a particular orthodoxy in Mansfield's classrooms, it is clear that school and community are congruent. The impressions generated by the qualitative data and by the questionnaire responses of teachers (tables 25 and 26) and other community adults (tables 10 and 11) substantiate this observation. Granted, students may differ from their parents and teachers in important matters of outlook and preference not included in these questions. Still, the socializing consequences of growing up in Mansfield turn out to be broadly, though not precisely, predictable from the values and perceptions held by Mansfield adults and teachers. This is the picture that emerges from the students' questionnaires in table 29.

Students differ from adults in understandable ways. They are much more definite about wishing they had more privacy; and their school strikes them as considerably less attractive, as do their churches. Their generally less positive view about the particulars of Mansfield is consistent with an adolescent inclination to minimize the goodness of the familiar. Yet, they are somewhat more positive than adults about a central myth of life in small towns—that small towns foster a pleasanter way of life than larger towns, and they are only slightly less positive about the desirability of a central fact—knowing everyone and being known. Finally, they clearly perceive the supportive quality of their community, believing that their families can count on help in times of need. Overall, student views about their community are more positive than negative—negative mainly in what I suggest are adolescent terms, but very positive on several critical points.

Feelings toward community are seldom discussed in school. Other than in unplanned situations arising when a teacher reaches out from a class discussion to the students' lives to illustrate a point, there are few occasions to examine local matters. In contrast, questions involving general values are very likely to be candidates for classroom exploration, formal or informal. The opinions shown in table 30 verify that on these particular issues student outlook is closer to their parents' than to their teachers', sharing their parents' conservative orientation, but to a lesser degree. Of course, some differences exist. For example, students are more conservative than parents and teachers on gun-control laws, more liberal than both groups about abolishing capital punishment, and more liberal than community adults on abortion. They reflect the more reserved mood of the past decade about patriotism—61.1 percent agreeing that it should not go out of style, compared to 90.9 percent of the educators and 86.6 percent of the other adults. But they leave no doubt that basically they share their parents' sympathies, reduced in percentage agreement by a measure of ambivalence that averages about 25 percent. On one issue on which students are as informed as their parents—life in Stanton—the results are almost identical in all three response categories. All three groups feel Stanton is not as pleasant a place as it used to be owing to the growth of its black population. Similar results are shown on the related issue of welfare: all three groups strongly agree that persons on welfare could work if they really wanted to. In fact, students are more ambivalent on most items than both adult groups, less ambivalent than parents only on the abortion issue, and less ambivalent than teachers on just the women's lib and Stanton items.

Students frequently refer to "getting out of Mansfield," saying it's a "dead town," and "gotta get away." This is the dogma of youth in small towns. Even those who see virtue in village or rural life can not easily picture themselves, while still a student, as rooted in Mansfield. Adventure looms after graduation; though its promise is not yet tested, it beckons and thereby lessens one's community attachment. Perhaps the clearest indicator (see table 31) of their age-related uncertainty emerges in the question "It is important to me what people in Mansfield think of me." Over 80 percent of the teachers and other Mansfield adults agreed, compared with 57 percent of the students; on no item did students express more ambivalence. Their 57 percent suggests a disposition to be tied to community, in the way that concern for public opinion weds one to local values, but almost one-third cannot make this commitment and another 10 percent do not care what Mansfielders think of them. Less than one-third (22.2 percent) wish they could move away right now, but 54.7 percent (about the same number as community adults) feel they could live happily elsewhere. Like teachers and adults they dislike hearing Mansfield insulted and they admire community loyalty; unlike both, they would be much less bothered if the town's name was changed (59.9 percent compared with 90.9 and 70.3). Finally, on a critical item in table 31, a surprising 46.4 percent attest they feel more at home in Mansfield than they ever could elsewhere. To be sure, this figure is almost matched (39.4 percent) by the number who disagree. However, since all but the strongest degrees of devotion to Mansfield are masked by this question, I conclude that more than this 46.4 percent are content with life in their community and that today's students constitute an ample pool from which to replenish the Mansfield mainstream.

7

What Else Goes On in School?
The Extracurricular Experience

> Everything was important when I was here in school; it really
> was. Where I teach now kids have got cars and everybody has
> jobs, and extracurricular activities are nothing. You pull teeth
> to get kids to join a club.

> I just don't know what it would be like without a parade or
> without football. There just wouldn't be anything then. It
> gives a special feeling to everyone. Kind of a spirit that makes
> people excited and feeling good.

The immediate answer to the question "What else goes on in school?"
beyond what happens in classrooms, is "An incredible amount," perhaps more than anyone realizes, and perhaps too much. Yet, if fewer
and less varied events took place, our high schools would be very different institutions, serving different ends and satisfying different constituencies.[1] In smaller school districts, the school's constituency is a
definite, identifiable group; most of what happens in school, in broad
terms, has its tacit support. Things go on because they have been going
on, and should nontrivial changes occur to disturb the status quo, the
constituency will be heard from. It is not so much an individual activity
or organization that is sanctioned as it is a rich, nonacademic, extracurricular program. Except for athletics, it is the program as a whole
that is sacred, not particular items. When the Future Teachers of America is canceled, no one protests; Medical Careers replaces it. If the
school experience were reduced merely to academic activities, a new
school board might be elected.[2]

Casual observation cannot capture the broad sweep of activities that
occur in or are sponsored by Mansfield High School during each academic year. Indeed, if every school event were chronicled, the result
would be a massive tome. I have selected daily announcements as the
primary basis for answering the question, "What else goes on in school?"[3]
These announcements are prepared from items submitted to the school
secretary each day by students, teachers, and administrators. They are
a fairly complete record of imminent and forthcoming activities: what
is omitted is hardly worth mentioning. This observation does not reflect

126

on the importance of academic matters, which usually are ignored in the announcements. After all, biology and home economics do not require an announcement except when they depart from routine and involve, for example, field trips. All items have one thing in common: they occur outside the classroom teaching-learning structure of the school.

Some extraclassroom activities clearly bear on the academic life of the school. But it is seldom rewarding to try to identify activities, whether labeled curricular or extracurricular, as "academic" in nature. That students may learn more about group dynamics and politics in student council meetings than in sociology or civics classes is not the point here. Nevertheless, it is apparent that some events relate chiefly to the classroom program—for example, the National Honor Society meetings, the Future Farmers of America field trips, and the essay contest inspired by the American Legion. In Mansfield the American Legion does not thrive, but its support for patriotic activities is well received; the annual essay contest is one sign of this. These events—those with classroom or direct academic connections—comprise the least of the school's extracurricular activities. Whatever else they may be, however, they join with numerous other activities to provide out-of-class diversion.

Some events reveal the rhythm of the school year and suggest where student and faculty resources are directed. For example, on the first day of school students learn they can pick up their yearbooks, joyful news indeed as they anticipate the round of autographing which will enliven their return to school. Also on this first day, the arrival of Mr. Archer the photographer is announced, signaling weeks of picture taking preparatory to the organization of the new yearbook. These pictures make possible another school ritual—the spring picture exchange, one of a host of activities that provide students with a measure for gauging their popularity.

Even the announcements of August 28, the first day of school, suggest the incredible range of activities that occur in any high school and the substantial efforts needed to coordinate them. Few teachers and students are immune to those mingled feelings of joy and expectancy that characterize the first day of school. The day and its feelings quickly pass, but not before the official prime movers of pep, the cheerleaders, have met, the seniors are launched on one of their largest fund-raising campaigns, and the Future Homemakers of America, their officers elected the previous spring, assemble for the first of numerous meetings of this busy organization.

At the other end of the year, the well-baked, satiated students and faculty are more than ready for the school year's terminal events. Only the seniors, for whom there will be no renewal next fall, may have tinges of sadness. Over several steamy days, everything collectible is counted and stored, "all extracurricular treasurers' books must be balanced and turned in," commencement preparations parallel the inventories and final meeting of cheerleaders with Mrs. Scott, and teachers end the year as they began it—with a meeting.

I have elaborated the events described in the announcements with information from several sources: transcripts and notes taken at the time of the event; printed programs; *Tiger Tidings*, the student newspaper; and invited student discussion. For most events listed there are no documents to provide elaboration, and thus one may get a distorted picture of an event's relative importance, especially those with a clear ideological message.[4] For example, the partial transcript below of the Teens for Christ meeting is not meant to suggest that it is a more influential organization than the Future Farmers of America, for which I have no comparable documentation, or moreover, that the view of Christianity presented is the one most generally accepted in Mansfield. Nor are the views of the Patricia Stevens representative necessarily acceptable to all teachers and parents.

Some Ideologically Oriented Extracurricular Activities

Many nonclassroom school events have ideological implications; those organized under religious auspices happen to be obvious candidates for this designation. Teens for Christ, the most energetic example, is directed by a local minister and always meets after school in a classroom; several of the church youth groups meet during the last five minutes of home room. These organizations are not school-directed in the sense that the Lettermen's Club, the Library Club, and the Camera Club are. Teachers invariably sponsor the latter groups, which meet more frequently than the religious clubs; otherwise the two types of clubs are not notably different in organizational terms. Several other organizations, for example, the Girls Athletic Association, Future Homemakers of America, and Future Farmers of America, listed elsewhere in this chapter, also inculcate notions of achievement, service, and the like. In short, activities with an ideological thrust are not confined to the following type of event.

> *October 9*
> Teens for Christ [includes ten persons] meets after school in the Audio Visual room. Everyone is welcome. The subject tonight is "Death." It should be pretty interesting.

October 30

On Wednesday, October 31, a representative of Patricia Stevens finishing school will meet with the girls in the A-V room; 3rd, 6th, and 7th periods.

Patricia Stevens Representative
[From my notes]

"I'm here because I want to talk to you about being a girl. After all, just because you wear old blue jeans doesn't mean you should forget how God made you. First of all, I want you to think about something. Do you want to be on welfare? Do you want to be humiliated because you can't take care of yourself? Well, I have a girlfriend whose husband died at twenty-six and left her with three little children. She married right out of school, never thought of getting any training, and now she can't exist without help. Even if she took the lowest type job, she still couldn't pay for baby sitters. She didn't know it would happen, and neither do you. That's why you must think ahead. Think ahead and prepare yourself for something other than staying home. . . . How many of you are going to college? [She counts twelve persons.] How many think you will finish? [Six hands are raised.] Watch it girls. If the guy is the right guy, he will wait for you. If not, maybe he's not worth it. . . . I'm a college grad, a nurse, a graduate of Patricia Stevens, and I know I can take care of myself. Would you believe that I make $1.00 per minute talking with you? . . . I'll bet you don't know that Stevens has a school that trains girls for many jobs, from typing to general office to modeling, etc. . . . Now, I want to talk with you about other girl things. About what can make you feminine. [She offers very specific techniques and suggestions.] Now listen to me, girls. I know your mother won't agree on some of these things, but remember that I'm right. Besides, do you want to look like your mother ten years from now? [The girls laugh and start chatting.] . . . Make the boy treat you like a lady. If he doesn't open the door, wait until he learns to do it for you. . . . Did you ever notice how your grandmother gets out of the car? Don't do it yourself. Remember, you're a lady. God meant you to be a girl, so for heaven's sake act like it. . . ."

Teacher Reaction

"It's good to have an outside person come in. I say the same things all year long, but it's different coming from someone else."

Student Reactions

"Wasn't she funny demonstrating how to walk?"
"Imagine, $1.00 per minute."
"I wonder how old she is; maybe she's as old as my mother."

The Patricia Stevens presentation points up the problem of trying to classify extraclass activities; almost any typology proves to be arbitrary. This talk, given three times during the school day, is no less career-oriented than that given by military representatives or than some of the field trips.

November 27
Teens for Christ after school today in the AV room.

Teens for Christ Meeting
[From my notes]

Minister: On the survey the first question is "Do you believe there are demons today?" There were 40 people answered yes, 11 people answered no. "Do you believe they are in the United States?"—40 yes, 11 no. The power of demons comes from Satan?—37 believe yes, 11 no. ESP and divine healing are the works of the demons?—19 yes, 31 no. "Do demons possess bodies?"—39 yes, and 9 no. "Can demons speak?"—31 yes, 18 no. "Can demons be cast out of a person?" —40 yes, 8 no. Describe a demon for me. Possibly that should have been on the survey, but was not . . . OK, Satan is not everywhere, but his what is everywhere?

Student: Followers.

Student: His followers.

Minister: So we could say the influence of Satan or the devil is everywhere in the world, but he is not everywhere in the world. Do any of you personally know of a person who has ever seen a demon? Anybody? OK, demons are not very popular today, needless to say, but I know a buddy who is a home missionary down in the hills of Kentucky and I was kind of depending on him to send a tape for us so that we could play it today. It did not come. One little woman my college professor told me about was possessed of a demon and they knew she was, so they were going to try and cast this out of her. She was probably five foot one or two weighing eighty or ninety pounds. And they said that it took five huge natives all their force to hold this lady down when this demon was fighting. And they prayed and prayed and prayed for this individual and for the demon to come out and the demon finally did come out. Now this leads us to the question whether the demons came from Satan—37 yes, 11 no. Most believe this; certainly I believe it. . . .

I admit I wouldn't have a seance for anything in the world because it's not just a little game. You're dealing with deadly powerful events when you have a seance or when you play with a ouija board. You say that's just a fun-type game. OK, what are you asking from that ouija board? For it to tell you something that you are not able to know in your own mind. Now, how can a hunk of wood, or whatever it's made out of . . . You know that that stuff doesn't have any smarts. And there's got to be something behind that ouija board because everyone I've ever talked to it's told them and it's happened a lot of times. . . .

Needless to say, the survey which provided the initial stimulus for the Teens for Christ discussion aroused no student or teacher comment. It was not distributed as such but was placed on a chair in a prominent location—the school's front hall—under a sign which encouraged people to pick it up. Almost one-fourth of the students in grades seven to twelve responded to the survey.

December 18
Annual Christmas Program: The band and chorus will per-form in the high school gym on Sunday, December 23. Every-one is invited.

The Christmas Program
[Distributed to persons as they enter the gymnasium]
The people of many countries light candles during the Christmas holiday season as symbols of faith. For long cen-turies in Christian lands candles have been placed in the win-dow on Christmas Eve to welcome wayfarers. The thought is that the Christ Child may be among those wayfarers as he walks abroad seeking to enter the hearts of men and women everywhere. . . . [The list of musical numbers for band and chorus follows this introduction.]
March 12
Any students interested in a "Youth Rally" held by the youth of the missions should meet at the Presbyterian Church in Forest at 7:00 P.M. tonight.
March 14
Will the Catholic Youth Group please meet in room 21 with Debby Osborne last five minutes of homeroom.
April 25
Church of Brethren Youth Fellowship members please meet in the last five minutes of homeroom today.

Homecoming

In the early days of the new semester, the clubs, the cheerleaders, and the classes gear up for the year ahead, electing their officers, planning their programs, and launching their money-raising ventures. However, no time is more eagerly awaited than the football season with its prac-

tices and pageantry, especially its association with the annual Homecoming festivities. It is as though the school were tilted so that everyone
is drawn (generally quite willingly) toward this October event. The
Homecoming program engages grade school children and adults, even
those with no special interest in school, since the decorated windows in
uptown stores bring home the occasion to all who walk or drive down
Mansfield's main street. Homecoming news warrants front page billing
in the *Mansfield Times*; school news, in fact, dominates the *Times* more
than news from any other source.[5]

The school year is replete with a series of climactic events. None is
more absorbing, none touches the lives of more students and community
Mansfielders, than Homecoming. Students and teachers plan, build, and
worry for several weeks before the officially designated Homecoming
week. All is busy-ness, all is mobilization, as this astonishing annual
carnival develops. First come the pre–Homecoming week preparations
that foreshadow the pageantry of the parading floats and the student
royalty who preside over the occasion; these are followed by a week of
mini-events organized to develop and sustain student spirit; and then
all culminates in the parade, football game, alumni banquet, and dance.
There is something for everyone; none but the most jaundiced depart
unsatisfied. If you can't abide a parade, there's a football game; if you're
past dancing and romancing, there's the nostalgia of the classes of '08
and '22.

September 26
1. Senior float and window committees will meet in Mrs.
Douglas' room at 12:30 today.
September 28
1. Homecoming queen and king candidates are as follows:
   Lenore Mann, Dolores Brend and Carol Kasel; Tom Ross,
   Craig Petterson and Ken Morton.
2. Homecoming attendants and escorts are as follows:
   Juniors: Donna Hacker, Judy DeLoache, Harry Korb and
   Jerry Clore
   Sophomores: Vita Browne and Mike Hass
   Freshmen: Carol Dweck and Jack Spaulding
October 9
1. The varsity and junior varsity cheerleaders and the pep
   club skit committee should meet in Mrs. Scott's room at
   12:25 today.
2. Juniors: Work on the float will begin at 4:00 after school.
3. Today marks the beginning of homecoming week. There
   will be many activities to get involved in—ways you can
   support your school and team. Try to keep posted on each

day's activities and *get involved*! Pick up a schedule of events in the main hall.

THIS IS HOMECOMING WEEK—WE NEED
EVERYONE'S SUPPORT TO MAKE IT SUCCESSFUL

Tuesday—Penny Day. There will be 5 marked pennies taped to certain hiding places. Everyone is asked to participate to find them. 1 megaphone will be awarded to each finder. Turn the pennies in to Liz Sheffield.

Wednesday—Poster Day. Every Class is asked to make posters to build school spirit. The gym will be divided into sections for each high school class. Be sure to get your poster in the right section. They will be judged and the winner will add $5.00 to his class treasury.

Thursday—Mystery Student. One student from each high school class is a mystery. Find out who it is and you will win a megaphone. Remember, pizzas are ½ price with these. If you guess who one of the mystery students is, tell Sheri Horton.

Thursday evening at 6:30—Bonfire. The annual bonfire and snake dance will start uptown at the post office and continue to the old baseball diamond for the bonfire. The freshman class will be in charge of the wood.

Friday—Hobo Day. Everyone is asked to dress like a hobo. Please wear old articles of clothing, such as shoes, shirts, and pants. Don't spoil all of the fun by causing any trouble. Suggestions: bib overalls, flannel shirts, etc.

Friday afternoon—Pep assembly. A pep assembly will be held during 8th hour. Many different surprises—prizes will be awarded for the previous contests, and the new homecoming queen and king will be announced.

Keep these sheets handy all week in order to know what is happening every day. Please help make this year's homecoming better than ever!!!!!!

Pep and Spirit

"Support your school and team," "Get involved," "We need everyone's support," urges the October 9 announcement introducing the Tuesday-through-Friday schedule of Homecoming activities. A display of school spirit is deemed desirable, and concern about its expression and magnitude is a recurring issue; pep and booster groups epitomize this concern. The maintenance of spirit, its renewal, its loss, and what remedies to pursue—all are part of the yearly cycle as demonstrated by the pep club meetings, cheerleader meetings, special programs, all-school rallies, and daily announcements such as "Football fans attention: Junior varsity intersquad game—come support the Tigers—we can't lose!"

Toward the end of January, Mansfield's avant-garde of spirit, the Pep Club, strives to shore up sagging enthusiasm by holding Greaser Day, a 1950s dress-up occasion planned "to bring out the big spirit of the basketball players to have a great game that night." There is a noticeable decline in overt expressions of spirit when the basketball season ends and the cheerleaders turn in their uniforms. Baseball games and track meets are announced without motivational reference to the results of the previous outing (as in, "By improving on their [the football team's] first game mistakes, they can come up with a win against Marsdale this week."). Despite the end-of-year waning of spirit-arousing efforts, the next year inevitably brings forth a new cadre of boosters like Bev Tarheel who on her own initiative issues a call to arms: "Please indicate in the space below whether or not you would be interested in helping to build the school spirit here at M.H.S.," and like the cheerleader who wrote in the March *Tiger Tidings* urging the "student body to try to get everyone to try out for cheerleader" because then "our school will improve their spirit."

Somehow it becomes mandatory that an elevated sense of school spirit prevail; that its presence or absence be remarked on by visitors; and that its course over time be noted, much as newspapers record stock market activity. And somehow the notion of spirit is fastened to the school's extracurricular aspects, as though it might be unseemly to be spirited in the presence of a book or of a teacher acting in her restrictive capacity as teacher. But perhaps of greater import for Mansfield, students, when encouraged to cheer for their school, learn of a loyalty that transcends their temporal designation as freshman or senior.

September 13
Reminder: Any student that wants to join pep club should sign up on the sheet outside of the library by after school today [fifty-three girls joined].

November 27
Any girl who failed to support the Pep Club Bake Sale should see Mrs. Scott during the noon hour—before the Pep Club picture is taken.

January 13
Pep Club meeting today at 2:15 in Mrs. Scott's room.

Pep Club Meeting
[From my notes]

Student: One of the main reasons for this meeting is people come to games but don't cheer. Some want to get rid of Pep Club; if we don't come and cheer I think we should get rid of it.

Teacher: How many of you plan to come tonight? Would you sit here in this bleacher if we rope off a section for you?

Student: Everyone sits with their friends.

Teacher: If you sit with your friends why don't you yell?

Students: What are the cheerleaders supposed to do when the band leaves and there's only three minutes left in half time?

Teacher: They could yell their hearts out. That's tough, but not impossible. If you bring friends, the cheerleaders wouldn't mind. . . . The most embarrassing part of the evening is when they introduce our players and coach and there's not a good cheer for them.

Student: We had a group of freshmen and sophomores at the last JV game and we did easy cheers, but they just sat there.

Teacher: That's past. Just forget it. . . . Would there be any chance, once after assembly or school, to stay for fifteen minutes and learn a cheer?

Student: We can't because of the bus kids.

Teacher: It's wrong to say that cheerleaders are responsible for pep. We have to get the whole school behind you; you can't do it on your own. It has to be a school project. If these people don't want to cheer, that's their business.

March 12
Both varsity and junior varsity cheerleaders and substitutes should meet with Mrs. Scott today at 12:30. It concerns the athletic banquet.

Attention Cheerleaders
[From *Tiger Tidings*]

As the basketball season comes to a close the cheerleading season also closes. Being a cheerleader for four years at MHS has had its ups and downs, its exciting moments and its disappointing days. But for Beth, Bonnie, Nancy, and Katy it's been a time to have fun for a week at cheerleading camp, meet cheerleaders from other towns, and view such exciting games as that football game between MHS and Harris, or that MHS basketball victory over Norville when Norville was on top in the conference.

Many times going out for cheerleader at MHS is termed a "Popularity Contest." Why? Maybe by having a selected number of teachers and students vote on the girls' performance would get rid of the term I mentioned. But I've thought of another solution. Maybe if more encouragement is given by the student body to get everyone to try out for cheerleader our school will improve their spirit, and many more girls might show they have the qualities of a MHS cheerleader.

Character-Building Activities

Educators and parents eagerly accept goals of character building, of establishing a sense of responsibility, and of getting along with others. Indeed, such purposes may be blessed by an ardent advocacy surpassing that applied to their academic counterparts. For the many who are untroubled by the muted voice of intellectualism, these purposes encompass growing up American. The claims of personality and character development resound; those of academic achievement are relatively silent.

The activities listed below, like many others, cut across several categories. They are simultaneously things-to-do events, money-raising events, and service-oriented, character builders.

September 4
Any girl in Future Homemakers of America [includes sixty-six girls] who would like to participate in the "Grandmother Adopted" project please sign the paper on the bulletin board outside the library door—before noon Thursday.

Student Discussion of Adopted Grandmother Program
[Invited student discussion[6]]

"My grandmother likes for me to come."

"Mine does, too. She just sits at home."

"You start off talking about something and my grandmother just keeps talking."

"I start off talking about something and she just sits there, 'Ah ha, ah ha,' and then she'll say something and I'll go 'ah ha,' and you just can't keep the conversation going."

"She likes it, but she hardly ever talks."

"Mine talks all the time."

"Sometimes you go over and you talk to them. I think it's something for them guys to do, you know, besides sitting around."

"And it's kind of fun to go shopping for them."

"Ah ha, you ask them if you can do anything for them."

"Everytime I get ready to leave she has to come over and kiss me. [She laughs.] That's embarrassing."

"She does. She smacks you right on the lips."

"That's the way I understand that she wants me to come back."

"But you should. . . . It's like your own grandma."

"Mine doesn't kiss me when I leave, she kisses me when I come."

October 5
Student Council will meet at 12:25 today in Mrs. Norwood's room. Important meeting.

Student Council
[Invited statement written by Student Council president]

A student council is important for every school. It gives each student, no matter what class they're in, a chance to become involved in what the school is doing. A lot of students don't have an interest in school morale, but a lot of them do. The students who do have an interest in what's going on, is what makes a success.

I, along with others, are becoming used to using rules to work by. The world is made up of rules, and when we graduate, abiding by rules will not be new. Serving in any organization, and as an officer, gives that person a responsibility to others. All during life we will be faced with our own responsibilities and will be able to handle them better. . . .

January 2
Future Homemakers of America meets today in Home Economics Room.

Future Homemakers of America Meeting
[From my notes]

Student: Oh, I wanted to explain about the receipts on the jewelry project. I haven't heard from those people and I have written twice asking that they let us know what we owe them. It would not be terrible if they never let us know how much we owe them, but I'm sure that it won't turn out that way. Right now we have over $700 that we owe. Our treasury stands at $900, which is good, but really isn't that good, because we have this problem of owing them without the bill. . . .

Teacher: OK, now I've got a couple of things I want to say about this grandmother's project. I think you all realize our grandmother's project is not just for gift giving and gift receiving. I know at Christmastime most of you received gifts from your grandmothers; many of you gave gifts to your grandmothers. This is fine; this is as it should be. I would like for you to tell me of anything that you might have done for your grandmother since school started. Has anybody called her and asked her if they could get her groceries? Or have you stopped off to see if you could carry out trash or mail a letter for her? OK, a few people have done this. Very good. Maybe you could shovel snow for her, now that we've been having plenty of that. Show some interest and concern and do something for her.

January 15
Today—Girls' Athletic Association—7th hour.

Girls' Athletic Association Meeting
[From my notes]

Teacher: I would like very much for you to tell me today if you think that you are going to be eligible for your next award. I assume that all the freshmen think that they're going to get a numeral. Are there any people in the sophomore, junior, or senior class that have not received their numeral?

Student: I didn't pick them up.

Teacher: Well, you have it coming to you. Any second-year awards? Freshmen? No? Go to my desk and you'll find one of those block Ms. If you have not accumulated twenty-four points in a semester you are extended an invitation from the officers of Girls' Athletic Association to resign. You never usually get an invitation to quit something, but that is our rule. In other words, if we enjoy you and you enjoy us, you must participate. This is one of the local requirements for Girls' Athletic Association members. It's not a requirement from the state office.

March 1
West Point Cadet will address students in assembly tomorrow. Attendance not compulsory.

Cadet Wilkie Visits Mansfield High School
[From my notes]

Cadet Wilkie lives in Brenton and he has stopped in Mansfield on the way home from West Point for his spring break. After his introduction, Wilkie says that he does not plan to give a talk but will answer questions instead.

He explains about discipline at West Point, that you can't give orders until you learn how to accept them. Plebes are hazed by the other three classes, they have to run between classes, and eat their meals in a prescribed way sitting only on the front six inches of their chairs. Cadets cannot use elevators between 7:00 A.M. and 5:10 P.M., and room inspections include white glove treatment of their door jambs. Further questions asked about demerits for unshined shoes, whether cadets can be married, reading of *Playboy*, if cadets serve in Vietnam (80–90 percent went), and the number of black cadets (8–9 percent).

Student reactions to Cadet Wilkie were generally negative: "That guy has got to be an A number one fruit. I mean living a life like that you gotta be a fruit." Teacher reactions were generally positive: "I wish my son had a chance to see this fine young man. We don't have many like that around these days." "That man knows discipline and there are worse things in life with which to become familiar."

"Now our students can see that life at West Point is just like in the movies; why it's even better in real life than in the picture shows."

Fund Raising

Perhaps no less applicable to out-of-school life is the outcome of frequent money-raising opportunities. Notwithstanding how the money is spent, the central fact is that while most extracurricular activities are sponsored by the school, they are not financed by it. Thus money raising is a necessity at Mansfield High School, and many national companies have a stake in this dimension of our school culture. These businesses rationalize their claims on student time by arguing that sales experience builds self-confidence, social skills, and financial acumen. Money-raising skills definitely transfer to Mansfield's adult organizational life, with its inevitable cookie sales, cakewalks, pancake suppers, and soup suppers. Money raising through voluntary efforts is valued for both high school and community projects: Does the school need a new scoreboard? The Crandalls' daughter special medical care? The town new baseball lights? In such cases, Mansfield traditionally mobilizes citizen generosity through informal, voluntary means, resorting, as the law requires, to referenda and the like for the larger concerns of new buildings and basic educational support.

As the item below indicates, the student council coordinates fund-raising projects at MHS. In previous years, clubs and classes had unlimited chances to raise money; now limits have been established that recognize the different needs of student groups for money. The remaining condition of consequence is that no school project can interfere with local businesses.

October 3
Today's activities: Student Council—4th hour.

Project Rules
[Prepared after Student Council meeting]
The following rules are set up to give each class and organization an equal opportunity to earn money.
Rules
1. A request form must be filled out in duplicate and given to the Student Council for clearance. . . .
2. Money-making projects are limited to two projects a year for freshmen, sophomores, and all club organizations. Juniors are limited to three projects and Seniors are limited to four projects annually.

3. Any money-making projects which interfere with the merchants in Mansfield will be vetoed.

Athletic Events

The one truly ubiquitous—some would say relentless—item in the daily announcements is sporting events. They begin with football practice two weeks before school opens and last well into May when the final track meet is held. In between, there is a tidal wave of athletics involving mostly males, as many as sixty different boys in the course of a year, but also ten female cheerleaders and an increasing number of female athletes. Approximately half the student body is engaged in interschool athletic events either as player, cheerleader, or manager. This proportion testifies not only to the interest such events hold for Mansfield youth, but also to the size of the school: the smaller the student enrollment, the higher the proportion of those engaged in competitive athletics. This high level of participation is spread among four sports for males—football, basketball, track, and baseball—and three sports for females—volleyball, basketball, and track. The Girls' Athletic Association (GAA), with over fifty members, also is involved in sports throughout the year, as is the Pep Club, with over thirty members. This number includes cheerleaders and girls who also are in GAA. Sports activities are so dominant in the high school that they reinforce a substantial post–high school interest in athletics.

The chronological listing below of sports events suggests but fails to capture their immense place in school life. Like matters of romance (see chap. 8), they slip with ease into all available corners of time and concern; they, not academics, are the rivals of romance. To shun them as participant or observer is to court being shunned. Other activities do thrive and even find a place in the popularity spotlight; none are as continually encompassing, captivating, and time-consuming.

September 18
1. The varsity football team lost to Summit 44–6 last Friday night. By improving on their first game mistakes, they can come up with a win against Marsdale this week.
2. The Junior Varsity football team plays at Summit at 6:30 P.M. tonight. The team bus leaves at 5:10 P.M. this evening.

October 2
Our Varsity Football Team plays Forest this Friday at Forest starting at 7:30 P.M. With the right attitude and hard work our team could be victorious.

October 19

Football players team bus leaves at 5:15. Also taping starts at 4:45.

November 5

1. Girls interscholastic volleyball practice at 3:35 today, Tuesday and Wednesday.
2. Congratulations to the varsity for their victory on Friday against Durango, 20–0.
3. Reminder: All those who have been out for football still owe $1.00 on their mouthpiece. Please pay this amount by Wednesday.

November 12

1. Congratulations to the varsity football team on their victory over Barland 42–30. The victory brought their record to 4 wins 5 losses.
2. Girls' volleyball team plays at Lowell tomorrow at 4:00 P.M. Students should be released from classes at 3:00 P.M. and bus leaves at 3:15 P.M. tomorrow.

December 5

Yesterday the varsity basketball team lost to Forest 71–65 and the Jr. varsity won 62–57.

January 29

The High School varsity team beat Grant 68–61 at the Ferris tourney. We are scheduled to play Harrison on Wednesday evening at 6:30 P.M. Anyone interested in a student bus contact cheerleaders today.

March 12

Barry Redfran was a unanimous choice to the conference coaches all star basketball team.

Interview with Barry Redfran

When we get to school we shoot free throws in the morning for basketball. And we had to shoot so many of 'em before we could go down, so many out of 10. We ended up making 9 out of 10. We're supposed to be here by 8 o'clock. All day long, it's mainly basketball I think about. Yeah, that takes a lot of time. We show our game films sometimes in study hall. They're good because you can see what you've done wrong when coach points out how you should be playing. I mostly get together with guys from the basketball team after school, in home room, during basketball, things like that; we talk mostly basketball.

March 14

The High School boys track team members [includes nineteen persons] are to report to the locker room the last 5 minutes of homeroom.

March 19
There will be a tv set available in the audio-visual room for the study hall groups and P.E. classes Friday in the afternoon to watch the state basketball tournament. Any teacher who wishes can make arrangements with their class to have a portable tv in their classrooms for the afternoon.

March 27
The girls' basketball team lost to Mantua yesterday 51–39. They will play again on Thursday with the bus leaving at 5:15 P.M.

Conversation about Girls' Basketball
[From my notes]

Teacher: Would you believe it, the girls were given two whole hours the other night for basketball. It took I don't know what to get that time though. Just imagine, the boys have the gym 99 percent of the time, and no one can understand why the girls might just enjoy having it. Girls and sports are pushed in the corner.
Student: I don't believe in all that liberation at home, you know where the woman does everything that the man does, but I think the girls should have more time for sports.

April 2
All High School boys interested in football next year will begin the weight training program Wednesday. Anyone with a schedule conflict please contact the coaches.

April 11
Today: If we follow our sport's schedule for today, the High School boys and Junior High boys track team members will be released from class at 2:00 P.M.

May 1
The frosh-soph high school boys track team will compete at the conference meet at Durango. The following team members [six students' names follow] are to be released from class at 11:15 A.M. The bus will leave at 12:00. The meet starts at 2:00 P.M.

May 3
High school girls track members meet with Mrs. Adams the last couple of minutes of homeroom in the girls' locker room.

The purported benefits of sport for character building and leadership are too debatable to discuss here. What is clear, however, is that Mansfielders value athletics as an essential aspect of the school. Both banker and unskilled laborer believe school is a more pleasant place because of athletics; they please everyone except the old fogies, grouches, widow ladies, and wrong-headed intellectuals. After the "basics," sports, to many, are schooling's raison d'être. In the Mansfields of America, they link generations and establish a focus for emotional investment that attaches people to the school. In fact, concern for one's school system may be the most powerfully integrative factor in small communities, the schools claiming the largest constituency of all community agencies. The school is Mansfield's most nonpartisan and inclusive community agency. By belief, tradition, talent, knowledge, and accomplishment no one need be left out. Accordingly, its affairs can and do embrace more persons than any other organization in the school district.

Activities for the Last Roundup

Junior high school students consider entry into high school to be an important event, but no special activities mark this occasion. In contrast, leaving high school is heralded as early as one's junior year in a school cycle with a two-year duration. On September 4, one week after the new semester has begun, eleventh-graders are informed they can purchase their class rings. Their year's social high point, however, is the spring junior-senior prom, for which they have raised money since entering high school. This dance unites them with the graduating seniors and anticipates their ascent to the top grade. The senior year, of course, is replete with special meaning because each game, meeting, and enterprise is the last of its kind for them unless they go to college. During this seemingly longest of school years this meaning is singularly marked by activities such as the purchase of graduation announcements, visits of college representatives, the senior play, and the graduation ceremony.

August 30
The seniors will meet in the library during 6th period today to meet with the Quality Magazine salesman.

September 26
All college bound seniors please see Mrs. Douglas concerning a new federal-type scholarship.

October 12
Seniors: Reminder: State University application deadline is December 15 if applicant wishes to be considered by the first notification date.

October 19
The American College Test will be given tomorrow at Sheridan University. Those seniors who are signed up for it should report there by 8:00 A.M.

December 5
Arnold Company will meet all seniors in the library sixth
period today.

The Arnold Company
[From my notes]

The Arnold Company is part of high school graduation tradition;
it contributes to the ceremony which surrounds this most national of
events. It not only rents caps and gowns, but also sells graduation
announcements ("order a few extra—saves embarrassment"), announcement covers ("enhances a fine keepsake"), name cards ("average—200"), thank-you notes ("mother may want some"), appreciation folders, memory albums, and class keys in school colors attached
to pendants, key chains, and key clips.

The Arnold representative did not sell his items; he gave no sales
pitch. (Perhaps none was needed. As one student said after prepar-
ing his order, "Well, you only graduate once.") He simply described,
carefully, how to fill out the order blank, since each order must be
in the student's own writing, and quoted the prices.

Male and female students sat at separate tables. Once the order
writing began, it spread like a contagious disease. No one was immune; the reluctant were unprotected.

December 18
Seniors: Will vote on 3 boys and girls they want as candidates for the Good Citizens' Award of the Daughters of the
American Revolution. From the three highest vote-getters, the
faculty will select the boy and girl as good citizen.

January 29
The Junior-Senior Prom theme and post Prom committees
should meet in Mrs. Scott's room at 12:30 today.

February 4
Senior class play practice tonight at 6:00—AV room—first
and second acts. First act from memory.

May 1
1. Pictures in color of couples at prom will be taken by Mr.
   Perry. A print is $1.00 for each 3½ x 5. Total amount of
   order must be paid when picture is taken.
2. The gym is now closed because of prom decorations. The
   band groups should go outdoors to get to the stage. The
   P.E. groups should go outdoors the next few days.

Career Guidance Activities

Post–high school opportunities are boosted throughout the year. They
often are tied to senior interests ("Any senior student planning a career

in government service please see Mrs. Douglas," says one announcement, or see her if you are "interested in the golden jubilee teacher education scholarship," reads another). Representatives of colleges, training schools, and the military make presentations. Health Careers introduces jobs within the health field; guest speakers and field trips acquaint students with its many opportunities. Knowledgeable persons address the Future Farmers of America, whose year-round activities are notably career-oriented. Even the experience of being student worker in the school office provides a chance for occupational exploration.

A vast number of career information programs exist as a routine part of the total high school experience. For most students, they are fairly casual events; for the seniors, each speaker, each field trip, each club meeting commands: Thou shalt decide! Being top dog in the high school comes at a price, though many students would gladly forgo the indulgent dimensions of the senior year and choose the independence of a full-time job unguided by Kuder, Patricia Stevens, or Mrs. Douglas, the school counselor.

September 18
Reminder seniors: Representative from Bradlow Junior College at 10:00 A.M. tomorrow and one from Sheridan Thursday at 10:30—give your name to Mrs. Douglas if you are interested.

September 21
Seniors: Any graduating senior contemplating going to the State University and interested in speaking with a midshipman concerning Naval ROTC see Mrs. Douglas today. Want to see a representative from Central? Do likewise.

October 2
A reminder to any senior planning to enroll in the dental hygiene program at Brown—December 1 is the deadline for application.

November 12
Any student who is interested in careers in history other than teaching should contact Mrs. Norwood.

November 15
Health Careers—1st hour [twenty-eight attended].

Health Careers
[From my notes]

Student: Our guest speaker is Mrs. Perham and she's going to speak to us about being an anesthetist.

Guest speaker: I work at Stanton Hospital and I've been there since 1951. To start my discussion, in order to apply for school in anesthesia you have to be a registered nurse and you have to be licensed in the state that you want to apply for anesthesia school. Anesthesia, I don't know if you girls know what it means, but when you speak of anesthesia you are relieving pain so that you can do a surgical procedure, in the maternity department so you can deliver the baby, or any place that you need to alleviate pain. . . . Are there any questions? What did you say, sweetie, I can see you moving your mouth back there?

Student: I was just wondering about being on call.

Guest speaker: Well, I am on duty twenty-four hours. There is really six of us who actually cover this floor.

Student: What's the needle with that big end, like when they have a heart attack or something? I'd think that would hurt the heart more than do it good.

Guest speaker: Well, no. Probably what you're thinking about is they inject adrenalin right into the heart muscle, and adrenalin is a real powerful cardiovascular stimulant.

Student: Do they pay pretty good?

Guest speaker: Yes, and it should be because you have a lot of responsibility. I don't know what it is to work forty hours a week; I've got forty-eight hours of calls and that means I'm in the hospital from 7 o'clock in the morning to 7 o'clock at night.

Student: Do you think they'll always need them?

Guest speaker: Oh, yes, because I don't think we'll ever have enough doctors to cover the field. . . .

April 2
See Mrs. Douglas to discuss results of your Kuder Preference Test.

Roy's Guidance Interview with Mrs. Douglas
[From my notes]

Mrs. D.: You've seen the results of your Kuder Preference. Did it measure you pretty well? Does that sound like you or somebody else?

Roy: Yeah, most of it.

Mrs. D.: OK, let's see what we have here? High in persuasive. Like to be a salesman?

Roy: Not as much as I'd like to do something else. I thought about being a politician. [He laughs.]

Mrs. D.: Outdoor life. Ever have any aspirations for forest ranger or . . .

Roy: No, I just want to work with animals.

Mrs. D.: You want to work with animals. Well, I guess that could be outdoors unless they start keeping the animals in incubators, too, like everything else. Music. What is it you play, Roy?

Roy: Trumpet.

Mrs. D.: A trumpet. Have you any plans to continue your music in college or anywhere?

Roy: No.

Mrs. D.: Just high school fun, huh? Social service? Are you interested in that type work at all?

Roy: Yeah, kind of. I'd like to help. I'd like to talk to . . .

Mrs. D.: I can see where you would fit in very nicely. Very personable person; you might enjoy that very much. So you think that reads you pretty well—clerical, likes math, keeping books, working with figures?

Roy: I don't like to keep books at all.

Mrs. D.: You don't like to keep books at all? That's what this says. No? Anyway, I think you did pretty well. Now, what do you plan to do after you graduate?

Roy: I plan to go to college and be a vet.

Mrs. D.: Sounds good. Well, I think you're on the right track. This test did measure you.

Finally, the high school is Mansfield's hub of activity, the place where when the lights are out in other public settings, save for the Laundromat and the taverns, there is very likely something happening. Being bored is the scourge of youth. Keeping satisfactorily busy is their delight, and Mansfield High School contributes significantly to this end.

Like a circus boasting "Come one! Come all! Fun for the entire family!" the school's out-of-class programs entertain and serve Mansfield. As noted, the grannies are adopted; grandpas presumably have athletics. Most activities place adults in the audience, though the Follies engage young and old alike as participants, not only providing one performance open to the entire community, but also involving the performers in hours of practice. The Follies, football games, Christmas program, and graduation exercises are designed for full community participation; many other events occur during the school day or immediately after school and are meant only for students, like the Projectionists' Club, the Library Club, or the Girl's Athletic Association. Still others, like the community carnival, are not even school affairs; community groups use the school's announcements to advertise their programs.

Although it is misleading to portray MHS as a whirlwind of activity, with frenzied students and teachers dashing from play practice to float building to soup supper, it does have abundant activity, varied to suit the tastes of most Mansfield youth. And while endeavoring to keep its students busy, it serves local adults as well.

It is no surprise to learn that Mansfield High School offers students more than academic experiences. Though Mansfielders occasionally grouse at the money spent on athletics, for example, and at student absences from class, they are pleased with the range and variety of their school's extracurricular activities. The program's adult proponents argue that such activities are no less important to student development than curricular activities, and its youthful advocates claim that extracurricular activities make school tolerable. ("Mansfield High needs more of this [Greaser Day] to help students enjoy school more than what they do now!") From all appearances, it is a stable program, endorsed by students, teachers, administrators, parents, school board, and taxpayers. The superintendent, in one announcement, reminds his teachers that *all* school activities are important and they must cooperate if a "full program" is to be implemented.

What are some possible outcomes of this vast array of activity? Well, if some degree of vanity is promoted by Archer's repeated appearances for yearbook picture taking, an activity which claims bits of student time throughout the year, so is humanity served when the Future Homemakers of America adopt grandmothers, sponsor an Indian child, and organize a host of service projects. And just what the residue is of numerous elections and committee meetings may be imagined but not readily documented. Those who see democracy growing strong with every hand-waving vote or secret ballot may be disappointed to learn that the Bill of Rights does not thereby automatically gain an advocate. But certainly a modus operandi that may apply to many out-of-school situations is experienced and reexperienced.

It would be interesting, though the data are unavailable and possibly unattainable, to document the size of the investment students and faculty make in extracurricular matters, defining investment in terms of time, money, energy, and concern. No doubt, more time and money go into academic activities, but where the balance of concern and energy lies between classroom and nonclassroom matters is much less clear. I am tempted to say that the cornucopia of doings this chapter presents comes out of the school's academic hide, but is this true? Even the most cursory exploration shows students leaving class day after day for extracurricular events, but it is not certain that if Mansfield students attended only academic activities that they would invest more of their resources in them. And it may even be unrealistic to argue that the balance between curricular and extracurricular matters is unsound or that the price paid to sustain the cornucopia is too high. Issues involving balance and price are questions of propriety, which is to say, questions of taste. At least in the United States we tend to act as if this were the case. Moreover, we leave propriety to be defined basically by each school district, influenced of course by state regulations (the compulsory inclusion of American history and physical education courses), federal money (the development of post-sputnik science, mathematics, and foreign language programs), and whoever else can get the school's "ear" (the American Legion and its essay contests.) In the circumstances, it might be that schooling in Mansfield without all the extracurricular activity would not mean a more vibrant academic experience, but rather a less vibrant experience in general.

If there appears to be keen competition between MHS's curricular and extracurricular components, I still cannot characterize the school experience as a straightforward confrontation between these two giants. Both provide the occasion, however unwitting, for a third factor which, like the smell of sulfur in a chemistry class experiment, permeates all aspects of the school—only with more pleasing effects. This factor is romance.

8

Romance and More Romance:
The Voice of the Students

The big thing was to drive around town and see where every-body was. There was a route you followed. You'd drive down Main Street. Go up by the nursing home, make a U, and drive back down Main Street. Then north across the railroad tracks by the old drugstore and make another U. On the way back, stop at the old drugstore and by the post office. On Fairlane, you drive south to where the street ends at the highway and back to the funeral parlor. Right turn there and out to the high school. Drive around the school, come back to the street, and drive through town again very slowly. After this, you're ready for the west side of town—past Good Shepherd Church and up to the Evangelical Church. You do this two-three times until you see somebody you want to see. Then you stop.

Mrs. Adams and *Julius Caesar* lead students to Watergate and affairs of national import; Mr. Blount strikes home with a series of questions probing personal religious practice and belief and Reverend Walter discusses the findings from the Teens for Christ survey about demons; a Patricia Stevens representative delivers homilies for personal and occupational success; and the Future Homemakers of America, pledged to service in a candlelight ceremony, bring joy to Mansfield's senior citizens via their Adopted Granny program. The organized elements of the school experience clearly abound; they are both exalted and mundane. One further element coexists with the Pep Club, chorus, and Chemistry class: it is unorganized and unscheduled, does not make the daily announcements, promises no formal credit or recognition, and is immensely alluring. It is the high school student's peer culture.[1] Educative in its own right, it fills the school's chinks of time and space like lava coursing down the side of a volcano, ubiquitous, powerful, inescapable. Its impact shapes student behavior: for example, to get by without appearing to do much work, to go out for football, to like teachers who are not too demanding, and to purchase a six pack. Student values and interests snare newcomers; only the insensible or the inordinately independent student could slip by their inevitable expression in the halls, alongside one's locker, at the lunch table, on campus, or in classrooms, school buses, gym bleachers, and shower rooms.

Occasions for meeting and talking and listening and observing occur at school all day, every school day. And, of course, they extend beyond the school's time and space to home and community during evenings and weekends. Like town gossip, the network of school talk assures that a student's behavior is public and thus known, while further assuring that what is said is also likely to be known. One student commented on Mansfield's effective communication channels:

In a small town everybody knows everybody else's business. You're always hearing whispers about somebody—somebody did this or did that. And pretty soon you're beginning to hear whispers about yourself, you know, and it doesn't sound too good when you hear it. After I'm married I really don't care what other people say. It's just right now, while I'm in school and everything. . . . Have you ever been involved in a rumor? Around small towns it'll go from one person, and they'll say such and such, they broke a window or something like that. Well, then, that person, they get it jumbled, and they go to another person, "Such and such tore the wall out." Finally you end up where he tore the whole building down or something. This doesn't happen too often, but then I'd say often enough. This gossip influences your life because you're almost afraid to go out and do anything because you're afraid somebody's going to talk about you.

My access to informal student talk was through diaries and a diary form which students wrote in response to the lead, "Today I was thinking about . . ."[2] Several themes dominate the diaries: romance, sports, cruising, drinking, and school as a bore.[3] The students' lives are busy and not necessarily with academic matters; in fact, school work is so seldom mentioned that it appears as a truly minor event in their lives. I suspect, however, that the diary form conduces to discussion of social events and that is why they dominate, though for many students schooling clearly matters less than meeting one's friends. That students are concerned about their academic activities is evident in the interviews in the next chapter, but their general disposition to discuss school work less than other subjects (for example, romance and sports) extends to their diary writing.[4] Their terse dismissal of school as a bore is a habituated manner of expression which obscures a greater range of feeling about class work than "bore" suggests.

Mansfield High School cannot be blamed for its students' affairs of the heart; it neither encourages nor discourages them. Because of compulsory education, it inadvertently provides the setting within which matters of romance are facilitated. Concern for whether a person notices, likes, loves, is true to me permeates the student body; it is not peculiar to any group. Mansfield has its share of student pregnancies and early postgraduation marriages, and the imminence of marriage often claims large portions of student time and energy during the senior year. But more typical for most students is a seemingly endless pattern of falling in love, falling out of love, and seeking new love. In the process, students may become informed about themselves and the nature of personal relationships; it is not clear from the diaries, however, exactly what is learned. Sheri Turner turns boyfriend into "X-boyfriend" and then anguishes over her deed; she provides striking counterpoint when she shifts from well-deserved good feeling about her adopted Grandma to vintage adolescent confusion over her ex. "Would you," she asks her diary, "wait for him [she is one year, three months, and fifteen days older than he is] or go ahead and have fun with this other guy until my X is old enough to drive?" Similarly, Bill Harwood trails his ex-girlfriend around Auburn, consorts with junior high school girls, and then comments maturely and insightfully on Mansfield: "Everything that happens in the newspaper is outside us. We are actually in our own little world . . . we haven't faced anything eye to eye."

Romance may dominate but it does not invariably preoccupy. In the midst of the most involved affairs, students still participate in a variety of activities: they continue their piano lessons, do their homework, attend play practice, and go to church. Indeed, they frequently refer to church and to religion. On the day before Christmas, Louise Maclane writes of killing herself because nothing is working out, but then continues, "if I did I would never get to heaven because I would have a very bad sin." On Christmas day, Janet Logan announces the new importance of Christ in her life.

Since cruising is confined to those having cars or access to friends with cars, it tends to be a pastime of older students. Students drive to satisfy recreational needs and to seek relief from their sense of confinement in Mansfield. Weeknight driving is around Mansfield, with Black's parking lot the central point for arrivals and departures; the weekend circuit encompasses towns up to fifty miles away. No specific destination is needed. The going is important and so is who you go with, though one always welcomes unexpected action as adding luster to an evening's cruising. Romance and alcohol, in a joining of themes, may accompany one's cruising, but it seems that a six pack in the car is more likely to be a males-only event. Student drinking is widespread.

If a drug problem exists in Mansfield, it involves alcohol—from Southern Comfort to beer—significantly more than any other drug. The school's solid citizens, as defined by local residents, find alcohol as attractive as those considered socially and financially marginal. Youthful excesses are not condoned; if one is caught, the law punishes ($100.00

for court costs if one is found driving with alcohol in the car), though not so severely as to discourage drinking. According to Mansfield students, smoking marijuana is common but not widespread. Drinking is less feared by parents and more preferred by students. "I was at this party and a guy offered me a joint. I told him to 'stick it' and got drunk," writes one student. Drugs harder than marijuana are seldom used. Recently, the high school was agitated by the rumor that a teacher had prepared a list of all pot smokers. One girl, not a diary keeper, wrote:

> When the dope list was going around school everyone was so upset because someone would tell them their names were on the list. Everyone of the kids were trying to find out if there was a list. Some that are on dope were sure they would get kicked out of school and the ones who were trying it were wondering if they would get kicked out or would they have to answer a bunch of questions like why did they try it, what satisfaction did you get, are you going to anymore, to a doctor or maybe the principal.

The poignancy of adolescence is not so much a theme as a quality of this period of life. It is expressed in different ways. Craig Lanton confesses he is "just plain chicken" for not displaying the expected machismo in the face of Mary Harble's clear invitations. Regarding his romantic complications he says, "I don't know what to do." After a fight with his girlfriend Billy Randolph tells her "where to go" and then is "about sick" with regret. Louise Maclane, in sad, short sentences, writes that she doesn't "really think anybody loves me or even likes me . . . let them feel the way they want to because I don't care." But no diary more sharply marks the mercurial behavior of the sensitive adolescent than Janet Logan's. She plummets from joy ("Beautiful! I loved every minute of today") to gloom ("I'm shouting for help"). Her briefly portrayed life strongly contrasts with Donna Victor's busy days of pig tending, hide-and-go-seek in church, kissing, smoking, musical performances, getting thrown in the boy's locker room, and homework, all taken in stride, all part of painless, effortless days. Donna even manages one brief outburst of moralizing about freshmen "making out" (kissing) in the hall by their lockers—"It makes people wonder if they do that in public just think what they do in private." Finally, Art Thompson, despairing that he'll never graduate, climaxes an awful day by running his car into a hedge and vowing to get good and drunk so he'll "feel like going to school" the next day.

Little more need be written about the importance of sports in Mansfield High School. The diaries confirm their overwhelming presence, since with few exceptions athletic activity is mentioned in each one.

Several of the girls play basketball for the school team; Donna Victor also plays on an outdoor court after church in what for her is a general entwining of boys and everything else she does. Billy Randolph writes through his New Year's beery haze that "he can't do without football," a sad realization, since after his next and final season he ceases playing organized football forever—no more cheerleaders, crowds in the bleachers, or lockerroom comaraderie. Bill Harwood not only plays on Mansfield's basketball team, he also attends the games of other nearby schools. "It was difficult," he confides, "being a small hero after the basketball game last night. That's the first real glory I've had for a while."

I assume that the content and tone of the diaries closely approximates the content and tone of student conversation at school,[5] though some diary statements are so personal (Janet Logan's, for example) that other students may seldom hear such feelings voiced, experiencing them more as moods than as manifest behavior. Thus the diaries tend to capture both latent and manifest behavior. And though Mansfield's students surely talk about other matters, some more trivial, others certainly more serious, than those discussed here, their peer culture is nevertheless largely shaped by these themes.

The Diaries

Louise Maclane, Freshman

Today I was thinking about:

December 16, Sunday. All the words to all the songs that I had to sing today. I was walking up to the risers to sing and I even forgot the titles. I was so worried, but I guess I made it.

December 17, Monday. Running away from home. But then after I thought about it for a while I decided it wouldn't be worth it. Because somebody would find me then I would be in trouble by the cops and my mom and dad.

December 18, Tuesday. When I was going to take a test in Health because the chorus was going to Auburn during that period and I was afraid I would not find time to make it up and I would get a zero.

December 19, Wednesday. Not going to school because of the weather. I kept listening to the radio hoping it would say Mansfield will not have any school today. But then after it did say it I wanted to have school. That way in the summer when its warm we could take our snow days.

December 24, Monday. Killing myself. Because nothing was working out. Everytime I did something it was wrong. I just can't do anything right. But then if I did I would never get to heaven because I would have a very bad sin. So I'm trying to think of another thing to do.

December 25, Tuesday. One boy from Bradlow. He's a senior this year, but I always thought he was too old. But we went to Bradlow and I went with him, my two uncles, and my brother and had a real good time. Now I guess he's not that old after all.

December 29, Saturday. What it would be like to be pretty. I was looking in the mirror rolling my hair, and I looked so ugly I wondered how people could look at me.

December 30, Sunday. The way people was treating me. I don't really think anybody loves me or even likes me. And all I can think of is just let them feel the way they want to because I don't even care.

Fourteen-year-old Louise, MHS freshman, is almost a caricature of the young adolescent. In uneven language she pours out two weeks of woe, just able to find the odd spot of joy in the "boy from Bradlow." Otherwise, she writes as though she had gone to a psychology textbook before starting her diary to discover what American teen-agers are supposed to experience. Over the same time span, classmate Sheri Turner single-mindedly pursues a boyfriend.

Sheri Turner, Freshman

Today I was thinking about:

December 14, Friday. What my girlfriend and I were going to do tonight. I also was thinking if I was still mad at my boyfriend and if I should quit him or not before he finds out what's going to happen tonight.

December 15, Saturday. What happened last night. I quit him last night and I know I hurt him, but he asked for it. I just keep wondering what life is going to be like ahead of me, if I meant what I said to my guy and I'm sure I did, because I've been going with him 7 months, 2 weeks, and 5 days, and he is 1 year, 3 months, and 15 days younger than me and things aren't working out at all because I want to go on dates and I can't cause I'm tied down to him. It seems as though he really never did care about me when we were going together, so it makes me feel a little depressed.

December 16, Sunday. I think everything is finished between me and my X-boyfriend. I guess if he doesn't care, I don't either. I keep wondering if I'll lose these 2 extra pounds I gained over the weekend?

December 17, Monday. How my X-boyfriend never did care or really liked me. The reason I feel this way about him is that today when he gave my ring back to me he called me a bitch (please excuse my prophanaty). There is no way possible he can get me back now. To change the subject, I went to the X-mas concert at the Grade School and I thought it was really good, no older than the kids were.

December 18, Tuesday. If I'll ever get over this little puppy love affair. I don't really think I can, cause my X-boyfriend seems like a part of me, but if I try hard enough I think I'll get over it. I'll tell you one thing he's got a lot of growing up to do. I guess I'm not the only one who has this kind of problem. Today my oldest brother and his wife got a new car and I was thinking to myself if I'll ever raise enough money to buy me a brand new car when I get to the age of 19 or 20. I hope so.

January 7, Monday. How I really made a fool out of myself. Boy, I have to say I was really played for a rockey [rookie]. I have a new boyfriend or at least I think I do. I went to the Jr. High Basketball game tonight and after it was all over with I was setting in the lobby waiting for my sister. He (my X-boyfriend) went and walked past me, but I kind of what you call gave him the cold shoulder. I'll tell you one thing after he (my X-boyfriend) told me he was getting tired of my kind-of shit, I'm not about to lead him on.

January 8, Tuesday. How it would be nice if I could get some good advice from someone for all these boy problems I have. Well, I think I've figured out what I'll do about my X-boyfriend. I'll still be nice and talk to him cause it shows how much more I have to do in growing up.

January 9, Wednesday. Boy, I had a real fun day. My sister and I skated all over town. We got our adopted Grandma's their mail. Boy, you wouldn't believe how happy they are when they see you and how glad they are to have you go get their mail when it's this bad out. May I ask you a question? What would you do with an X-boyfriend, that has everything a girl like me would want, but is a little more than a year younger than me and he couldn't drive yet and I want to go out on dates with, but I can't cause he's not old enough? Would you wait for him or go ahead and have fun with this other guy until my "X" is old enough to drive?

Donna Victor, Sophomore

February 28, Wednesday. Seventh hour Janet and me went down to practice our solos but we just goofed off. Berner had to go to the grade school for Jr. High band so me and Janet went out and had a cigarette. After school Steve called and we talked for about an hour and a half. My lambs are a month old today. Jerry Hart called me to talk about Janet Rolf going back with him. He was drunk.

March 1, Thursday. After choir me and Janet went out and had a cigarette in Sarah's car. Then we went down in the dark room where Steve and Geri were making out. It was really sick. She's supposed to get married when Al comes home from service, she's going steady with Hank and dates Steve. One of these days she'll learn. Nina, Tom, Maris, George, Bill and Joan were all making out at the end of the Frosh Hall. Sterling came down and caught them. There's other places to go besides school to show their affections for each other, if you want to call it affection. It makes people wonder if they do that in public just think

what they do in private. At about 6:00 I babysat and the baby got sick
and barfed all over the floor.

March 2, Friday. Had to practice in the Jr. High boys' locker room.
It stinks down there. Practiced my solo second hour. Geri is going to
the university and stay with her sister and smoke grass. Went down in
the shop fourth hour with the guys and goofed off until noon hour.
Seventh hour we had an F.H.A. meeting. In eighth hour we had a missionary from our church that spent a year in Argentina. They speak
Spanish there so he showed us slides and tried to teach us new things.
After school all 19 of the little chickens got out. Danny's mom came
over and wanted me to go home with her so she wouldn't have to stay
by herself. We made candles and put a puzzle together. She is so sweet.

March 4, Sunday. Got up and went to church. Fran and I couldn't
listen to the sermon because we had to keep the nursery. After church
I went home, changed clothes and went up to play basketball. Me and
Willie went up for a rebound at the same time and when we came down
we tripped each other and I landed on top of him. At 4:00 mom and
dad came by and we went out to do the chores.

March 5, Monday. Directed the choir first hour. After that me and
Janet went out to Sarah's car to get our books and had a cigarette.
Second hour I went to practice my solo. I don't have it memorized yet
and it has to be memorized by Saturday for contest. Sixth hour we had
GAA, and then went to seventh hour P.E. After school I had to play
basketball. I played three quarters and made 5 points.

March 6, Tuesday. Was supposed to go to the game at Oakfield with
Geri, but she decided not to go so I went with the Sanders. We tied
about 100 times. The refs kept jewing us, most of the players and almost all the kids and cheerleaders were crying. We finally lost by 4
points. We went riding around a while, then took everybody home. I
owe each of them 10 kisses apiece because they made more points than
I predicted. It was really a raunchy night.

March 10, Saturday. Got out to the high school about 6:30 A.M. After a lot of confusion we finally got on our way. I was the first soloist in
my room and I was scared stiff. I got a second. I missed a first by one
point. Sarah was sick so her dad had to bring her. I had to take some
pills to settle me down. We had to wait on Tommy Harris about 20
minutes because he was so drunk he passed out. After I got home I
went to bed. I have to be in Sarah's wedding. If I keep this up while
I'm sick I'm going to be dead by the end of the weekend.

March 11, Sunday. Sarah got married today. After the wedding I
went home and then later on went to Janet's and then the Evangelical
Church to play hide-and-seek with the guys.

March 12, Monday. Mr. Berner was really in a bad mood. Lately,
he's always grouchy. He takes his personal problems out on the kids
and that's one thing that I think makes a good teacher go bad. A

teacher is for teaching kids to do things, not to take their problems out on. At noon hour me, Janet, and Hank went riding around with Ted and smoked some pot out of a pipe. Hank decided to skip this afternoon so he could go with Ted and smoke some more. Sixth hour me and Janet gave our report on coronaries. I think we got an A on it. Seventh we did stunts in P.E. again. Eighth we had a Spanish test. Me, Babs, and Bonnie graded each other's papers and wrote in a few answers. If we hadn't all three of us would have flunked it. Ate supper and then went up to meet the guys so we could play hide-and-go-seek at the Evangelical Church.

Donna Victor's diary entries provide a fairly complete picture of her days. Thus we learn that she misses little of MHS's in-class and out-of-class activities. Two years from now, when she graduates, the record beside her yearbook picture will attest to her energetic involvement in school affairs; it will contain no hint of the drive that extended after school to necking and hide-and-go-seek at church, chores, and babysitting. She cheats, practices hard for solo contest, and keeps Danny's mom company "so she wouldn't have to stay by herself." The contradictory facts of Donna Victor's days would distress the adults in her life. They are denied access to her contradictions; their lives are simpler without such knowledge.

Vita Adams, Sophomore

March 19, Monday. School was boring today, like it always is. Right after school, Hank picked me up. He took us to Helen's house and told me he would be back. He came back about 8:30 and went riding around until about 10:30. He didn't want me to go to Auburn with him because he was AWOL. I got home at 10:30 and the old lady was bitchin' like always.

March 20, Tuesday. Hank picked me up after school today. We listened to tapes and drank coffee. This Johnny Cash tape was playing, and Hank was singing a song and every time a certain part would come on he would sing it louder and look straight at me. I told my mom tonite that I was leaving this summer. Nina and I are going to live with her mom in Arkansas.

March 21, Wednesday. A lot of things happened today. Joan told me that Bill and George took off and Helen took a bunch of pills and she is in the phsko [psycho] ward at the hospital. Jesus! It all had to happen in one day. What a bummer! After school my little brother and I cooked supper, for my mom. After supper Nina and I went horseback riding. About 9:00 Hank came down. We went riding around. He told me that his recruiter called and he has leave until Saturday.

March 22, Thursday. School was better than usual today. Nina and I walked to uptown today and we really saw some tuff guys. They were riding around town so we went to Jeffersons [Cafe]. About twenty minutes later, they came in. Saturday Joan and I are going to babysit for her little brother and sister and if her older brother, Bill, comes home, we can't let him in the door. Her parents said not to. I don't know why.

March 23, Friday. School is terrible today. I had a drivers ed. test that was real hard, made cookies in home ec. that tasted like rubber and flunked my Biology test. Now I am in Study Hall, and Mrs. White came over here nosing around. I told her I was writing a diary.

For Vita Adams, the school part of her day is to be tolerated—no more, though she records some variation of feeling. It is OK, boring, and pretty good when the Brenton College Band and its "tuffer guys" play for an assembly. She awaits the complexities of her after-school life with absorption. In contrast with Vita Adams, Sheri Turner and Donna Victor emerge as innocents. Donna appears to like basketball about as much as kissing boys; she is not shy about either activity. Sheri's affair of heart has a "he loves me, he loves me not" quality. Vita's love life is constant in intensity and variable in feelings: in one astonishing eight-day period, beginning March 24, she looks for Hank on his last day home, finds him flirting with Helen, and gets drunk on Southern Comfort. "I guess there is a first time for everything." *March 25:* Hank is AWOL, he has a date with Lola, while Vita goes out with Larry Sams. "I much rather have been with Hank, though." *March 26:* Hank and Vita meet on the highway, each driving in a different car. Vita joins Hank and "This song, 'I Think I'm Falling in Love' came on and I was looking in the mirror at Hank and he turned and looked to. Boy, our eyes met and we both turned our heads real quick." *March 27:* Hank's car breaks down while he is driving with Joan. The police come by, Hank is "busted," and Joan gets three month's probation. "Joan thinks its all her fault and it can't be. I am not pissed at her but she knows I love Hank." *March 28:* Joan's brother Bill returns from somewhere. "I really wouldn't mind having Bill back. I do like him a hell of a lot but: Hank, it seems like he's always there. I'm just gonna forget about Hank and get Bill back." *March 29:* After school, Vita takes the family truck and heads straight for Bill's house even though her mother thinks Bill "is some kind of freak."

March 31, Saturday. Today was really boring but about 7:00 at night was another story. Nina-n-I went into Jeffersons and was drinking a coke. We drank about ½ of it and filled the rest with Southern Comfort! Wow! Then we left! We walked down by the tavern and then we started to walk back and there came Bill and their whole family. So Bill's dad told us to get in and take them home then Bill and Joan could come back. When we got out there the muffler was loose so Bill was tightening it up. Bill got finished underneath the car and he got up and said "So you don't believe I was in California, huh?" I said, nope. He said, well, I wasn't. Then he told me why he left and everything. Then he asked me if I wanted to try it again! I mean to go back with him. So I said okay! After we left I had a couple more gulps of Southern Comfort and I just barely remember the rest.

Janet Logan, Sophomore

November 30, Friday. At ten after 6 I went out to the ballgame. It was awful boring, maybe 'cause I was so depressed. No one knew I left and when my brother got home he said people wondered where I went.

December 4, Tuesday. I'm in heaven again! Had a really great day for a change. We got out of school at noon and I came home and worked. Bruce was here. He is going to the concert Thursday with us.

December 5, Wednesday. A bunch of us kids from the church went over to see a really funny play. Coming home I went to sleep on Ray's shoulder and he said he'd take me to see 2001 if he had his ring back. Betsy got the bright idea that I liked him. That was one short-lived rumor. I like him for a good friend. He has helped me a lot with my problems and believe me I've got enough.

December 6, Thursday. I discovered that Tony has an awful lot of personality and character. He's in my class at school but that was the first time I ever really talked to him. I'm really glad Bruce went with us. He gives me a feeling of security. He broke up with me a little over three weeks ago. If I had been keeping a diary then all anybody would see would be squiggly marks. I even lost six pounds. I didn't eat anything for three days but three cokes. It took me three weeks to get over him. I still try to remember it wasn't a dream.

December 8, Saturday. Something kind of funny happened today. Bruce went by and honked and I went downstairs saying "Bruce honked, Bruce honked." My little sister Connie says "Oh no, not again." I about died laughing. Boy this week has been so busy. I'm feeling really good.

December 17, Monday. I went to a volleyball game. Bruce is back with Barb—again. He just keeps going over the same girls. I come three from now. I think that is hilarious!

December 22, Saturday. I remember once I didn't want to get out of the car when Bruce brought me home and he asked me why. He said "Is it because you don't think I'll come back?" I said yes. Then he said "Don't worry, I'll *always* come back." Well, I can see my memory will bother me today.

December 24, Monday. Well, it's Christmas Eve and Santa comes. This Christmas something else is added that wasn't present in my life last year. That something is mainly Christ which led to everything that happened to me. I've got so many happy memories but then again I've **got too** many sad ones.

January 1, Tuesday. Yesterday morning and the day before I cried because I had so much fun last year and so many things happened to me, but now that it is a new year and I can't stop time, I am glad and my resolutions are to make this year better than last year, since last year was the best I can remember. My other resolution is to lose about 30 pounds. I have lost 20 so I know I can do it.

January 5, Saturday. For some reason I want to stand up and shout. I'm not shouting for joy though, I'm shouting for help. Another Saturday night I sat home. No one even called to talk. We had practice at the church today. I was just sittin there thinkin and I started crying. Everytime I want to say something or talk to someone they never hear. Maybe they just don't care. I know I'm a loner but that doesn't mean I should be lonely. I feel like everyone is always talking about me and always laughing at me.

Last year the Women's Club had a tour for Honor Roll students. I was sitting in the second seat from the back on the left side of our school bus talking to Bruce. A rabbit went running across a field and I pointed it out to Bruce. We were the only two people who saw it. That was the first time I really met Bruce.

I'm not going to fight my memories. I'm going to let them carry me away. Everything has a dark haze on it carrying me downward.

HELP!

From Wednesday to Saturday, ebullience to depression. Janet Logan's moods swing pendulumlike along a continuum of concern for Bruce. Bright, articulate Janet does well in school, though her diary reveals no more awareness of it than Vita Adams's. Both experience the longing of lost love, but Janet's life is marked by an introspective brooding like freshman Louise Maclanc's, only more sophisticated.

By some calculations, the culmination of brooding and longing and, occasionally, fulfillment is Sarah Hayward's experience. Beginning her diary shortly after the new year, she states in her first entry that she "woke up feeling crummy" and continues to report daily on the state of her health until it is clear that this pert, healthy senior is not sick but pregnant. Sarah marries Rod, has her baby, and returns to school one day to show off the child to students and teachers. All this occurs after she has stopped keeping her diary. At no time in the course of her diary writing do the strands of her adolescent life become unraveled. However tumultuous her love life, her curricular (band, psychology, and constitution test) and extracurricular (GAA and play practice) participation remains robust. Pregnancy, of course, is not the inevitable outcome of youthful enchantment with romance, which for most students seems to vary in intensity from high to higher, but few are either unenchanted or disenchanted. Beth Hoffman, the final female diarist, best exemplifies a low-intensity case. She disposes of Bill, a left-over from her junior year, the day after Valentine's Day and settles down to almost two weeks of parentally wholesome days. In her Southern Comfortless life, she likes basketball and "Etomology" as much as she likes Bill. Four years later as a college senior Beth cringes at the memory of Bill, recalling that in high school it just seemed necessary to have a boyfriend and for one year Bill was her candidate.

Sarah Hayward, Senior

January 11, Thursday. Woke up feeling crummy but had to go to school for Psychology semester test. Well, I think I flunked it but that's okay. History was all right today. Mr. Doddson is *so* tuff! All together school was a bore. After school, I went bowling for GAA. I bowled my highest of 136. I'm so proud of myself! Janet and I decided to go to the game at Auburn. Mom let me drive. I let Janet and Donna off and went to Brenton to Rods. [Rod attends a nearby college. His family lives in Forest where he grew up and went to school.] I don't know what to do, I love him so much and he loves me. I could get pregnant or run off and get married but those two are so wrong. We are just going to have to wait until I'm 18. What a bummer of a night.

January 12, Friday. Woke up a little late but made it to school on time. Took the rest of the Psychology test. Yeah!! They cancelled play practice so I'll have to call Rod after school. Wanda didn't want to be on our volleyball team and kept bitching and got mad and walked down to the shower room. After sixth hour Mrs. Douglas griped me. I'm super mad! I was coming home from school and Lee Cobert hit my car and bashed the side in. I cried.

January 13, Saturday. I have to wash my hair and get ready for my date with Rod. Rod came at 7:00 and we went to Chubbs party. I felt sick but thought nothing of it. I drank and got sick and puked all over the place.

January 14, Sunday. Woke up with bad hangover and made a lie up to mom why I was sick. I had to take Helen and Donna home at 2:30. Didn't go to church and stayed in bed until Rod came down. He stayed until 10:30, when Mom told me I better go to bed. He got mad because he's a big 195 lbs., 6'2" body that is 18 years old! I cried a little and went to bed sick.

January 15, Monday. Still sick so stayed home. I hate to miss school but would rather do that then be sick at school. Today is my birthday. I'm a whole 17.

January 16, Tuesday. Still sick but went to school at noon. It was crummy of course. I have to stay 30 minutes after school for Mr. Doddson Friday. Went to the game and Rod came. We came to my house and talked about the chance of me being pregnant. We are both a little upset but not too worried. In a way I hope I am, but yet, with no money, it will be hard to live with Rod going to school not to mention supporting a wife and a baby.

January 17, Wednesday. Came to school and took a test eighth hour which I probably flunked. Steve just asked me to go to the show with him and I said no. I got in trouble in P.E. study hall for talking. I didn't flunk my English test. I only missed 6. Studied for at least 3 hours for my constitution test. That is the test I'm afraid of flunking.

January 18, Thursday. Woke up at about 7:30. It was hard to get ready because I was so tired. Had band then the constitution test. I don't think I did too bad on it. We went to Auburn after school and ate and then had play practice from 6:30–8:00. Came home and watched a good show with James Stewart in it.

January 19, Friday. Came to school and had band. Spent all third hour changing from study hall to psychology. It looked pretty funny, me, Dave, and Rob walking the halls all hour. Typing was very boring. Especially since I know I had to stay after school for 10 minutes and we got out at 2:30. It really isn't that bad since I had to stay in Mrs. Scott's room and I really like her. I guess you could say she's my favorite teacher. Rod came over and watched T.V. then went to his apartment and talked about our problem. We both agreed it was O.K. except telling our parents.

January 21, Sunday. Went to Sunday School and church. Play practice was awful.

January 22, Monday. Went to school. Had psychology. We have a pretty good class. Went to play practice. Got home at 10:30 and put my clothes together for picture taking Tuesday.

January 23, Tuesday. Woke up feeling sick but rolled my hair and got all my clothes together and came to school. We took pictures all day. I only had History and Typing. Mom said something to Janet about me not starting [menstruating] yet! Oh, I wish I could see Rod. On weekends just isn't enough. We haven't decided how we are going to tell our parents yet. I'm scared but so unsure. Maybe I'm just too worried to start. I better go to bed before I drive myself crazy.

January 26, Friday. Mom asked me about the fact I haven't started but I lyed out of it.

January 27, Saturday. His parents and mine have heard that we are getting married.

Beth Hoffman, Senior

February 13, Tuesday. Today didn't turn out as I wanted it to. Mrs. Taylor came in during my study hall and said that ours was the last class to have a Senior Class Trip. When I asked why she said we didn't have enough money and that only a few people did all the work in the class, but that seems true in almost anything that is done. I almost forgot we had a Medical Career meeting today. I'm positive now that I am going to do something in the medical field.

February 14, Wednesday. During 1st hour today I went to a meeting where any of the interested Juniors and Seniors could go. A recruiting officer came to tell us about the Army. He really made it sound interesting, but I know I would never join. Bill came back at noon hour. I told him I thought he had quit school, but he said he hadn't, he had been sick. I also noticed he had his ring back so I asked him if he had broken up with Terry. He had. I then decided I would talk to him, but now I realized that was a dumb move. I really don't know why I listened to him I knew he was feeding me a bunch of lies and I soon found out I was right. When we dated before he was so kind and sweet to me.

February 15, Thursday. Well, I told Bill off so that'll be the last I'll see of him. They offered this year a new course with Latin 2— Etomology. Only the Latin 2 students would take the 1st semester then any one could come in during the 2nd semester. I really like it. You learn so many new words. I really didn't like the way Mrs. Douglas taught Latin 2, but you couldn't ask for a better teacher for Etomology. Sometimes she's so spacy its funny. Like the other day she came in and started testing us on Lesson 4, but we weren't even completed with 3 yet.

February 16, Friday. Finally, I thought Friday would never come. Today at noon hour the Pep Club is supposed to have a meeting.

February 19, Monday. I didn't have all my English done, but hardly anyone did. We're studying about Walt Whitman and we had to read some poem that was 6 pages long! The one thing I can't stand to do is interpret poems, but Mrs. Scott makes them interesting. I didn't have to go to work until five, so Peggy and I went riding around. When I got home Kerry came over so we could do Algebra together.

February 20, Tuesday. Had a usual day at school. All my classes went just as always. Some of them I would become bored in, but maybe the next day they would be the most interesting one.

February 21, Wednesday. We had our Etomology test today. I really didn't study much for it, but the way I look at it you either know it or you don't. There was about 100 points on it and I got 100. We sang at Auburn this afternoon at the Nursing Home, then Mrs. Taylor let us get a drink at the D.Q. [Dairy Queen].

February 26, Monday. School wasn't boring at all today. 3rd hour a man came to talk to us about reptiles. He brought all kinds. He had a python, a boa constrictor, poisonous lizards, and spiders (etc.). I only had 1 class in the morning and 1 class in the afternoon too.

February 27, Tuesday. Today was a great day. Nothing much happened at school, but about 5:00 things started to roll. Our GAA team played Forest. We lost, but it was a good game. The referee said even though our team was losing it was the best game she had ever seen girls play. At the 1st half we were behind by 13 or 14 points, but the 3rd quarter we started scoring and lost by 4 points. It was a very clean and fair game. Monday night we play Harris here. I can't wait cause I love to play basketball.

Billy Randolph's diary is the first of four written by male students. He is a junior involved in sports, trapping, drinking, and romance, though much less of the last than many of the girls. Mansfield's rural location easily satisfies this young man's hunting ambitions and on December 23 he has "one heck of a day." (More of the country flavor of Mansfield is captured in a senior boy's late spring musings: "If I could, right now I'd be sitting on the river bank fishin'. I've done it all week. We've been talking about getting fish fever. You set in school, see how nice it is and everything, and you want to go fishin'.")

Billy does not ignore his school work, even during Christmas vacation, the period covered by most of his diary. His writing is terse, like Louise Maclane's, but lacks the anguish of her pointed entries. As though advised to "keep it brief," he skips on with usually fewer than fifty words per entry from one "nothing day" with hunting and trapping to one sad day with a girl to one "WOW!" night with cases of beer. Suffering boys either do not keep diaries or, possibly, when they do they less readily convey their pain. That they experience it, however, is made clear by each of these four diarists. But what might have inspired Janet Logan to lament her loneliness one day and to be enraptured the next, evokes relatively moderate expression, for example, from Fred Jay. On December 14, after photographer Archer delivers the yearbook pictures, he is upset when fellow students fail to clamor for his photograph. The next day, a clamor having set in, he expresses his luck "to have as many kids wanting them."

Appearing conscious of more in himself and in his school experience than Billy Randolph, Fred Jay also writes of sports, girls, and trapping. Not too sure of his own athletic prowess, he bristles at teammate Gardner's ball hogging. His commentary on romantic matters carries a bit of that swagger and bravado which seems to be the norm for some young Mansfield males. Sheri Turner's "X" calls her a bitch, Billy regretfully tells his girl where to go, and Fred Jay's Michele is "not a bitch like *most* of the others."

Billy Randolph, Junior

December 21, Thursday. Last day of school. I didn't have my Eng. III Research paper done, but I did it during the Christmas party. Went to Bert's nothing going on so I went home and went to bed.

December 22, Friday. Did my Christmas shopping, ordered my New Year's Eve cheer and didn't do anything all day.

December 23, Saturday. Had one heck of a good day. Hunted all day, killed a pheasant, my first of the year, a quail, and a rabbit. Went out and played ping-pong with Paul till about 11:30.

December 29, Friday. Well this is a nothing day. Hunted all day and saw nothing. We lucked out and pulled our traps before the rivers all flooded.

December 30, Saturday. Had a fight with a girl, and I am about sick. I like her but don't want to go steady. I told her where to go and now I'm sorry.

December 31, Sunday. What a day. The day wasn't so great, but the night. WOW! We had three cases of Millers for three people. I lost count at 9 and passed out after awhile.

January 1, Monday. I feel like hell this morning. When I woke up the light about killed me. I have a hangover you wouldn't believe. I can still feel the beer in me and I didn't eat all day. Went out that night and drank six screw-drivers and my hangover went away. I watched the football games, then worked on my Black Lit and went to bed. What a day.

January 2, Tuesday. What a drag. School started and I couldn't hunt today. I hated to go back but I had to and it wasn't so bad after I got there. New Year's Eve when I was plastered, I realized one thing. That is I can't do without football.

Fred Jay, Junior

November 29, Wednesday. It was difficult being a small hero after the basketball game last night. That's the first real glory I've had for a while. Black Lit. is seemingly tougher because Scott gives us too many papers to write out. Norwood changed the monotony of Economics by taking us up to the bank. Tonight Hart and I are going to Michele's to play pool. Got back from Michele's house. Still can't make my objective. Michele is the kind of girl I've wanted. She's not a bitch like *most* of the others.

November 30, Thursday. Had a very easy practice last night. I really wish it would be hard. Wrote my paper for Black Lit. Once I got started it was easy to finish.

December 1, Friday. Boring day at school. We didn't have our Pep Assembly because of the jerks at Tuesday's game. Didn't have Chemistry because of the FHA and FFA meetings.

December 4, Monday. Held Student Poll in school today. Wasn't too good of a turnout. Nothing else happened except practice was very slow. Everything was slow.

December 5, Tuesday. Only had a half a day of school. Teacher's institute today at noon. Went home and played Ping-Pong and slept till around 4:00 p.m. Had to get up before the game. We finally beat Forest. I only scored two points but I rebounded a lot better.

December 7, Thursday. School wasn't too bad. Noon hour was more exciting. Had more fun than usual. Found out from Hank that he's finally getting some off Geri Portle. I figured he was. I just hope he doesn't ruin her. I've been messing around with a couple of 8th graders. I'd better lay-off. They're both kind of young.

December 8, Friday. School Pep Club is having problems. If they don't yell tonight the club will dissolve. I have been lucky to have no homework at all this week. Beat Harris 52–48. Damn Gardner is a real ball hog. If he doesn't straighten up, he's going to get told off.

December 9, Saturday. Worked this morning at the store. Wasn't too bad. Slept most of the afternoon. Tommy and I went to Brenton to Patterson's apartment and got drunk. Ride home wasn't too bad. Switched into Tommy's car and went by Chuck Folsom's party. Cops were watching it and Ferris stopped us for loud mufflers. I was a little scared when he searched the car because I didn't know what Tommy had in it. It was a close call.

Like many small communities, Mansfield has one full-time policeman who begins work in the evening and remains on duty during the night. One of his main jobs is to enforce a curfew for school-aged youth. Thus one challenge of the high school student is to break curfew and to avoid getting caught; another is to drive with an open can of beer and to avoid getting caught. The policeman is a local person and likely to know what curves to watch for speeders and which houses and cars to observe for youthful revelers.

December 13, Wednesday. NO SCHOOL again. Ralph and I brought some more traps. Took them out and set them. I think he is cheating on me. If he is, I'm going to get all my traps and sell them. I don't like the idea of getting jewed.

December 14, Thursday. Exchanged pictures today. Didn't get too many book. It kind of pisses me off. Steve and I are going to screw around with a couple of 8th graders tomorrow night. It is going to make me a laugh but what the hell. I don't care.

December 15, Friday. I've got to get some more pictures. I'm lucky to have as many kids wanting them.

December 16, Saturday. Got up and worked till noon. Nothing going on at night. Rode around Auburn. Bev (my ex-girl) and her boyfriend were riding around.

December 25, Monday. Merry X-mas. Christmas was boring. Went to Teri's and talked. Followed ex-girl and her boyfriend around town a little then came home.

January 4, Thursday. First hour study hall is the same as usual. Riggs doesn't let anything go on. One can't even whisper there. When she leaves the room all hell breaks out because we can't talk with her in there. Second hour Black Lit is getting more boring everyday.

January 5, Friday. The school day here is usually kind of dull. Nothing happens that is unusual. Everything that happens in the newspaper is outside of us. We are actually in our own little world. Us kids are trying to keep away from the responsibility we will have soon. We don't know the actual things that go on. We know that it is happening but we haven't faced anything eye to eye.

January 8, Monday. Classes are so boring I try to find some way of making them more exciting or interesting. Whether I talk about something off the subject or not. I'll do almost anything to make the class not seem so boring. That's why I get my good grades. The kids all give up too easy.

January 9, Tuesday. This morning Tate gave us a lecture on school attendance. He was saying that the future would be the time when it would show up. Which is true. I more or less laughed because I don't have that problem. It's the dum-asses that do. Maybe they don't realize what will happen later on.

Craig Lanton, Senior

The people whom I will be involved with are people who live in this area. Some I like, some I don't. My opinions on some things are bound to be biased but since it's my diary that's the way it's going to be. It will mainly deal with the school day, peer relationships, and what I do for entertainment during my free time and weekends. I will tell it how it is and I won't leave out any facts.

Craig Lanton, good-natured jock and restless senior, is at loose ends between basketball and track season. Like many older students with cars, he takes advantage of the continuing, post-season athletic activity to attend the series of games that eventually lead to basketball nirvana —the state tournament. Contrary to his own introduction, he writes little or nothing about his school days or about his peer relationships except as they involve the romantic complications which occupy his "free time and weekends." His four-day diary opens calmly with a general reflection on his senior year. He ushers in the aura of excitement and confusion of the next three days with his first sentence, "Well, last night I went over to the Regional Tournament"—where he sees Mary Harble. The aura continues with a profusion of sentences each beginning with an explosive "Well." It is as though having released this little burst of sound, he can then go on to express his thought.

March 1, Wednesday. Since this is my Senior year I can't help from feeling that at last it's finally here; my last year. The only thing that I look forward to is graduation. I really can't figure out why it's so boring. I guess I'm just anticipating getting out. Today, not much happened. Just like usual. Since basketball is over I don't have anything to do until track starts. Tonight I think I'll go to Summit and see Auburn and Harris play in the regional. I really don't care about the game. I just want to go over and check up on this girl from Auburn named Mary Harble.

March 2, Thursday. Well, last night I went over to the Regional tournament. Bill Howard went with me. On the way over we stopped at Shelton and I went into the tavern and got a six pack of Budweiser to drink on the way over. Well, you remember that cheerleader I was telling you about, Mary Harble? Well, she looked up and gave me a big smile so I decided right then and there to ask her out. Well, the game ended and Auburn won, and I never did get a chance to talk to her. But those big smiles of hers were enough to keep me hopin! Well, on the way back we came up behind Auburn's student bus and who do you think was in the back seat? You're right, it was Mary. Well, she really started wavin' and smiling so then I was really determined to ask her out. Well, we got back in Auburn and started riding around when we saw Mary and her sister Nancy walking; so I pulled over and asked them if they wanted a ride. Well, they hopped in and Mary scooted right over next to me. It took me by surprise so I liked to shit in my pants. I think it was one of those times when I was at a loss for words. All I could do was stutter. Well, we got to Shakey's and I got a coke and sat down. She came over and sat down also. Well, then I started to take them home and she got in and scooted over next to me again. Then I really made up my mind to ask her out. Well, we got to her house and her sister went in and then it was just me and her. We talked for about 20 minutes when she started to get real cuddly. This whole situation took me by surprise, so I didn't quite no how to handle the situation. I'm really very shy if I don't know the person. Then I walked her up to the door and she was acting really nice. Then I got a brainstorm. I decided to play kind of hard to get. So I said good night and didn't ask her out. As I started to leave she asked me to come down to her house tomorrow night which is tonight. I'll probably go, but I feel I must tell you the real reason why I didn't ask her out before I close for the day. I was just plain Chicken!

March 3, Friday. School day wasn't to bad, since it was Friday, but Friday night was really a bummer. Our choir had to sing at the Brethren Church. That was kind of enjoyable because it wouldn't hurt me to go to church more often. Well, I guess I'll start with the bad part. I had Julie with me but we got into a big fight so I told her either to shut up or I was going to take her home. Minutes later . . . on the way to Auburn (by myself) I decided to go down to Mary Harble's house. Well, no sooner I got in Auburn when she pulled up in her car so I hopped in with her and went riding around. That's about all I did Friday, not much action over all.

March 4, Saturday. This day was a real heller. I got up around 9:00 and then went and cleaned my car out. Well, that afternoon my friends and I from Auburn decided to go to Bradlow. Left at 5:30 P.M. and first stopped at Brenton to get a case of Budweiser to drink on the way up. Well, we got in and got some beer and listened to the band until 9:00 then we left. We were all pretty drunk. We made it back to Auburn around 10:30 and went to a party in Harris. It was pretty wild.

This Saturday was a lot of fun, but I have a feeling better ones are on their way. Oh, Jesus! This school week has been terrible. All's that I have been doing is mostly girl trouble. It's like this. I broke up with Julie to date the cheerleader from Auburn I was telling you about, Mary Harble, and then I decided I shouldn't have because I found out I really liked her (Julie). Well, Julie has a cousin in Auburn, Joyce, and she is at the root of all my problems. She fed Mary a bunch of crap about me and Julie really got upset. Then Joyce tried to fix it so Julie wouldn't go out with me. She just about succeeded. In the meantime she was getting Julie fixed up with this kid from Auburn. They were just literally trying to screw me up royal. I don't know what to do! I have a feeling that I might lose them both, but what the heck, I'll get over it.

Craig Lanton and Art Thompson, the next diarist, have been classmates since kindergarten. Both played football, are bored with school, and enjoy drinking; otherwise, they have little in common. Craig is part of Mansfield's mainstream. By all local standards, he is successful in and out of school. Art, to the contrary, is bright, sensitive, and alienated from Mansfield's school and community. He has never become socialized to prevailing norms. His hair was long before it was fashionable and therefore acceptable to have long hair. For some years his father has been gone and his mother, left to raise three children, has "a reputation." Like Vita Adams, he has local friends, but the focus of his day is outside school in a serious attachment to his Dar, a non-Mansfielder to whom he is engaged at the outset of the diary and later marries. Once Art settles down in marriage, school resumes importance. He appreciates the need for a diploma, wants no more than this from MHS, but is unable to comply sufficiently with Mrs. Scott's expectations to feel assured of graduation. Mrs. Scott is the favorite of most students. Perhaps because it is not their school and community, the Art Thompsons of Mansfield are not reached by Mrs. Scott and her fellow teachers.

Art Thompson, Senior

Before I start my diary I wanna give kind of a character sketch of some of the people I might mention in this diary. Just please excuse the spelling and grammar. I never was good in writing. I hate English.

Dar = Darlene is the girl in my life. There's been others, but no "one" like her. She's special (we're engaged). Dar is 18. She's got a real nice personality. I would say she's easy to get along with. That is we hardly ever fight (but when we do, we do). There's only one problem Dar has that is she can't get along with her mother. I can understand why. When I first started dating Dar she "Hated" me. Simply because of my long hair.

Billy = Billy is our little angel. He's 11 months old and one of the cuttist little baby's there is. He can't be any sweeter. [Dar and Billy live with Dar's mother until Dar and Art get married.]

Simp = Dan Cartwright. Simps just cool. He goes to Mansfield Tech [a mildly derogatory name for Mansfield High School], and he's one of my best friends. He's wild!

December 7, Thursday. Today was basicly the same as any other day. I got up and went to school. School was the same. In 7th hour P.E. we played dodge ball by the rules called jail. When you get hit you hafta go behind the opposite lines and to get out of jail you hafta touch a ball then run.

I then (after school and supper, about 6:30) went down to the Marathon Station and shot the B.S. Then I decided to drive to Brenton to pick up my girlfriend for our daily talk. My day isn't complete without seeing her. But I've got to stop seeing her so much because I'm not working any more and mom can't afford too let me bum that much gas. After I'm 18, I'm gonna try to get a job. Lots of things are gonna happen then. Wait and see.

December 8, Friday. Friday was a regular day. It started out O.K. that is. I reckon it ended that away to. I got up and went to school. School was the same old line of B.S. After school I went bombing around in my car. I sold concessions at the ball game. After the ball game I headed for Dar's house. I left her house at 12:30 and made it home 20 minutes later for curfew.

December 15, Friday. Today was the same as yesterday. Nothin happened. I went to school then ran around a little after school, went home and ate supper. Then I went out ice-skating at the old plant. It's a riot except I haven't got any ice skates. Simp broke them for me.

December 20, Wednesday. Went to school today. I worked on the potters wheel. It's something that takes a lot of talent. I didn't get anything of it. I stayed in Mansfield tonight. So naturally I was bored!

Started Diary Again March 6, Tuesday. Things have changed for the better since I last wrote in this diary. By changing I mean my life. I'm now happier. Nothing was wrong with my home or anyone there. I really got along well with my mom and brothers. I just didn't like it. I really like married life. I love my wife and son. I've only got one problem that really bothers me. That is, school. My grades in English, geography and history are really low. I've really got to crack down to graduate. I've done decided that if I don't graduate that I'm not coming back next year. I'm going to get my diploma but not through Mansfield Tech. I'm living in Auburn now. I got a job but I lost it because I can only work second shift.

March 7, Wednesday. I didn't go to school today because I didn't get out of bed until 10:30. Dar did the laundry and she drove my car to work. Nothing really happened today, with the exception of "get this" I actually did homework. "Really"!!! It don't sound like anything unusual for someone else. But Me!! I haven't done any homework since seventh grade. And that's the truth. This world's gotta be coming to an end. I'm not sick, just depressed because of school.

March 8, Thursday. Well, I went to school today. I have to put my hours in there. I've gone to Mansfield Tech for just almost 6 years. I really didn't mind the first four. But the last two are really starting to get to me. There's one certain teacher I can't stand. I don't know where she got her college diploma. Maybe K-mart on some credit card she stole off some old lady up around 90 years old. She's really bad. Mrs. Scott is the one. She sat behind her big desk today and told the class that we didn't have to be there. Bull, what good chance does a young kid have without at least a high school diploma. You have to at Mansfield whether you like her or not because how else are you gonna get that year of English required for graduation. You can't because there's only 2 English teachers. The teachers make the kids quit. Mrs. Scott has just about accomplished the very same god damn thing. Last night I missed a curve and ran through a hedge. It wasn't to bad after I got back down to earth. I'm gonna go get good and drunk. So I'll feel like going to school tomorrow!

These diaries exemplify what students are likely to think and talk about while they are in school. They suggest several themes which comprise Mansfield's student peer culture. The impact of this culture intersects with the curricular and extracurricular life of the school and influences a student's response to the "business" side of school. Can we doubt that Janet Logan behaved differently in school during her heartbreak days when she drank only three cokes and lost six pounds, or that Sarah Hayward was distracted by her morning sickness and consequent anxiety over her parents' response to her pregnancy?

For most of the Vitas, Louises, Billys, and Arts, who describe the more private aspects of their life, things will never be the same again after leaving high school. Their diaries portray this incredibly indulgent period when through their constant contact with many other young men and women they are enabled to engage in continuous romantic fantasy and interaction. Moreover, the period of adolescence contained within the high school years has hedonism as its hallmark.[6] To be sure, there is a work side to this picture, both in school and out of school, and all pleasure seeking does not result in fulfillment. But having a good time is central in a student's life.

Elsewhere I wondered about the relative investment that students make in curricular and extracurricular affairs. Such estimations are complicated by those informal, unscheduled matters which suffuse the school day and which, as the diaries verify, are profoundly absorbing.

Since these matters do intrude into the school, it is only appropriate to identify them in this picture of Mansfield High School.

However, very few diaries refer to still another experience which affects a student's life in school—his after-school job. Since Fred Jay works only on weekends, he manages to attend all required basketball practices. Art Thompson goes to work after he gets married. Other students, none of whom volunteered to write a diary, concentrate on their jobs and merely pass time in school doing what is needed to graduate. They often own new cars and must work to make their monthly payments. Art is a good example of that student who, though school has lost its meaning for him, yet hangs on, knowing that job prospects are dismal without a diploma. He scornfully flouts Mrs. Scott for telling his class they did not have to be in school. "Bull," Art says, "what good chance does a kid have without at least a high school diploma." In fact, he fails to graduate with his class, though he eventually gets his diploma after making up his English deficiency in an out-of-school program designed to help persons like Art graduate.

Few students are as close to being "settled" as Art. To the contrary, most are hesitant and uncertain about the decisions they face. Of course graduation soon resolves the perplexities of some seniors. Their perplexities reflect not only the spirit of the time—what is "cool" and what is "tough," but also the peculiarities of their locality. Meanwhile, the students have been socialized in, by, and, possibly, for Mansfield.

God and country, sports, pep, voluntarism, romancing, drinking, and cruising—these are some of the major dimensions of growing up American in Mansfield. The community's high school provides occasion, setting, and reinforcement for these beliefs and behaviors which join with feelings about community and village life to produce the contented small-town citizen. Before this stage is reached, however, the turmoil of the senior year must be experienced, when the customary urge to "get away from this place" merges with countervailing sensations.

9

Views from the Top:
The Seniors' Perspective

Among all students the views of seniors bear most heavily on the adolescent peer culture; they are a high school's elite. Seniors undoubtedly have a limited perspective on school and community owing to their youth and lack of experience with other places and cultures. Their opinions and points of view, however, may never again be as instrumental in shaping the behavior of a large group as they are this one year. The seniors whose statements illustrate this chapter belong to one graduating class.[1] Many common feelings and views permeate this group.

The high school years are a long rite of passage for American youth, after which childhood should be left behind. For some, college represents a grace period, but the choice of further schooling still should represent a decision of responsibility rather than a mere prolongation of the youthful, carefree side of adolescence. To be sure, good times are not a thing of the past just because one graduates, but there is a quality of good times that passes with graduation.

However much the graduate may look back later at his senior year as not all that much of a watershed, at the time feelings of finality prevail. It is a time for lasts—the last occasion for being together with a group known since kindergarten, the last dance, the last football and basketball game played or attended as a student, the last split performed as cheerleader, the last illegal smoke in the washroom, the last class cut, the last forged note, the last class joke, and, possibly, the last time to be part (albeit involuntarily) of an organization so singlemindedly devoted to the well-being of its members. Ruby remarks:

> This year's prom is going to be most meaningful to you probably because it's the last one. And graduation. You're always, from the beginning, counting weeks and weeks. And then when you graduate you wish you were back in, you know.

> The year has gone so fast I can't remember it [observes Maryann]. I think it has because each thing happens, like the last Homecoming, or something, and you say, "Well, I won't be here next year." That's the biggest thing, that this is our last this or this is our last that. I know I'm a senior, but I don't feel that much different. Till May 29th

comes. Then I can say what it's like to be a senior—not being able to look forward to next year here.

Seniors generally do not doubt that it is good to have reached the final year of high school. Some have reservations: "I'm going to miss school when I get out. I know that. I will. I don't want to graduate really; this part of my life is so long. I don't know how it's going to be after I get out." More feel like Helen:

> I know I'm gonna have to graduate. I know I'll be in tears that night. It's gonna be pretty sad to have to leave good ol' MHS. I'm always griping about it, but I really like it. I'm excited about going to school and meeting all the new kids and then decide what I'm gonna do the rest of my life. I think that's sorta exciting.

They believe that MHS is basically a good school, failing mostly because it lacks a student lounge where cokes, snacks, and smokes would be available to mitigate the tedium of tiring days and to add zest to good ones. "We kids been trying to get a student lounge; you know, a place to smoke." But, says Ruby, "I think the teachers have a love for the kids here. It's just that people gripe. What they have they don't like."

Seniors are impatient to be free of routines that have become boring; yet it is the routine that some students will miss.

> Being with the kids and having that school to go to day after day, . . . well, it's just sort of, it's the routine. I know that's where I've belonged for thirteen years. That's where I've gone every day. I think that's what I'll miss: that routine of get up and go to school, this is where I'll be, this is who I'll be with.

Summer vacation provides respite to the routine that with pleasure is reestablished each fall. Seniors are distressed with "bossy" teachers who speak down to them, who fail to appreciate that seniors should be treated with consideration and respect. Hugh says, "Some teachers think they run this school. They try to boss you around. Fifty percent of 'em are like that." And Jerry agrees. "Teachers here think they're so great. If they want to run over us, they could run over us. It don't really matter what the student will say."

Like expectant mothers, seniors anxiously count the days until graduation—"Three or four more days," says Tony, "three or four more days." Yet they are unsure that the days of their forthcoming freedom will be as happy as the ones they soon will complete. Some are pained by the terrible wisdom that they cannot go back to do it over and do it right. And they are alternately nostalgic about the last (lost?) every-things created by graduation while cheered by the firsts that graduation makes possible. Being a senior in high school is the culmination of those years which at first seem endless and then pass by all too soon. And, sometimes, in the midst of their final year, when the end is very near, students may blast forth a sad mixture of anger and disappointment like buckshot fired at an unknown target. Listen to some senior girls:

"Well, that's what I mean. All your life you look forward to being a senior, you know, think it's a big shot. And then once you're a senior there's no big deal."

"Yeah, I'll be glad when I graduate."

"This whole school sucks. I hate every bit of it. I don't care. That's what I feel."

"As a student body I think we're a part of this school. I think we should be informed of what's happening in it, too."

"It's not that we should have more freedom, but we should know what's going on."

"And I'm sick and tired of the seniors being treated like sixth-graders."

"Like you go in the office. They say, 'What are you in here for? Do you have a pass? How long do you plan on being here?' and all this stuff."

"When I come to school I know that's just the less days I'm going to have to come later."

"What I'm going to like about graduation is we get away from Mansfield."

"You get to get out and be out on your own."

"You can't have those certain few telling you what to do."

"There'll always be somebody telling us what to do, like if we get a job. But it ain't going to be like any of the people out here or I won't work for 'em."

"I'm going to miss some things, though, like cheerleading."

"Well, I'll miss football days and stuff like that."

"You can always come back to the games."

"Yeah, but you can't participate."

"You're outside looking in then."

In Mansfield, high school graduation is an important event. It marks the end of formal education for most people in a community where youth are urged, usually, to acquire a diploma as their ticket to work, less often, to college; where the majority have less than four years of high school education themselves; and where education is valued for teaching the basics and for its vocational implications. Clarence supports the basics idea, albeit in language less elegant than his elders on the school board:

Well, to me the main thing you actually need is writing, arithmetic, multiplication, division. All you need is reading and writing and the basic facts of arithmetic. It's all right to know that history, but to me it's not going to do that much good when you get out. They teach the stuff that's actually supposed to help you when you get out, but history isn't really going to help you in any job. I'm not after that much of a job, probably. I'm not going to college and I'll just probably be a factory worker. I haven't got the grades to go to college anyway. I only make about Cs. In my book, all you need are the four basic things—reading, writing, and arithmetic. What else is there? Reading, writing, and arithmetic, and maybe English.

And the necessity of a diploma for getting a job has become entrenched as conventional wisdom, as several senior girls note:

"I'd quit now if I didn't have to come."
"You have to get an education or you can't get nothin'."
"When you go someplace, they say, 'Did you finish school?' And if you say 'No,' that means you're not dependable."
"You're lazy."
"You're a dummy. You don't want to work."
"And you have a hundred other people who have a diploma who are applying. Yeah, that's realistic."

These days, most Mansfield youth do reach and complete their senior year, though not without unease for some, turmoil for others. It is the bittersweet year. Now, at last, one is looked up to as the epitome, the senior. Mystique blends with myth, supported by a bedrock of prerogatives granted and assumed. Undeniable is the seniors' age and experience, which for a brief time do count for something. "A senior," says Ruby, "is allowed to do a lot more than the rest of the students are. Like when a teacher wants something done, they'll usually look towards the seniors." Tony agrees: "I think the school runner sort of falls to the senior class. I'm the top one now; see, I'm on the top."

Somewhat obscured for lower classmen is the press of decisions to be made at the close of the senior year—job, school, marriage, and where to live, decisions which in the seniors' unsettled state cloud the air like swarms of horseflies on an otherwise beautiful beach. A year later, forgetting the flies, one recalls the beach with satisfaction; not so at the time. Take the case of Hugh:

You hear all these kids can't wait to get out of school. I used to say it; I know I did. But you get up here now [the senior year] and you don't know what you're going to do when you get out. I'd like to have about two more years of school instead of graduating. So many different decisions.

Seniors generally keep their uncertainty to themselves, not sharing with often equally perturbed peers their doubts about succeeding in college or moving to a new, larger place, and their concern as to whether they will be accepted after leaving the comfortable confines of Mansfield school and community. "It's not hard to be involved here," observes Wayne, "because of the clubs and that stuff, but when you graduate it's all over. I got about thirty-eight friends here. It's not easy to say forget about 'em all and go out and meet new people." Of course, students like Mary feel they would "rather go on": "It can't last forever. When I get older and look back my high school is just gonna be a very, very little portion of my life." But many share Linda's confusion:

> I don't know if I want to get out of school 'cause I don't know what I'm going to do. I don't say anything to anybody else about it. Everybody seems like they want to get out of school real bad, and I don't.

She has more company than she knows, including those like Cynthia who recognize the social loss she will experience when she no longer has the school to unite her with her friends.

> OK, I'm a senior, right? Like next year everybody's going off to college or getting married, and like all your friends and things are going to go astray. Just to get to go to school, you know, and get with people and your friends and everything, that's something to look forward to, too. Even on three-day weekends, in a little town you don't probably see your friends very often. Because they all have guys, you know, and they all go with their guys and then you never see 'em till Monday morning. Like next year there's not going to be that school to bring us all together every Monday morning.

The sons and daughters of Mansfield's farmers and factory workers do value their school experiences. Mike, for example, extols the virtues of bookkeeping, occupational information, shop, and English, pleased with Mrs. Norwood's insistence that he read books which were slow going at the outset. And Jeannie mentions several teachers who influenced her decision to go to college.

> I plan on going to school because of teachers I had, like Mrs. Scott and Mrs. Norwood. They went to school and stuff; they're just freshly out of school. The teachers that I've always had before were older. Yeah, they were mostly about, I imagine, in their forties or fifties, at least.

Surely, Elmer exaggerates when he claims that U.S. history teaches him nothing he did not learn in eighth grade and his friend Jack simplifies when he states that school mainly is "to help build up your character." Notwithstanding that schooling is lauded, a distinguishing feature of

MHS is the students' and faculty's modest academic expectations. Even capable students fail to perceive value in the more abstract aspects of education. Julia, an exception, meant to maximize the academic possibilities of high school and was encouraged by her father: "Dad told me when I started high school, 'You just get out what you put into it.' And I wanted to get out a lot because I have a lot of plans afterwards." But the brightest students often disdain hard work or the need for it to achieve acceptably well (that is, make the B honor roll). Helen speaks for many students when she summarizes her position on academic affairs:

> My mom always wanted me to be on the B honor roll 'cause then she knows that I'm at least studying. No, I never was pushed. I just didn't wanna be one of the dumb kids in the class. There's not that much competition. It doesn't really matter to that many kids, I don't think. I mean just so you got your B average. I didn't work very hard last year and I had like about As except for one class. I'd rather go out 'cause I think you learn more from people than you do from books. That's my own philosophy.

Wayne, now a university student, admits he could have worked harder, but "Who wants to sit at a book for each class an hour a night? It's no fun. There are too many other things going on." Mike believes,

> A lot of people, they like to be an A student. I think a person should relax. I don't see how they can really relax and enjoy theirselves and be an A student. Well, I think the high C to B student, I think they're gonna be better off when they get out of school than a lot of A students 'cause they're more relaxed.

He concludes that the people who get As stay at home so much they don't learn how to communicate with people, rationalizing his lesser efforts with, "There's more to life besides grades." Mary finishes near the top of her class, regretting, as she contemplates her questionable preparedness for college, that she did not try harder.

> I'm number four in the class and I could have easily been one or two. I'm sure I could have. For a lot of tests I didn't study; just from listening in class I could pass. That's why if I would have studied I could have done so much better. In classes everybody just does the bare minimum to get by.

But, she explains, "School wasn't that important to me." Ruby and others admit that they do not have to work hard to get good grades because their courses are easy. She can't complain, she says, "because I know I don't mind them being easy." Yet she adds, "I think it would help a person more on going to college if they were harder and you had to study. Like sociology I'm taking now. I like the course but you're just in there making grades and doing nothing." Finally, students in the National Honor Society are said to have airs (perhaps like those Jessica feels college students have). "You can tell who's in it and who's not because they act like they're higher than everybody else," says Helen. She prefers fun to study—"I'm more the easygoing kind; they study, study, study"—and settles for being on the B honor roll rather than being a "real brain." The National Honor Society chapter regularly fails to find its quota of eligible recruits.[2] The requirements are a 3.5 grade point average or better (on a 4-point scale) plus above-average character. Five percent of the senior class can be considered for membership each year.

It seems that the school experience often provides more than those who do not intend to go to college want, but no more than the college-bound wish to work for. Somewhere between these modest points Mansfield's teachers pitch their intellectual tents, accommodating themselves to a level of success with which most participants learn to be comfortable.

The senior's olympian view of high school embraces different pasts and prospects. Amanda, married in her junior year, faces imminent work, an immature husband, care of her child, Tommy, and, until she graduates, the daily perverse and paradoxical position of what strikes her as a generation gap. Since she has been married, her peers think of her as much older and no longer share their intimacies with her. Linda, with firm plans to marry after graduation, manifests the ambiguities of adolescence, unsure of parental wisdom, but persuaded when it comes from her boyfriend's mother. "When Butch's mom says it, then I know the thing is right. When my parents say something, I don't always agree with them." Gene has no firm plans and thus has resolved to go to college until he discovers what he likes to do. The one thing he is confident about is his desire to leave Mansfield.

It seems like the people who stay in Mansfield don't get anywhere. They have to go outside for an education to make anything of themselves. You know, a lot of people stick around here and work at Vulcan's; that's all they do the rest of their life. And I could do that, but I don't want to work at Vulcan's. I don't stay around here unless I have to. One thing that really surprised me when I came here was everybody thought how important a car is. "What kind of car you got?" That's about the first question they'd ask. And after a while I could understand it. A car is the only way you can go someplace to get out.

Some college-bound students, like Gene, consider moving away from the community, though not necessarily to places either distant from or even much larger than Mansfield. Chicago or St. Louis are attractive in the way that a fantasy is. ("You know, having never lived there [Chicago] it's kind of the ideal place right now. I don't know that much about it; it's just the idea of a big city." This same student, now at college, is homesick and hopes to move closer to Mansfield.) Seldom, however, do seniors refer to settling in places much larger than Auburn (approximately 5,000); even Stanton (over 50,000) is too large. Dorothy mentions several of the factors motivating her to prefer a place larger than Mansfield:

> A town like this, it's good, but it's kind of, not secluded, but the people are limited that you can really get to know. It doesn't bother me that I'm leaving Mansfield to go on to school. I mean I like living here. I know I'll come back, but I won't live here. I wouldn't live in a big city, you know, like Chicago or St. Louis, if I was married and had children. I don't know if I were single, that brings on a different thing, but if I had children I'd settle probably in a middle-sized town, a little bigger than Auburn, where children would have a chance to still meet people and have opportunities for 'em.

And Auburn, a metropolis compared with Mansfield, is Helen's preference, though she focuses more on the attractiveness of Auburn's larger school than on Auburn:

> Yeah, I'd like to have grown up in a bigger town because I don't like everybody knowing my business. Just take this morning. A girl went out with a different guy over the weekend and that's the news first thing this morning. I'd like to have went to a different school. About Auburn is the size. In Auburn they don't know everything about you. That's what I like. Also, there's more things to do there than here.

Those who perceive Mansfield school and community as providing restricted social and academic opportunity are matched by others more contented, who fear the seeming anonymity of larger places. Both are reasonably realistic about what Mansfield can offer, though less so about the urban school and community. The seniors, in their characterization of Mansfield, show the impact of having grown up in a rural setting. On the one hand, they wish to get out ("seems like people who stay in Mansfield don't get anywhere"), and, on the other, they welcome the comfort of staying close to home. There is still a third group who without rejecting Mansfield are fascinated by the larger world around them that they have slowly come to know.

> I like living here [says Dorothy], but I have to get out to go places like Stanton because it's so much different than Mansfield. They talk different and it's sort of hard to talk to 'em because their language is so different from ours. Our language is like a couple or three years

behind them. Auburn isn't that different; it's getting to be like Mansfield. I've known Auburn for two years and I'm getting to know everybody there. It's just about like Mansfield, but Stanton is a completely different world. I don't think I could live over there because they drive so fast.

Wayne, a Mansfield loyalist, reflects the distress of many adults over the prospects of school consolidation. He volunteers the view that the recently passed tax referendum was a good thing. Otherwise, "they would have had to consolidate. I didn't think that was a very good idea because it would put together Auburn, Oakfield, and Mansfield, and then you're gonna have a big school." And, furthermore, that sense of the school as the center of Mansfield is decisively recognized by students. Jeannie, for example, writes:

> As far as living in Mansfield, if you don't go to school here there's not that much to do. Most of the whole town revolves just around the school activities. Like I know some people that graduated a couple of years ago who work in factories and live in Mansfield. They're left out a lot more than when they were in school. A lot of mom's older friends come to the ball games and stuff. I know my parents will come to ball games and talk to their friends.

Wayne and Jeannie share the sentiments of Elmer, who, better than most students, conveys the special quality of life in Mansfield for those who belong. Elmer concludes that,

> I think sort of deep down the people of Mansfield care for everybody. I think it's really a good town. I think everybody cares for each other and I think that really deep down like if something big came up in this town, that everybody would join in and help each other.

These feelings, frequently expressed by local adults, are not shared by all Mansfielders, but they are a salient community characteristic.

Eventually, some seniors, emboldened by college or work experience, will acquire the social and intellectual skills appropriate for areas larger than Mansfield and Cunningham County.[3] Meanwhile, for many in stable, intimate Mansfield, the grip of early socialization loosens slowly; for some, only partially, at best. Despite the seniors' frequent trips by car to Auburn and Stanton (places psychologically still part of Mansfield), as well as to Brenton and Bradlow, Mansfield community and environs is all most of them really know well; it is their domain of mastery, security, and acceptance. Lesser known outside places are faced with some diffidence.

In the following commentaries, seniors continued their reflections on being a senior, the school experience, and the future.

Interviews with Seniors

Wayne: "An Athletic/Everything Split"

"I've always liked Mansfield because it was small and I knew most everybody. In larger schools, all the kids don't know everybody in their graduating class. It's sorta enjoyable to know who is walking down the hall. It's just nice. Next year I'm going to the university to study business. My mom, she thinks its OK. I've got an aunt that is about to drive me crazy, though. She doesn't think that I ought to go up there; thinks it's too big."

Like Mr. Browne, MHS shop teacher, Wayne shows the influence of socialization about size. Somewhat reminiscent of the child who, in getting the measure of himself and his world, constantly compares his size to that of objects and persons in his environment, the rural resident learns about size. He comes to understand what size is just right, as viewed by others significant in his life—parents, relatives, friends, and neighbors. No judgment could be more subjective; it results mostly from having literally tried on the size of "things Mansfield" so that they seem either to fit or not to fit.

"In school I've taken about everything offered except typing and stuff that doesn't make any difference. And I'm pretty satisfied with what's happened so far. I play clarinet in the band and I really enjoy that. You can go down there and relieve all your pressures. And the teacher is a pretty nice guy.

"There's a lot of friction right now over band and money, because band hasn't had one cent since about two years ago, and the athletic department gets about $1,000 every year. In this school there's an athletic/everything split, especially boy's athletics. I mean everything lines up after that, because athletics always gets all the money. Teachers here can't see that, can't see one place getting more money than everything else. There's nothing I can do about it. I join the athletics. You gotta have money; that's the kind of thing you've gotta have money for. Anyway, I think schoolwork could have been a little more demanding and sports could have been a little less demanding. Sports is more demanding here I think than the academic because the small community always likes to see the football team play and stuff like that.

"I took black lit a while back. I'm still prejudiced. I'm prejudiced and it's hard to change my mind. Everybody came in thinking the same things as when they went out. I think that the class tried to make you less prejudiced; I don't think it succeeded. I've never been close to 'em for any length of time, even to talk to 'em. I don't think I've ever talked to a black person except a saleslady in somebody's store. So, you just have to go along with what other people say—stereotypes, rumor, stuff like that; that's all you can go on. You don't know for yourself."

Hugh: "The School Is the Town"

"Yeah, I enjoy being in school 'cause that's about the only thing to do in Mansfield. The school is the town. They don't really have nothing else. But I wouldn't like to live in a large town like Stanton. Oh, Auburn, that'd be OK. That's where you have to go if you want to do anything around here.

"Some classes, I don't know why they send you to them. You're not going to use it. I don't believe that anyone learns their English in grade school. They learn at home before school ever starts how to talk and how to say things. I don't see how three more years of English in high school is going to help when you get out of school unless you're going to college and be an English teacher. I talk usually the way I want to. I phrase it; I don't use no adverbs.

"Other things like welding, woodworking, and mechanics—that's something you can use after you're out of school; or art, you could use it when you're out of school. There's certain things you should have when you're in high school, like math, science, biology. I learned an awful lot from just those classes. They're kind of fun. Mainly in your freshman and sophomore years you could take everything you're going to need in high school."

Tony: "Not Just a Number"

"I like it where I am. We don't have many kids and you're not just a number. And the teachers are more personal towards students. They try to help a student that's failing a course to make him pass. In a big school they just—Oh, he's flunking. That's your own tough luck. Take the athletic program. There's not so much competition and everybody that wants to play can play. Anybody that goes out for a sport here is on the team; there are no cuts. Like one year we had over fifty-five people out for football and they all stayed. No one is ever turned down for sports, band, chorus, or anything.

"You know, I think it's kind of boring to some people to study. I think some people are studious and other people, like me, they just, well, I'll study enough to get through. I have studied, I mean when like finals come up. Finals are just really terrible. I don't like 'em at all because I don't get any personal life.

"I'm not going to college but I am going away to study auto mechanics in Kansas City. I want to get away. My parents like the idea 'cause I think they were afraid I wasn't going to go to school. And really I didn't think they wanted to see me work in a factory the rest of my life. And I don't. What I want to have some day is my own shop."

Dan: "No Room for Change"

"Living in Mansfield, well, like you have to hold up a certain reputation because it's such a small town, you know. Like from the time you start kindergarten all the way till you graduate you can't change your personality. There's no room for change in Mansfield or in the school. I'd say the kids around you put you in the slot; the teachers kind of do it, too. If you get a bad grade in one class, a teacher thinks that, well, he must be a poor student, so he doesn't really look for him to do better. You have to fight really super hard to get a grade up because they don't think you can and they don't think you're trying so they're not paying that much attention to you."

Mike: "Being on the Outside Looking In"

"I got job applications in at Durango Products, Vulcan, Thompson, Argo—most of the big factories in Stanton. Right now I'm working part-time in the gas station. I won't leave unless I get a better job. My dad never put any pressure on me to work. He said if I wanted to work to go ahead. He said you might as well enjoy yourself now 'cause later when you leave school you're not gonna be able to.

"I thought about going to school, but I'm not really that good of a student. So I figure it'd probably be better off first thing to get a job. I've thought about college a bit, though; until my sophomore year I thought a lot about it. Then I decided I'm not really that good a student. My counselor said that maybe a junior college would be better for me; he knew I was about an average student.

"If I do go to junior college I'm gonna take vocational stuff, welding or something like that. I haven't thought much about doing anything else. We took these Kuder preference tests, or something like that, and on the salesman's I got pretty high, way over the ranking where you could be it.

"If I had it to do over again, I'd probably take English IV. I never did find English really hard because, well, English I, II, and III, I just went through 'em like anything. In English I could have been an A student in there if I'd wanted to. It was so easy I didn't have to study for it and got Bs. Some others like bookkeeping is kinda hard in places so I have to study it some, but I'll get C or B out of it. I didn't really care to study that much, and with my job I don't have too much time for it anymore. All the way through, football and baseball took up most of the time after school. I'd get some studying at night, but not a lot because practice didn't get over until like seven o'clock sometimes. During the winter, that's when my grades would be the best. In between sports the grades are the best.

"I would say I've got a lot out of high school. Like right now I'm in occupational information. They teach you how to fill out job applications and we learn about different types of work, factory worker, social worker, etc. Mrs. Norwood I thought was a really good English teacher 'cause a lot of those books I thought I wouldn't like. The first chapter or so really drug, but she kept telling me to read, and I'm glad she did 'cause a lot of books she gave me to read were pretty good. And then bookkeeping. You always are gonna be making money and you're gonna have to keep a record of what you spend and how much you're spendin' on what. Shop I like but right now I don't think it's gonna help very much. I took biology and botany both. I thought they were a lot of fun. I don't think they're gonna help me too much when I get out of school, but I enjoyed 'em.

"I'm gonna miss it, high school, I know I will. Right now I guess I won't; come about August, that's when I'll start missing it again. I'll miss the football games. A lot of the teachers out here I get along with real good; I'm gonna miss seeing them. And a lot of kids out here besides seniors are my friends and I won't see them too much after I get out of school. It's gonna be different. I'm used to being out in June and July, but then about August 25th . . . It's gonna be different being on the outside looking in."

Jessica: "Bogged Down"

"I don't dread coming to school. I like to be with the kids and the teachers, but my schedule this year, it just bogs me down. Like shorthand. All you do is write shorthand every day and every day. I know it isn't possible, but I think I'd like to have, you know, different classes and in different order. They just go on and on and on every day. And I think, too, one reason I get so bogged down is because I only have two different teachers for my four main classes. And mostly the kids are the same in all the classes, too; that can get sort of boring.

This is a notable small-school problem. Because the faculty is so small, most teachers must teach several subjects. Consequently, it is possible for a student, like Jessica, to take four different courses, but to have only two different teachers. Also related to size is the relative lack of diversity among students. Because the student population is so stable, many students have been together for twelve years by the time they become seniors. Jessica shows those contrary senior feelings—tired of the same old faces, but "I'll miss it; I know I will," after she graduates. The constraints imposed by size—social, occupational, and psychological—motivate Mansfielders to migrate. Alternatively, small size clearly abets the development and maintenance of a sense of community.

The implications of smallness are reflected in other student observations. The positive feeling of many boys about athletic opportunities at MHS, as well as those of students who took joy in being part of a school so small that teachers knew you by name, is balanced by Dan's view that if you get pegged as a particular kind of person, then it is very hard to break out of that slot; and also by the feeling, mostly expressed by girls, that Mansfield's gossip and restricted school offerings make a larger place appear more attractive.

"I still like school. In fact, after I graduate I'll miss it; I know I will. After graduation, I'm not sure what. Right now Barry and I don't know anything for sure about our marriage. I've taken all the business courses and made good grades. I don't really want to jump into a secretary's job, but I'd like to have like a receptionist's job and then, you know, work up.

"Ever since I've started high school I always really didn't want to go to college even though I've made the B honor roll almost all the time and lately I've been getting on the A honor roll. I don't know, I don't dislike it, but I just have sort of a down look on college because anybody can go to college now. And so much is happening on the college campuses. Oh, the coeds, I don't agree with that because of my religion. You know, the boys and girls rooming together. Isn't that what it's called, 'coed,' where they're living in the same room?

"When you go to college everybody thinks they're top man. 'See, I'm in college and you . . .' My cousin went to a junior college and she just picked up the way college kids are. She'll come by the house and try to talk to me about how big she is and how I don't know anything. Yeah, I just never have wanted to go to college; anybody can get a diploma."

Julia: "I Have a Lot of Plans"

"A lot of kids say you shouldn't study in high school or something, you know, but I've put a lot into it and got a lot out of it. I have a lot of plans. I know a lot of kids say, 'Well, I didn't study, I just studied to get the C or the passing grade,' but I like to see that report card at the end of the nine weeks and I like it when my mom and dad see it. I look to teachers as the person who knows. If you're gonna get out and know it afterwards, then you are gonna have to do this. A lot of the kids might think of me as weird because of that, but I liked the four years."

Linda: "Free to Do Anything You Want"

"Well, today I went to sociology class and we discussed about sociology. I don't really like that class. I don't like the teacher. He just thinks he's better than anybody else so I don't care for him too much. And I have art. That's my favorite class out of the whole day 'cause I like to paint and draw and stuff like that. I get good grades in there. Oh, one thing I like about art is we listen to the radio and it's just like you're free to do anything you want and you get to talk. Well, there's discipline, but if you don't go out of the range, then there isn't any. Mr. Smith, our art teacher, says that seniors have priority in his class, because he was a senior once and he knows how it is to be a senior. That's all he ever said. And fourth hour I have economics. That class is OK but I don't get to talk too much because I'm one of the only girls in the whole class and the boys are talking all the time. In sixth-hour study hall I can do anything I want. Me and Bonnie Ray, we can be all by ourselves. There's no teachers in there to tell us what to do. Seventh hour I have P.E. and I can't stand P.E. No, I just don't care very much for sports unless my boyfriend's playing. That's the only time I like it. And then last hour I have home management. Mrs. Neilsen, she's real nice. I mean you don't think of her as a teacher, more like a friend she is. We get to pick what we want to make and if you want to cook, you can cook. It's better that way instead of telling you that you have to do something. What you want to learn, you can learn; and what you don't want to learn, you don't have to."

Mary: "I'm Glad It's Over"

"I don't like the school system here. I want my kids to go to a little bit bigger place, about like Auburn. Mansfield's too small; it doesn't offer enough. I think high school kids need more of a choice in what they wanna do. Auburn has that work program and in Stanton they only have to go to school half a day.

"I learned the most in science because that was something I was never exposed to at home. I didn't really learn that much in English because I picked up most of that in junior high. As far as reading novels and stuff like that, my mom's influenced me there because she reads a lot. The best things in school are FHA and GAA and the friends I met. The courses I liked best were economics, biology, and some English classes.

"Graduation! It's just not real yet that I'm gonna be gone. It won't seem real until August when the first day of school begins and I'm not around. I'm glad it's over, though. My boyfriend, he'd rather come back because he really liked going to school. He thinks this is the big part of his life and I don't think it is. I guess that's because he liked high school better. I look to what I'm gonna be doing a couple of years from now and he looks at what he's did."

Amanda: "I'm the Generation Gap"

"Well, I got married the beginning of my junior year. I came back to school and everybody said, 'Hey, Amanda's pregnant, she had to get married.' My junior year was pretty hard because it was like everybody was afraid to talk to me. Well, I don't know how to explain this, it was like if you associate with somebody that had to get married, you're next on the list. About the middle of the year, though, it was sort of like being accepted again; almost like coming to a new school.

"It seems like sometimes in the class somebody wants to ask me how it is, and what I feel; nobody does. I think they're afraid to. It seems like a lot of kids that I used to run around with are now on drugs, even here in school. And, you know, I wasn't supposed to find out about it because they're afraid now. I'm the generation gap here in school.

"I like school, being around people, and everything. If I had to stay home all day I'd go crazy. I don't know, I don't really think I'm learning all that much. It seems like now I'm reliving what I've already learned because I'm not taking, say, any higher classes, whatever you call it. Now shorthand, that's something I plan on putting to work when I get out. But classes like economics and sociology, it's just discussing what's happening today, and, you know, what happened before, like the depression and stuff. Sociology is about people in society and I already went through that, getting married and having Tommy, so it just seems like a rerun. In economics you learn how the economy goes up and down; this dollar does this and this dollar does that. You're not really into it till you're out of high school; then you see for yourself, you know. In class you don't really think about it; you sit there and you discuss it. I don't think the kids are fully aware of where their money goes. For that they have to get a job and support theirselves. When you're out of high school, you're on your own. It's no more, 'Hey, I know where I go tomorrow, I go to school.' Yeah, electricity, just turn the switch on. It seems like a playground for teen-agers or something, I don't know.

"I feel like I'm twenty-five years old right now. I really do. I feel like I've got worldly knowledge; I mean I seem like so much older than my classmates. They're all for this fun and games: 'Hey, where're you going Saturday night and who you got a date with and how many roses did you get on Valentine Day?' And I mean that stuff is important to me, but, you know, no more wild dates, no more wild parties. It's 'go home and take care of your kid.' "

The Coming of the End

In one's senior year, as in all previous years, the first day of school begins with a sense of satisfaction at seeing old friends not seen much during summer vacation, and with an effort once more to settle down to work. Football players already have begun practice, and later, in November, as the seniors play the season's last game, the special aura of this final year becomes palpable fact. The fact is further pressed home as Homecoming, the Christmas program, senior play, prom, and the purchase of graduation announcements slip by, until all that remains is the last week of school. By this time, the dropouts have long since gone, the unfortunates who failed English III are left behind, the married ones focus on babies and work, and survivors face six days that look like this:

Friday, May 25:	End of semester exams
Sunday, May 27:	Baccalaureate, 7:30 P.M. to be held in the high school gymnasium. The invocation will be given by Reverend Father Samuel Hoffman and the message by Reverend Herbert Walter. The chorus will provide a number and Billie Sue Hornsby will provide processional and recessional music. The benediction will be given by Reverend Thomas R. Sattler.
Monday, May 28:	No school.
Tuesday, May 29:	Awards presentations (after assembly).
Wednesday, May 30:	High School Commencement. No school.
Thursday, May 31:	Report cards. School dismissed 10:30 A.M.

To be able to leave in good standing, seniors are advised that:
1. All students who have obligations must take care of them in the office by the end of school Tuesday.
2. Obligations cover book rental, shop, lab and library fees.
3. All reports from third quarter must be turned in by Tuesday.
4. Library books must be returned by Tuesday.
5. Band uniforms must be returned as soon as possible.

Having been urged to leave a clean slate, seniors also do some leaving of their own—their thoughts, for example, about what they will miss most, told to inquiring reporters from *Tiger Tidings*. Their sarcasm, never veiled, is announced with quotation marks as in my "counsellors" advice or Mrs. Lemmon's "enjoyable" lecture in world history. Seniors also make their traditional bequests, leaving younger students, especially the juniors, next year's chiefs, with treasures and experiences that reflect feelings of friendship or a desire to wound, and reminding teachers of events that either teacher or student found embarrassing. Accordingly, John leaves Mr. A, the principal, a new pad of admit slips and Sid leaves Coach B a book of rules for volley ball. One need not be an insider to know that John overdid cutting class and Sid had a spat with Coach B. Seniors inevitably leave their ability to get in trouble, nicknames, athletic supporters, motorcycles, and good times, in one more class's last will and testament.

A recent school board decision eliminated midterm graduation. One senior, a good student who was not attracted to the early escape that a February completion offers, approved this decision, saying, "You miss all the fun if you graduate in February. Then it's almost like not graduating. The last year is the one everyone waits for." Well, not quite everyone, but by overcoming one's erupting impatience and controlling the frayed nerves that develop as the semester finally passes winter's hump and winds slowly through spring toward the final day, one eventually feels that the year was worth enduring. And then, at last, Wednesday, May 30, arrives, the new clothes are donned and hairdos are in place, loving parents, friends, and relatives assemble in the gym, get their programs at the door, take their seats in hard chairs or in the bleachers, and begin to wave programs in a futile effort to cool off. It must be hot on graduation night, the seats must be hard, and the commencement address must be long and trite: it is thus that discomfort reaches the level required of a rite of passage.

And so it is this most recent graduation night. The maroon-berobed seniors occupy the first two rows of chairs. Once the audience settles in place, the dignitaries, who have waited patiently in the lobby, self-consciously march the length of the gym and onto the stage. Facing the audience and the graduates-to-be are two school board members, the superintendent, the principal, a minister, and the commencement speaker, who, the program claims, will present an "inspirational address."

After the band has played "Panis Angelicus" and "Pomp and Circumstance" (just a bit on the squeaky side, since many of the best musicians are seniors), after the national anthem has been sung, and after the Reverend Charles Ardmore has given the invocation, Superintendent Tate welcomes everyone. He thanks the ninety-second graduating class of Mansfield High School for its gift of $100 toward new stage curtains. Ardis Bane, class historian, then recalls the high points of the past thirteen years (twenty of thirty-three seniors have been together since kindergarten). The commencement address is given, but not even its designation as "inspirational" could bring it alive to those impatient newcomers to adult life down in the front rows. (Perhaps such addresses are really meant to reassure adults of the continuity of their society's values.) And, finally, the president and the secretary of the school board combine their efforts in handing out diplomas to the expectant, well-rehearsed seniors, who leave and return to their seats according to the time-honored system. Amid popping flash bulbs and restrained applause (all have been urged to save their expressions of joy until the end), seniors approach the school board officials and reach out for congratulations with one hand and for their diploma with the other. With scroll in hand, each senior waits, standing at his seat, until all are assembled and ready to sit down. Then the program winds down and out with a trembling-voiced student's farewell address (moms and grandmas dab their eyes), more music, no lease squeaky than before, a benediction, and, at last, the grand march. Merciful grand march! Tired, hot, pleased graduates rise to join a partner in the center aisle where the coordinate steps to parade back toward the lobby end of the gym. As in a wedding reception line, they line up against the gym wall (which on other occasions is covered with heavy mats to protect rambunctious basketball players unable to stop their charge to the hoop) to await those same loving parents, friends, and relatives who offer kisses, presents, handshakes, and good words. Female graduates hug each other; some sob uncontrollably. Then six hundred bodies move out of the gym on their way to celebrations. The graduates stay at their parentally prepared festivities long enough to preside as guests of honor and to count the cash. Then they slip away to parties of their peers, where talk turns to whose punch contained what alcoholic content, their gifts, and how glad they are that "that" is over.

For Mansfield High School and for Mansfield, however, "that" is not over, only its ninety-second installment. By annually repeating this educational exit ritual, Mansfield High School demonstrates its capacity to respond to the schooling needs of its support community. Indeed, the ritual also reconfirms the community's capacity to empower the school to respond to its needs. Only viable communities continue to meet this test of potency in a ceremony that symbolizes the success of both school and community.

These statements of the seniors suggest that they have grown up as Mansfielders, sensitive to the particularities of the place they generally seem pleased to call home. Many students know their school has been central to their lives, and thus it is hard to leave it. Some even recognize their school's central role in Mansfield. For them, as for many of the school's previous graduates, a Mansfield without its high school would be unimaginable.

10

Paradise Maintained?

"I'll never forgive them for this. Forcing me out."
"Why?" I asked. "Most people who have the money *want*
to live in the suburbs."
"You could never understand," he said. "I'm a townie.
I lived all my life in Charlestown. You know, we got something special here. There's only one Bunker Hill in the whole
country."—Joe Klein (1975)

The Case Reviewed: Something Special in Mansfield

Mansfielders do not claim to live in paradise—indeed, some might ob-
ject strenuously to this religious allusion—but it is clear that many hold
strong positive feelings about their school and community. Many others,
of course, hold strong negative feelings. The experience of growing up
in a small, cohesive community is felt deeply, for better or for worse.
In any event, this study has focused on those with positive views who
feel they belong in Mansfield. Belonging is a powerful, precious sentiment, an invariable attribute of community; it moves people to strongly
defensive behavior and supports the feeling that even beyond one's
family one is not alone. Mansfield provides this sense of belonging.
    Mansfield's ethos, "the guiding belief . . . the spirit that motivates
the ideas . . . or practices of a people" (Webster), has been formed
partly in response to the realities of small-town rural life and partly
in reaction to the predominance of urban society. It incorporates the
conviction that people live a good life in small towns, and that Mansfielders are more at home in Mansfield than somewhere outside the
community. Other beliefs, generated by contrasting urban and rural
life, characterize Mansfield as a preferred place where people are safer
and more secure, uncrowded, better looked after, friendlier, independent, and God-fearing. Tim Browne believes that people in bigger places
"don't give a damn how you are."[1] Believing that people give a damn
is central to Mansfield's ethos; it unites school district residents. Mansfield High School is central in an outlook which claims uniqueness for
Mansfield only as one of a class of unique places—rural communities

—although Mansfield may be unique in itself for persons like Nancy Parker, third-generation native, who acknowledges, "I belong here as I would no place else."

The Nancy Parkers of Mansfield form an important part of the high school's support community, but this is more than a school-related group, a congeries of people with the school alone as a unifying factor. It is a community in sociological as well as geographical terms. That is, within a given area its people share common interests and loyalties, not through singularities of language, race, or religion, but through shared outlook, history, occupations, institutions, and purposes. It is a community with integrity and identity. Its small, white, fairly stable, mixed blue collar–farmer population is the group whose property is taxed, whose children attend the school, who buy the cakes at bake sales, who attend Homecoming parades, and who elect the school board. Not just textbook stuff, its history is carried forward by living people whose tastes and values emerge from this history to influence the present. Although those tastes and values are moderated by the forceful messages of the nation's media, they continue to instill in each new generation visions of a safe, secure Mansfield.

Generally similar communities are found in some suburbs and cities as well as in other small towns. The residents believe their school belongs to them and that the well-being of their community is tied to their school. In short, more than merely personal interests are involved. Thus, while all schools have a group of parents and taxpayers, places like Mansfield have an adult constituency with special, enduring feelings that may become dramatically manifest when an irritant or threat arises with the power of altering the school in some unacceptable way. Since Mansfield has not actively faced such threats (consolidation at this time is a potential, not an actual issue), this portrayal of her high school within its community framework focuses on a system in relative equilibrium.

Football is king in Mansfield as it is under thousands of lighted fields around the country each September, October, and November. The Pep Club ardently urges its less-spirited peers to cheer for the home team. *Julius Caesar* commands the time and interest of sophomores in lessons enlightened by parallels drawn from contemporary events. Biology, if not current events, blends the scientific and the theological in a locally acceptable way. Students are examined on unit tests with questions that challenge their capacity to recall. Many students acknowledge minimal pressure to excel, and teachers seem reconciled to a comparatively relaxed academic environment.

Seniors' misgivings about leaving school reflect both the uncertainties they will face and the shortcomings of what they have undergone. Their retrospective musings contrast sharply with the ramblings of diary writers who often portray the anguish of adolescent romance common anywhere in America. Students, not consumed wholly by romance, have ample resources to spare for an abundance of activities that well introduce them to the voluntary nature of fund raising in America and to their subsequent roles in the world of work.

Educators in Mansfield contribute to a relationship between school and community which satisfies both themselves and Mansfielders; the school system is adapted to local orientations through the mechanism of local control. While financial support and educational mandates come to Mansfield from outside the school district, significant prerogatives still are exercised within it. Most notably, Mansfield hires all educators and selects all instructional materials.

Some board members are concerned about the stress on sports and winning, but neither they nor any others associated with the school seriously question the staggering array of nonacademic activities that form part of the high school experience. Indeed, the reflections of students, teachers, and board members upon their school convey the impression of an imperfect but basically acceptable system.

Children who grow up in Mansfield tend to develop an identity that differs from identities developed in other social settings in the United States. To be sure, the Mansfielder is a readily recognized American—patriotic, believing in God, independent, sports-loving, and unalienated, but one who is peculiar to Mansfield and similar places. His identity does not incapacitate him for living elsewhere, it inclines him, rather, toward Mansfield. Thus Mansfield's children not only grow up American, they grow up in a way that contributes to the survival of Mansfield. Like their parents they fit into their community. Through preference and habit the Mansfielder has not only accommodated to the requirements of small-town agricultural life, he is committed to perpetuating the very qualities that distinguish that life.

But other than generally stated school objectives about good citizenship, nothing in the school's curricular documents indicate that anyone seriously expects the school to be responsive or contributory to the communal interests and needs of Mansfield. Educators and parents give first priority to individual student needs and then, a distant second, to national well-being. Community interests lag far behind. It is this order of priority that dominates the thinking of legislators and educators about the worth of small schools and their future. Given a school's contribution to personal identity and community maintenance, however, it is appropriate to stress the importance of schools to their support constituencies, particularly those located in settings with already fragile communities.

The Emergence of School-Community Congruence in Mansfield

Mansfielders know that Editor Matthews's era of 1890–1912, the coal-mining period which ended in the early twenties, and the slower-paced, more neighborly world of the pre–World War II years no longer exist. The villagers own television sets, read newspapers from Stanton, and travel throughout the state and the country. Nor do they pretend that the outside world does not exist. Village leaders and school board members respond regularly (though often uncomfortably) to directives and authority from non-Mansfield sources.[2] When asked what their school system should do for their community, beyond educating their children, Mansfielders reply with uncertainty. In effect, they do not conceive of MHS serving communal Mansfield needs; it serves, rather, to help individual children acquire "the basics" and develop competencies useful for employment or success in postsecondary institutions. They hold no expressed vision of the school as a community agent directed toward survival, notwithstanding the widely held belief that Mansfield's future is uncertain.

No one—educator, parent, or village leader—associates their school with the tasks of developing talent useful to Mansfield's economy. Preposterous indeed, so it would be argued: few jobs are available and those few are held by unskilled women or members of the families that operate local businesses. Farm jobs also are scarce, the days of the farm laborer mostly a memory, and even sons of farmers cannot count on succeeding their fathers. Thus, if we seek consciously articulated connections between schooling and community survival, we cannot identify occupational ties. Nor, for that matter, can we identify political ties. In short, the community is not the focal point for study in school. The school's overt orientation is, on the one hand, individual and, on the other, translocal—clearly and significantly national more than state or regional. Moreover, aside from the school's valued contribution to Mansfield through its payroll and local purchases, and its effect on bringing parents to town[3]—all contributions of consequence to Mansfield's survival—neither educators nor lay persons expect the school to teach content, develop skills, or promote an outlook that will improve Mansfield's chance for a viable future.

Therefore, Mansfield's close school-community relationship is not due to any effort to orient the curriculum to local needs and interests. In fact, the shaping of the high school results from the accumulated impact of countless things done and not done, grumblings, votes cast, vacations taken, telephone calls made, homework encouraged or discouraged, magazines and books read, and movies and television shows watched. These actions create the social environment to which Mansfield's educators must respond, never exclusively or mindlessly, and always with dispositions derived from their professional training and personal inclinations. The effects of homogenizing national forces do indeed reach Mansfield's teachers and administrators, but they always filter through these rural-oriented educators.

Accordingly, those whose decisions affect the nature of the school have been habituated to making the "right" responses. These arise out of the sensibility that Ben Matthews, his newspaper successors, and numerous current community adults display when they urge fellow Mansfielders to shop locally or when they agree that teachers ought to live within the school district. It is not planned action that establishes the school-community fit in Mansfield, it is the natural behavior of persons for whom localistic orientations are compelling. Extralocal views are of consequence, but they exist within a strong community-oriented context.

Most significantly, the farmers who dominate the school board have deep roots in Mansfield's past. Sensitive to their role as community guardians, they take account of the impact their decisions have on community well-being. They are appropriate agents for the mainstream Mansfield orientation. For example, the school board rejected an admittedly bright, energetic candidate for school superintendent because his "city" ideas would not suit Mansfield. Instead they selected a man whose views and values appeared to be reassuringly compatible with their own about how to work, spend money, respond to innovation, and discipline students.[4] The board members felt so good about their choice that they described him in the most flattering way they knew— he was "country."

Both as a consequence of teacher self-selection and the choice of teachers made by Mansfield's school leaders, rural-oriented educators are hired. They have been raised in small towns and have attended the smaller branches of the state university system, and typically, they have grown up in Mansfield or its environs. Recently, when jobs were scarce and teacher candidates numerous, local persons seemed to be preferred, a fact all the more interesting since no school official gave priority to such persons. No board member, for example, credited local origins as an important criterion for employment. Yet Superintendent Tate said privately that if qualified teachers were available within the district, why should he let them get away to other districts?

Mansfield's stable cadre of teachers prefer small-town life. By virtue of their background and experience, teachers need not be coached as agents of a particular outlook. Their own upbringing has socialized them to reinforce locally appropriate levels of intellectual attainment and a substantial degree of student participation in out-of-class activities; in short, to be fitting representatives of this rural school district.

Though cognizant of the need for Mansfield's youth to qualify for occupational and educational opportunity beyond Mansfield, they appear, nevertheless, to teach in ways that are comfortable for the community, as if living in Mansfield was in fact the conscious target of their educative efforts. Given local control, could it be otherwise? And given the behavior of local students, need it be otherwise?[5]

We see, then, that the results of two truly major decisions—selecting the superintendent and selecting the teachers—tend to reinforce Mansfield's ethos.

In regard to the level of academic discourse and the balance of academic-nonacademic activities, Mansfield's educators do not make conscious decisions. The prevailing modus operandi emerges from the type of educator hired and that person's interaction with other educators, students, and parents, within the framework of what the school board finds allowable. To be sure, several school district documents contain policy statements, but they are not referred to except in concrete matters (involving expulsion or the junior-senior prom, for example), and they are couched in typically grand language. Only one item in the school board's *Rules, Precedents, and Procedures* reflects the sort of policy that would underline the school-community congruence indicated here: "The teacher should have a respectful attitude toward the standards and the accepted patterns of behavior of the community in which he is employed." That teachers actually possess a "respectful attitude" is not attributable to this statement, but to their own upbringing and to the process of recruitment and self-selection which eventuates in the employment of a certain type of teacher.

Over the years, formal community participation in educational policy making has been minimal because the same people, in terms of disposition and family background, tend to form the support community today as in past generations. During most of this century migration rates have been moderate, and many families have remained in residence from generation to generation. Neither internal nor external factors have created a disjunction between school and community that would stimulate energetic community participation. Like-minded people usually replace one another on the school board and they comfortably reflect the school district's stability. Hence factional dispute is rare and instances of displeasure with the school can be dealt with informally. Telephone calls to board members or exchanges in the restaurant or the post office usually suffice to make the point.[6]

On the face of it, Mansfielders do not ordinarily expect their children to follow parental footsteps. Most believe their children will seek opportunities outside the school district. Thus they do not disparage those who become urbanites, and decidedly not those who "do better" than their parents. Such success fulfills the American dream. And since the school was never calculated to serve the ends of Mansfield's preservation, it is not criticized when the sheep stray from the flock. However, an impressive proportion of "sheep" stay home or very close to home, ostensibly living the lives of their parents, having realized that Mansfield is more than just a place to be raised in.

Actually, once young adults are past the stressful, restless, impatient junior and senior years of high school, when the town crowds in on them uncomfortably, when they often ache to get out, and when intimacy is not security but a breach of privacy, they do not invariably dash off to exotic places. Like their teachers, the college-bound go to smaller institutions in the state, while the noncollege youth stay home or move to one of several neighboring small towns, commuting in either case to Stanton, Auburn, or Forest for work. The brain surgeons and the engineers move away, often returning for Homecoming each fall; their departure may not represent a rejection of Mansfield's life style or values so much as a desire to seize opportunities defined by occupational preference.[7] In short, many move-aways and stay-at-homes alike retain abundant affection for Mansfield and small-town life, looking back fondly on their high school days, unaware that they had been deprived of notable opportunities of any sort. For both groups, Mansfield is home, where they are known and know everyone, where anyone's death may be a personal loss, regardless of whether the dead person is a family relation. Small-town living conduces to a generalized caring about all persons accepted as belonging. Looking after elderly citizens was a Mansfield tradition long before the Adopted Grandmothers came on the scene.

The Dilemmas of Congruence

If Mansfield's school-community congruence produces many salutary results, it also creates dilemmas that cast a shadow over these results. For example, while the school experience does not preclude occupational and educational success for Mansfield's graduates, it is still comparatively limited. From an external perspective, this is clearly a real price that is paid. In other school districts, parents, students, and teachers place more emphasis on academic achievement and press for more resources to be directed toward intellectual goals. Consequently, some children in this and other states are better taught mathematics and science and better informed of their nation's political and economic complexities. Mansfielders strive to hire not the best teacher, in an intellectual sense, but the teacher who will best serve Mansfield. This is an important distinction. They would reject teachers as unsuitable who were "too intelligent for this community" and therefore "more than we want," just as they rejected Dargan, a candidate for the superintendency. From these facts emerges the first dilemma: if education is perceived as best when it attempts to maximize the intellectual potential of a child, then MHS may be faulted. But if in places like Mansfield the schools contribute to a sense of personal identity and to low alienation,[8] then something of compensating value may have been gained, especially since we are frequently informed that modern society has become "a dust heap of individuals without links to one another" (Homans, 1950:457).[9] If Mansfield's children lack educational opportunities equal to those available in larger cities and suburbs, they are not denied these opportunities by virtue of race or national origin, but by virtue of Mansfield's size and prevailing ethos, which establish the limits of excellence. MHS graduate Nancy Decker recalls:

> I wanted to take world history, but the principal said there wasn't enough kids for it so I had to take shorthand. And I wanted to take sociology and economics, but because there weren't enough kids for them either I had to take home ec.

Yet if other standards were instituted for academic performance, the selection of educators, and the balance of academic and nonacademic activities, Mansfield High School no longer would suit Mansfield. It would not be the local institution it is, doing the bidding, however uncalculated, of Mansfield's citizens. Such standards would have to be imposed from outside, for they would find little support at home.

The close fit discussed here promotes intergenerational stability in Mansfield. Neither by learning nor by aspiration are the community's children sharply distinguished from their parents. The shared feelings between young and old about where to live and what to believe suggest a second dilemma: in Mansfield, maximizing intellectual achievement and high intergenerational stability are probably incompatible. In fact, any school that fosters intellectual development beyond the level of the local community contributes to intergenerational instability, whereas, schooling that merely reaches the community's comfort level encourages a measure of control that tends to keep people in place. Ironically, reform efforts designed to raise the educational level are often resisted because of their cost and their alien ring: many communities, accordingly, have self-imposed inhibitors to their children's mobility. To say of such communities, "If they're happy, let them be" is a possible but not very satisfying reaction to this situation. "If they don't hurt anybody else, let them be" is no better. And it may be too obtrusively interventionist to adopt the educational equivalent of a fire code, which drastically restricts a community's behavior regarding its own property. With appropriate qualifications, all three considerations contain an element of rationality worthy of note in decisions about the limits of what is good at individual, community, and national levels, but how sharply one is torn by attending seriously to the imperatives derived from each level of good!

Although Mansfield has no black citizens and the possibility of busing does not exist, the community harbors antiblack sentiment. Thus it socializes children with values that conflict with national ideals, albeit disputed ones. No school policy supports this sentiment, but the school is a forum for its expression and its reinforcement by peers. This points to a third dilemma: Mansfield's harmonious relationship between school and support community is maintained at the cost of compromising some national ideals. In this dilemma, particularism, in the form of the local community's sense of the good, is pitted against universalism, in the form of the nation's sense of the good, both of which inspire essential activity, the former to human dignity and well-being and the latter to national integration and survival.[10] Clearly, the interests of any individual community may differ from those of the nation as a whole. Moreover, what is good for a community is not inevitably good for the nation. It is unpleasant, however, to contemplate a society so insecure that it cannot believe itself the richer for its subgroup enclaves, each with its own identity. Yet if the outlook of some subgroup (and some majority groups as well) became dominant, national integration and social justice for all would be threatened.

To some degree, it is immaterial that outsiders, whether Mansfielders or non-Mansfielders, reject Mansfield's way of life, because a majority of its residents value it highly. It is not immaterial whether or not their ethos is compatible with national ideals. Yet if schools and communities are compelled to fit a template of national values which eliminates their singular outlook, they cannot serve their preferred ends. A banal national ideology would descend like a pall to smother heterodoxy. Indeed, it is hard to see good coming from a winner-take-all situation for either community or nation. Avoiding the horns of potential dilemmas is the policy maker's continuing challenge.[11]

These dilemmas of local control follow from the fact that each good social organization has boundaries to its goodness. That community autonomy has limits was dramatized by the 1954 desegregation decision of the U.S. Supreme Court. Thus at the same time that we value the harmony of Mansfield school and community, we must be prepared to honor principles of justice and equality and to condemn what we have praised, if the price exacted by this harmony is judged intolerable. Who is to judge? And when is it to be declared that the cost of good-

ness for some has become intolerable for others? These are especially
complex and controversial questions.

A final dilemma involves consolidation. To those with roots in Mansfield's past, to those who resonate with their little school's special balance of academic, athletic, and other nonacademic activities, school
consolidation is anathema. Incorporating a small school within a larger
network of schools and other communities undermines particularism.
Yet consolidation is an increasingly likely solution to the problems of
the Mansfields of America as lower enrollments necessitate the elimi-
nation of courses and schools fall victim to declining economies of scale.
Residents react to the imminent loss of their school with a passion comparable to that of people who feel their cultural survival jeopardized
when their native language is threatened.[12] "Over my dead body" was
a Mansfielder's response to the mere prospect of consolidation; he is
one of many who realize their school is invested with more than educational functions. Mrs. Wilmot said, "Consolidation—I don't think I'd
like that. I think that children live differently in different towns and
. . . Oh, I don't know. It might not be that different. I can't put it
into words." But she has already done so. Her feeling of belonging is
bounded and somewhat exclusive. In limited yet telling ways she feels
distinct from others living in ostensibly similar communities.

Mansfielders may admit to the advantages of a county-wide high
school system, but consolidation evokes such a deep sense of loss that
the promised broader and richer curriculum of a larger school does not
compensate for the loss of its school. Interestingly, the customary interest in schooling's vocational payoff is set aside when the question of
consolidation is raised. When asked about the purposes of schooling,
Mansfielders focus on what is best for their children. When asked, to
the contrary, about consolidation, they focus not on what is best for
their children, but on what is good for their community and acceptable
for their children.[13] To Mansfielders, Mansfield High School remains acceptable. Defined as a quandary between the best, affordable education
for one's children and the continued well-being of one's community,
consolidation issues are packed with emotion and difficult to resolve.

The continued existence of a school that can contribute to subgroup
maintenance, to the integration of its support community, is inversely
related to the application of two universalistic principles: fiscal rationality, which argues for school reorganization, and academic excellence,
which calls for the employment of educators and the promotion of
curricular reforms deemed unsuitable for Mansfield as currently consti-
tuted. These principles are espoused by educational organizations ranging from state teachers' unions to state school board associations.[14]
They are therefore strongly supported. A countervailing force is cur-

rently rising among diverse groups which urges resistance to the increasing scale of contemporary society.[15]

The Case Generalized: Serving a Support Community

Schools traditionally are thought of as places specially for youth. But despite disagreement about the ideal and the actual role of youth in giving shape and direction to schools, schools act in behalf of a community's adults and their organizations. This association is evident in Mansfield. For the most part, it is not children who either mandate or sanction what occurs in school, but some set of adults with needs to be fulfilled and purposes to be served. This is as true for learning within institutional settings as for learning in primitive societies where children are raised in the most informal circumstances. What governs is an adult group's sense of the elements of survival in a particular culture's terms.

To be sure, many adults dream of their children developing competencies that lead to social mobility, but such dreams seldom extend beyond material matters. Aspiring parents do not so much want their children to become different human beings as to become richer ones. Pressures and aspirations for educational experiences to enhance social mobility, greater earnings, and a better life do not contradict the essentially conservative tendency of schools in places like Mansfield to maintain continuity between generations. Such schools basically transmit rather than modify critical matters of belief and outlook. But the point of special interest here is that the school as *our* school engenders a deep feeling of possessiveness that other community institutions rarely evoke with equal fervor.

The level of my understanding of the school-community relationship might have rested at this point, emphasizing, in my judgment, a critical though narrowly general conclusion confined to Mansfield and places like it elsewhere in the United States. By chance, however, I had an experience that extended my case beyond a rural setting and small towns. For a moment, I return to a personal note.

In the year following my fieldwork in Mansfield I served on a university committee involved with bilingual-bicultural studies. After several months of meetings, I attempted to clarify my own feelings about such studies and the nature of the commitment a university should make to their development. These efforts led me to several colleagues who had attended schools for black youth in the pre-integration South. Their description of such schools and their relationship to the black community sounded just like Mansfield. Both types of schools, those for black children and those for rural white children, were so controlled by their respective communities that the schools looked, felt, and sounded as if

they were designed to fit a certain constituency. Though far from perfect, the schools were comfortable for both children and their parents;
in local terms, they were appropriate, albeit limiting, institutions.

Once I understood that the school-community relationship observed
in Mansfield existed outside the white rural Midwest, I understood more
than just the issues that perplexed me about bilingual-bicultural education. I could see that the problems and apprehensions prevailing in
Mansfield existed in many other places too. Daily newspapers had been
informing us about places where a perceived threat to schools was pain-
fully manifest.

Throughout 1974, for example, schools in Kanawha County, West
Virginia, were embroiled in dispute. Stimulated by church leaders with
a fundamentalist orientation, parents protested the use of textbooks
which (though acceptable to educators) they labeled "antireligious,
communistic and pornographic" (*Newsweek*, 1975:7). They rejected
the classroom practice of treating values as issues open to discussion
rather than as certainties deserving inculcation. Picketing, strikes, and
bomb throwing attended this controversy.

Stormier reactions followed the 1975 busing of black Roxbury students to South Boston High School, where an Irish subgroup had long
been dominant. White Bostonians vigorously resisted the busing in of
children whose presence they felt would modify the climate of *their*
school.[16]

In the 1960s, black communities in New York City worked to establish local control of the schools that served their children. In the 1970s,
the Latino community in America spearheaded a similar movement on
behalf of themselves and other ethnic groups. They urged the creation
of bilingual-bicultural schools that would honor the culture of their own
subgroup as well as that of Anglo society.[17] Some state legislatures
acknowledge the claims of this movement by mandating that instruction
in a child's mother tongue must be provided by school systems where
a certain number of children, knowing too little English to permit their
being adequately educated in that language, exist in one school.

Through the Supreme Court, the federal government also intervened
in another related case. The Amish, a small Mennonite sect living in
various locations around the country, base their social order on religious
beliefs that separate them from most modern Americans. They reject
many changes that distinguish us from our eighteenth-century forebears,
preferring a separate, religious, pastoral existence that they feel is en-
dangered by "too much" secular schooling. Up to a point, the Amish
tolerate their children's public school education. Protesting, however,
that compulsory schooling to the age of sixteen interferred with their
own religious training, they eventually took their case to the Supreme

Court. In 1972, Chief Justice Burger declared "that enforcement of [Wisconsin's] requirement of compulsory formal education after the eighth grade would gravely endanger if not destroy the exercise of . . . [Amish] religious beliefs" (Keim, 1975:98).[18] And in one more example of a private institution designed to provide its clientele—religious, white-flight, or aristocrat—with an educational milieu that fits its own notion of propriety, the Amish have recently begun to establish parochial schools.

Although each of these instances is otherwise distinctive, they share at least one prominent characteristic: each involves a support group aspiring to sustain a school or school system that reflects and reinforces its own particularities. Such schools are not meant to suit all students of any origin. They are meant to have a feeling, a flavor, a stamp that is all the more distinctive the more stable the school-community relationship and the more singular the subgroup comprising the community.

Yet, surely, the point of distinctiveness can be pressed too far. To an important degree, we have a national system of schooling, such that tenth-graders, for example, should be able to transfer with relative ease from one school district to another. A generally common educational and cultural heritage is reinforced by textbook companies, teacher-education programs, and accreditation associations, whose impact serves to create some degree of uniformity among school districts. This uniformity is useful to maintain national integration in political and social terms.[19]

The linking of a national perspective to that of the community introduces one final consideration. For it is unequivocally true that since our schools exist in a complex and generally open society, they are subject to being influenced by the interests and values of a host of concerned agents. In a large democratic society, schools cannot escape being a battleground. Moreover, the question of whose views about schooling should prevail has more than ordinary consequence for Mansfield, since Mansfield is linked to the state and nation by indissoluble ties, and its children must be competent to cope with the world beyond its borders. But the nature and limits of competence are defined by the mainstream Mansfielder, just as the community is essentially defined in his terms. For better or for worse the school serves those whose views dominate. And like a good shoe, Mansfield High School fits mainstream Mansfield.

Whom Shall the Schools Serve?

A school's community-maintenance function takes us beyond general principles of educational success and fiscal rationality. People comprising a support community will defend their schools when alarmed by "dangerous" textbooks, the presence of black children, or units on sex education. Mansfield may never experience the turmoil of a first day of school when parents and children protest bused-in "outsiders." Yet Mansfield has its outsiders—people with city ideas and people who would spend too much money or take away their school. When hiring a superintendent they demonstrated their sense of inside-outside; universalist criteria did not operate. Though different in detail, this community-maintenance behavior of Mansfielders belongs in the same category as Kanawha County protests, busing resistance, and the organization of private schools. These are natural though not necessarily desirable behaviors of persons in our society. Those who enjoy the congeniality and comfort of an existing good fit between school and community reject the outlook of others who would disrupt this fit in the name of what to them are extraneous principles, however well-sanctioned by the Bill of Rights, scientific findings, or established behavioral conventions.

At the heart of resistance to changes that would undermine school-community accord are a community's special qualities—intimacy, belonging, and nurturance. When overlaid with feelings of territoriality they generate a sense of being part of a special people, school, and town. This sense may be in the mind of the beholder and hence inaccessible to critical scrutiny, but it exists as fact for mainstream Mansfielders. And though these qualities are always in flux, they are treasured as eternal goods, irreplaceable and priceless, the marks of an unchanging (or, at least, very slowly changing) order.

That Mansfield school and nonschool agencies can join to socialize Mansfield's youth in particularist ways is not unusual. What is unusual is the midwestern rural American that adult Mansfielders mandate their schools to promote. In actuality, many historical precedents support the peculiarities of one school-community configuration or another, each of which discriminates in some negative sense. A single school-community design never has dominated, though some models more than others always have been favored by the dominant, white, middle-class American. The rural fit has been one of the latter type, profiting from nostalgia for our rural past and also, until recently, from rural-dominated state legislatures. Other types, enjoying less political clout and no historical halo, are less secure.

An endorsement of school control by support communities can be interpreted as encouragement for certain potentially harmful practices. It is not always clear which idiosyncratic behavior and which sacred belief will prove acceptable to a community or to the law. Paradoxically, at a time when the protagonists of prayer in school are still not reconciled to their defeat, bilingual-bicultural advocates are encouraged by state legislatures and the federal government to stress their sense of the sacred. Consider the Kanawha County textbook issue. It exemplifies an attempt by adults of fundamentalist views to insure that their public schools do not undermine cherished values. What is admirable behavior to its advocates constitutes censorship to its detractors,[20] a retrograde move with serious implications for maintaining an open society and the principle of freedom.

Textbook controversies occur frequently. Kay Bartlett describes another contemporary case in Island Trees, New York. She aptly quotes several spokesmen to demonstrate how such issues are defined: indoctrination versus critical thinking, on the one hand, and parental versus nonparental control of children's values, on the other (1977:15).

Now, the censoring of books offends many who accept the idea of religiously separatist schools—Jewish, Catholic, or Lutheran. They forget that such schools choose educators and curriculum materials both to promote their graduates' vocational success and to imbue them with particular views. Parochial schools engage in censorship to the extent that they do not offer equal access to competing belief systems. Many other private schools expect their students to grow up American in generally recognizable ways, but distinctively American in other ways that follow from the reasons the school was established in the first place. In Mansfield the process occurred naturally as the unplanned creation of people who settled down where land was good and the water potable. Those who engendered the school system had occupation and location as common statuses. The etiology of private schools usually is different, but the issue is the same: "how far local control can go before violating the First Amendment" (Bartlett, 1977:13), and how far any school can serve the special interests of its clientele. A vast gray area of uncertainty embraces the issue of the school and its responsibility to different publics and to varied ideals. Legally the schools belong to the state; traditionally they are controlled by cities and local communities; interest groups seek their support; and professional educators, their outlooks in conflict, speak to a multitude of ends. In fact, schools serve many masters. In Mansfield, it seems right that its schools in large measure serve Mansfield.

The concern to maintain school-community congruence should not be interpreted as support for any brand of antifederalism which promises salvation with the return of resources to nonfederal units of government. Too much of value in the United States results from congressional programs (Commager, 1973:47). Yet the idiosyncratic local factors associated with decentralization also merit perpetuation in what must be a continuous examining and defining of the balance of power between two loci of authority—the national and the local. There surely are midpoints which allow a particularist ethos to prevail in school and community, tempered by and supportive of national needs, and responsive to truly critical fiscal realities. Of course, no school system should be supported if it is unable to meet certain academic standards, though it is far from obvious what these standards ought to be. I believe educators and noneducators alike must recognize that schools do more than educate children; they also maintain communities. Thus, is it not preferable, as small school districts struggle to solve financial problems and to meet academic standards, that they be imaginatively assisted to overcome their deficiencies rather than disappear as the price of those deficiencies?[21] Specifically, the factor of community good should be allowed to compete with the factors of educational and financial good in the issue of school consolidation. Similarly, the factor of community good should be allowed to compete with the factors of educational and national good in the host of related cases (Mansfield or South Boston) involving a high degree of school-community accord. Applying simple, monolithic policies to the fate of schools and communities is objectionable.[22]

Note the complexity of specific cases. While the nation agonizes over busing and desegregation, white communities resist what they perceive as destroying their particularism. At the same time, the nation increasingly supports bilingual-bicultural education, which aims to foster particularism. It is difficult to sort out the good from the bad cases once one gives credence to establishing and maintaining a close fit between a school and its support community.

Moreover, the universalist notion of promoting full intellectual and emotional growth, whatever this may mean, or of attaining efficiency through cost-benefit analysis challenges the particularist notion of community maintenance. Actually, people settle for a quality and type of schooling which suits them even though it may not promote to the fullest their child's personal development and social mobility. They are not indifferent to these outcomes. But there is more to schooling than meets the eyes of teachers, legislators, and academics who conceptualize purposes for schooling not fully shared by those who constitute a community. There is a school's noneducative, community-maintenance function, which usually becomes apparent to its support group only when it is threatened. Given our tradition for local control of schools, the dispositions of communities should not be ignored. And given our commitment to cultural pluralism, however faint-hearted, there is further support for idiosyncratic school systems engendered by idiosyncratic communities. Of course, this view may encourage educational policies that are at odds with national interests, if not with those of politically and economically disadvantaged minorities. My concern is not to diminish the response to these interests but to underscore those of communities, wherever they are found, as a factor in educational policy making.[23] I am concerned that the conditions of modern society be congenial to the survival of communities and wisely respectful of those collectivities whose "quest for community" has not been denied.[24] And I am struck by the tension between antagonists of ways of life that have "gone modern" and those who deny "the virtues of small town life." Surely our conception of human rights can accommodate both perspectives![25]

In my portrayal of a rural school district, I mean to support the survival of communities, the easy ones like Mansfield, which have a homogeneous mainstream group, and the less easy ones like Kanawha County and Island Trees,[26] which face the profoundly complex task of maintaining a school system in which some residents want their schools to reflect the absolutism of their religious doctrine or personal creed, while others want their schools to reflect the Bill of Rights. If interpreted rigidly and narrowly both positions undermine community.

I have tried to be sensitive to the romanticism which attaches such blinders to an observer's eyes that he sees only that reality which squares with his preconceived notions.[27] Mansfield is not paradise either to me or to many of its inhabitants who for different reasons remain outside the charmed circle of acceptability. It is a community in a psychological sense, and like all such communities it is inevitably somewhat exclusive. Although not everyone feels or can feel he belongs there, I find Mansfield appealing because it embraces those who, in a manner of speaking, will submit to it. Believing that such rewards are uncommon, I value places where they are available.[28]

With its particular brand of instruction, its ideological orientation, and its stress on sports and money-raising activities, Mansfield High School is not a school for everyone or a model for other communities. Given local control, it could not be; nor is it meant to be. But it does belong in Mansfield. As one teacher observed after reflecting on the school's strengths and weaknesses, "I guess it's as good a school as you can expect Mansfield to have." Under the conditions of local control, her comments are essentially accurate. She did not intend to be patronizing. As a Mansfield native, she knew what kind of school the desires and expectations of community adults would support. Given the people, the school is appropriate.

In a highly mobile world of transient personal relationships, where social commitments are ad hoc and alienation is common, Mansfield seems not so much an anachronism as a haven. Admittedly, it can stifle or restrict behavior of consequence in other settings. Still, it is a place of rare intimacy. Bearing in mind the dilemmas they raise, cannot a nation's Mansfields be nurtured rather than threatened by modern society? Must we equate goodness with largeness, mindlessly allowing all the dimensions of life to increase without regard to the quality of the life that results?

From external perspectives and criteria, the school can be judged more harshly than my narrative suggests. But as I assured my Mansfield hosts, I did not come to conduct an evaluation. I planned, rather, to examine the relationship between school and community in a rural setting. I found the relationship to be mutually beneficial. The two are joined in the maintenance of a significant American subgroup, one that I do not see as prototypical for all of us, one that is flawed, but one that is worth treasuring—if the price paid by Mansfield and the nation is not too high.

Appendix A: Tables

TABLE 1

Distribution of Operating Local Public School Systems
and Number of Pupils, by Size of System, 1970

| | Systems | | Pupils | |
Size of System	Number	Percentage	Number	Percentage
25,000 or more	191	1.1	13,493,237	30.0
10,000 to 24,999	557	3.2	5,041,609	17.9
5,000 to 9,999	1,104	6.3	7,626,270	17.0
2,500 to 4,900	2,018	11.5	7,036,096	15.6
1,000 to 2,499	3,448	19.7	5,634,730	12.5
600 to 999	1,976	11.3	1,541,080	3.4
300 to 599	2,410	13.8	1,056,883	2.3
Under 300	5,794	33.1	607,762	1.3
Total	17,498	100	45,037,667	100

SOURCE: This table is adapted from Lewis R. Tamblyn, *Rural Education in the United States* (Washington, D.C.: Rural Education Association, 1971).

TABLE 2

Age Distribution in Mansfield School District by Sex, 1970

| | Male | | Female | |
Age[a]	Number	Percentage	Number	Percentage
0–4	76	6.9	63	5.8
5–20	352	32.2	290	26.9
21–34	182	16.6	158	14.6
35–64	350	31.9	370	34.3
65+	134	12.2	197	18.2
Total	1094	99.8	1078	99.8

SOURCE: Census data for school districts in "Cunningham County," 1970.
[a]These categories follow those used in the 1970 census data.

TABLE 3

Educational Achievement of Mansfielders,
25 and Older, by Sex, 1970

	Male		Female	
Years Completed	Number	Percentage	Number	Percentage
0	1	0.2	20	3.0
1–8	204	33.9	166	25.2
9–11	127	21.1	162	24.6
12	211	35.1	243	36.9
12+	58	9.6	66	10.0
Total	601	99.9	657	99.7

SOURCE: Census data for school districts in "Cunningham County," 1970.

TABLE 4

Family Income in Mansfield School District, 1970

Family Income Annual	Number	Percentage
$1,000–$4,999	103	16.5
$5,000–$9,999	252	40.3
$10,000–$14,999	187	29.9
$15,000–$24,999	51	8.1
$25,000–$49,999	31	4.9
Total	624	99.7

SOURCE: Census data for school districts in "Cunningham County," 1970.

TABLE 5
Population of Cunningham County, Mansfield Township, and Mansfield Village, 1890–1970

	1890	1900	1910	1920	1930	1940	1950	1960	1970
Cunningham County	14,481	15,224	14,630	14,839	13,247	13,447	13,171	13,635	13,263
Mansfield Township	2,245	2,134	2,011	2,507	1,991	2,047	1,815	1,777	1,818
Mansfield Village	767	815	1,011	1,479	1,121	1,215	1,152	1,200	1,303

SOURCE: Census data for the indicated decades.

TABLE 6

Number and Size of Farms in Cunningham County, 1860–1964

	Number of Farms	Total Farm Acreage	Average Farm Acreage	Value per Farm (Dollars)
1860	518	103,441	200.0	—
1880	1,935	207,246	107.1	—
1900	1,692	203,946	120.5	—
1920	1,501	206,781	137.8	93,847
1930	1,446	206,146	142.6	82,175
1940	1,278	201,122	157.4	91,685
1950	1,227	210,126	171.3	106,216
1959	996	205,096	205.9	142,328
1964	832	204,745	246.1	166,588[a]

SOURCE: "County Agricultural Statistics," a bulletin published by "Cunningham County" in November 1969.

[a]Figure for 1967, not 1964.

TABLE 7

Mansfielders by Status

Status[a]	Number	Percentage
Newcomer	11	4.6
Transitional	28	11.7
Local	85	35.5
Native	105	43.9
Total	229	95.7[b]

[a]These labels represent self-designations.

[b]Percentages in this and other tables will not always equal 100 percent because of missing data.

TABLE 8

Community Roots in Mansfield

Generation	Number	Percentage
First	68	28.4
Second	29	12.1
Third	67	28.0
Fourth	28	11.7
Fifth	14	5.8
Total	206	86.0

NOTE: This table represents the number of generations respondents' families have lived in Mansfield: that is, if one or both parents lived there, the respondent is listed as a second-generation Mansfielder.

TABLE 9

Relatives outside Respondent's Immediate
Family Living in Mansfield Community

Number of Relatives	Number of Respondents	Percentage
0	40	16.7
1–5	58	24.3
6–10	39	16.3
11–15	23	9.6
16–20	15	6.3
21 and over	64	26.7
Total	239	99.9

TABLE 10

How Mansfield Adults View Mansfield Community
(N = 239)

	Agree		Neither agree nor disagree		Disagree	
	%	N	%	N	%	N
1. Mansfield is a safe place to live.	91.6	219	5.9	14	2.5	6
2. People in small towns like Mansfield are better able to live the kind of life they prefer than people in larger towns.	54.0	129	22.2	53	22.6	54
3. One of the most important things in Mansfield is its good school system.	69.9	167	15.9	38	13.0	31
4. I like living in Mansfield because you know just about everybody and everybody knows you.	56.9	136	23.0	55	19.2	46
5. One of the most important things in Mansfield is its good churches.	66.1	158	21.8	52	11.3	27
6. If you or your family had some misfortune, you could count on people in Mansfield to help out.	75.3	180	14.2	34	9.2	22
7. To me living in Mansfield is somewhat like being part of one big family.	33.5	80	26.8	64	38.1	91
8. People are no friendlier in Mansfield than they are in larger places.	29.7	71	14.2	34	52.7	126
9. Mansfield is a specially good place to raise children.	66.9	160	22.2	53	8.4	20
10. I basically feel that we are at least as well off as most other towns our size.	76.1	182	7.9	19	13.8	33
11. I wish a person in Mansfield had more privacy.	31.0	74	43.5	104	22.2	53

TABLE 11

How Mansfield Adults Stand on Contemporary Issues
(N = 239)

	Agree		Neither agree nor disagree		Disagree	
	%	N	%	N	%	N
1. Perhaps most people of working age on welfare could work if they really wanted to.	72.4	173	20.5	49	7.1	17
2. This country would be better off if it had stricter gun laws.	35.6	85	25.1	60	37.7	90
3. Abortion should be legal.	32.6	78	23.8	57	42.3	101
4. We may be very worried about energy problems and the financial situation, but communism is still the number one problem facing the United States.	53.6	128	9.6	23	36.0	86
5. I believe that capital punishment should be abolished	19.2	46	20.0	48	59.8	143
6. I can't get excited about what's happening around the world. There's too much to worry about at home.	19.7	47	18.0	43	61.9	148
7. The United States should continue to provide financial aid on a regular basis to foreign countries.	17.6	42	14.6	35	65.7	157
8. I feel the women's lib movement is mostly a good thing.	25.9	63	30.5	73	41.4	99
9. Stanton is not as pleasant a place to live as it used to be.	63.6	152	25.5	61	8.4	20
10. One thing that should never go out of style is good old-fashioned patriotism.	86.6	207	7.1	17	3.8	9
11. The American way of life can't be beat anywhere in the world.	74.1	177	13.4	32	9.6	23
12. I think it is important that a person believes in God.	88.3	211	5.9	14	3.3	8

TABLE 12

How Far Mansfield Adults Identify with Mansfield Community
(N = 239)

	Agree		Neither agree nor disagree		Disagree	
	%	N	%	N	%	N
1. I probably feel more at home in Mansfield than I ever could some place outside the Mansfield community.	52.7	126	18.8	46	28.0	67
2. I get mad if I hear somebody insult Mansfield.	74.5	178	17.6	42	7.1	17
3. It wouldn't bother me if, for some reason, the name of our town was changed from Mansfield to some other name.	14.6	35	15.9	38	70.3	168
4. It still makes sense to me to be loyal to one's community.	60.3	144	16.7	40	23.0	55
5. It is important to me what people in Mansfield think of me.	81.6	195	12.6	30	5.0	12
6. It is hard for me to think of living happily in some place other than Mansfield.	25.1	60	23.4	56	50.6	121
7. I wish I could move away from Mansfield right now.	11.7	28	21.8	52	66.1	158
8. Even if I had the opportunity to move from Mansfield, I would prefer to stay here.	47.3	113	24.7	59	25.1	60

TABLE 13

Sales Tax Receipts in Mansfield, 1951–71
(In 1967 Dollars)

	Type of Tax[a]	Number of Taxpayers	Total Tax Receipts
1951	A	40	$ 30,059
1956	A, B	—	21,287
1961	A, B	41	20,493
1966	A, B, C, D	43	23,362
1971	A, B, C	29	22,157

SOURCE: Annual reports of the "City of Mansfield."
[a]A = Retailers' occupation tax; B = Use tax; C = Service occupation tax; D = Service use tax.

TABLE 14

Comparative Financial Data on Cunningham County School Districts, 1970–1971

School District	Total Enroll- ment	Enroll- ment Rank[a]	Total Tax	Tax Rank[b]	AVPP[c] $	Rank[d] AVPP	Effort Rank[e]	OEPP[f] $
Auburn	1,470	319	2.324	337	23,978	635	396	883.34
Oakfield	528	628	2.436	303	36,834	342	555	1,098.79
Mansfield	550	618	2.599	229	32,476	407	483	999.01

SOURCE: "School Statistics," published by the governor's commission on schools in March 1973.

[a]Out of 890 schools of all types.

[b]Out of 393 schools organized in unit districts. There are 436 unit districts; the lower number of 393 results from ties.

[c]AVPP is assessed valuation per pupil, or the amount of taxable wealth available to a district for the local support of education.

[d]Out of 1,072 schools. There are 1,084 school districts of all types; the lower number of 1,072 results from ties.

[e]Out of 1,084 schools. Effort rank is a correlation between a district's potential wealth, as measured by AVPP, and the degree to which that district draws upon its wealth for the support of the schools, as indicated by the district's total tax rate.

[f]OEPP is operating expense per pupil, or the amount of money a district actually spends to educate each of its students.

TABLE 15

Selected Educational Expenditures, 1972–73

Instructional Program	
1. Salaries (excludes administrators but includes teachers who coach)	$121,165
2. Contractual services (repairs)	275
3. Supplies	
Textbooks	150
Library and audio visual	2,459
4. Other instructional supplies	
Home economics	350
Vocational agriculture	300
Industrial arts	500
Music	800
Art	400
Physical education	400
Science	699
Math	150
Business education	350
Driver education	200
English	150

TABLE 15 (Cont.)

Latin	75
Spanish	75
Social studies	75
History	100
Supplementary reading [probably includes elementary school]	500
Workbooks [probably includes elementary school]	2,450
Photography	250
Auto mechanics	600
Journalism	350
5. Travel	
Vocational agriculture	275
Home economics	70
Scouting and athletic meetings	250
Teachers conference workshops	400
Lunch supervisors	200
6. Other	
High school language and math entry fees	20
Music—state band and chorus contest and awards	380
Athletic entry fees and tournaments	120
Total	$134,631

Athletic Program	
1. Salaries	$ 4,750
2. Contracting services [largely officiating, repairs, and tournament costs]	
Football	790
Basketball	890
Baseball	120
Track	100
3. Materials and supplies	
Football	1,495
Basketball	1,233
Baseball	150
Track (boys)	1,019
Track (junior high girls)	150
4. Other	
Awards	400
Athletic needs	50
Medical supplies	300
University football game	25
State sectional tournaments	150
Dry cleaning	25
Total	$ 12,649

TABLE 16
Mansfield Teacher Salaries Compared with State Median Salaries, 1971–74
(Annual Pay in Dollars)

	Nondegree[a]		B.A.				M.A.			
	No Experience	Maximum	No Experience		Maximum		No Experience		Maximum	
			Mansfield	State	Mansfield	State	Mansfield	State	Mansfield	State
1971	6,620	7,740	7,300	7,500	9,300	10,087	7,700	8,200	10,700	11,920
1972	6,920	8,110	7,600	7,600	9,800	10,400	8,000	8,324	11,250	12,280
1973	7,000	8,575	7,700	7,900	10,200	10,825	8,100	8,668	12,000	12,800
1974	7,400	8,975	8,100	8,400	10,600	11,600	8,500	9,207	12,400	13,665

[a]Statewide figures for nondegree teachers were not available.

TABLE 17

School District Staff Experience in Mansfield, 1964–70

| | Years Experience in Mansfield | | | |
	0–5	6–10	11+	Total N
1964	10	4	20	34
1965	11	3	20	34
1966	10	3	20	33
1967	9	5	19	33
1968	8	6	23	37
1969	3	6	23	32
1970	9	7	21	37
Mean percentage	25	14	60	100

TABLE 18

Years of Experience and Number of High School Teachers by Earned Degree, 1972

| Years Experience in Mansfield | Degree | | | |
	None	B.A.	M.A.	Total
0–5	1	6	2	9 (50%)
6–10	1	2	0	3 (17%)
11+	0	2	4	6 (33%)
Total	2 (11%)	10 (55%)	6 (33%)	18 (100%)

TABLE 19

Student-Teacher Ratios and Student Enrollments in Grades 7–12, 1964–74

	Number of Students	Number of Teachers	Student-Teacher Ratio
1964	252	15	1:17
1965	265	16	1:16
1971	267	19	1:14
1972	260	19	1:14
1973	248	20	1:12
1974	234	18	1:13

TABLE 20

Number of Students and Teachers in Mansfield School District, 1964–74

	Number of Students	Number of Teachers
1964	619	34
1965	620	34
1966	607	33
1967	626	33
1968	604	37
1969	574	32
1970	569	37
1971	549	33
1972	541	31
1973	500	35
1974	474	33

TABLE 21

Courses and Their Enrollment for Selected Years

	1968	1971	1974
English I	45	49	35
English II	45	43	43
English III	38	42	39
Short story	—[a]	—	—
Black literature	—	—	9
Speech	30	26	—
Creative writing[b]	—	—	—
British literature	—	—	—
Journalism	—	19	15
Total	158	179	141
Latin I	—	10	—
Latin II	—	—	—
Spanish I	23	12	10
Spanish II	10	8	8
Spanish III	—	—	—
Total	33	30	18
Biology	48	45	24
Botany and zoology	21	12	14
Chemistry	13	21	11
Total	82	78	49[c]

TABLE 21 (Cont.)

	1968	1971	1974
Practical math	24	24	23
Elements of Algebra	—	18	—
Algebra I	24	20	19
Plane geometry	17	20	12
Algebra II	14	14	15
Modern math analysis	3	7	—
Total	82	103	69
U.S. history	40	45	38
Occupational information	—	—	—
Current events	—	—	—
Minorities history	—	—	11
Consumer economics	—	—	—
World history	—	—	—
Civics	15	—	—
American government	—	16	—
Geography	—	—	8
Sociology	23	—	22
Economics	—	12	—
Total	78	73	79
Shorthand	8	7	18
General business	—	20	8
Bookkeeping	13	20	19
Office practice	7	16	12
Typing	55	40	43
Total	83	103	100
Vocational photography	7	—	5
Auto mechanics I & II	13	14	12
Art I & II	15	10	37
Total	35	24	54
Introduction to industrial arts	—	—	—
Industrial arts I	15	18	17
Industrial arts II	—	—	10
Industrial arts III & IV	9	7	7
Total	24	25	34
Vocational agriculture I & II	14	8	15
Vocational agriculture III & IV	14	17	7
Total	28	25	22

TABLE 21 (Cont.)

	1968	1971	1974
Home economics I	12	15	10
Home economics II & III	13	15	16[d]
Home management IV	—	6	20[e]
Total	25	36	46
Grand total	628	676	612

[a]The dash indicates the course was not offered in that year, though it was taught in other years not shown here.
[b]Enrollment figures not available.
[c]This decline was due to a temporary reshuffling of teachers.
[d]II only.
[e]III and IV.

TABLE 22

Funds in the Accounts of High School Classes
and Extracurricular Organizations

	Cash Balance June 30, 1972	Receipts	Disbursements	Cash Balance June 30, 1973
Class of 1972	$ 50.93	$ 173.00	$ 224.03	—
Class of 1973	762.17	5,081.73	5,843.73	—
Class of 1974	573.66	1,726.78	2,071.97	$ 228.47
Class of 1975	551.53	628.55	308.16	871.92
Class of 1976	139.54	1,464.64	1,074.25	529.93
Eighth grade	—	668.10	437.68	230.42
Band	48.78	379.18	404.28	23.68
Camera Club	115.64	38.53	136.80	17.37
Future Farmers of America	1,158.57	1,414.77	1,741.87	831.47
Future Homemakers of America	116.58	541.03	415.56	242.05
Future Teachers of America	6.95	—	—	6.95
Girls Athletic Association	179.66	498.60	445.27	232.99
Lettermen's Club	259.69	223.20	194.00	288.89
Library Club	14.05	—	—	14.05
Pep Club	1.83	657.14	650.80	8.17
Projectionist's Club	28.21	44.50	14.45	58.26
Student Council	155.62	1,341.94	1,209.18	288.38
Total	$4,163.41	$14,881.79	$15,172.20	$3,873.00

TABLE 23

Class Standing, College Attendance, and Place of Residence of M.H.S. Graduates for Selected Years (1947–65)

Graduation Class	Top of Class[a] Attended College	Top of Class No College	Bottom of Class Attended College	Bottom of Class No College	Top of Class In Mansfield Area[b]	Top of Class Out of Mansfield Area	Bottom of Class In Mansfield Area	Bottom of Class Out of Mansfield Area	Total Attended College N	Total Attended College %	Total Living in Mansfield Area N	Total Living in Mansfield Area %
1947 (N = 14)	3	4	0	7	4	3	4	3	3	21	8	57
1948 (N = 14)	5	2	0	7	2	5	7	0	5	36	9	64
1949 (N = 14)	4	3	1	6	3	4	3	4	5	36	6	43
1950 (N = 22)	7	4	2	9	6	5	9	2	9	41	15	68
1951 (N = 18)	1	6	2	6c	6	3	7	2	3	17	13	72
1956 (N = 14)	5	2	0	6	2	5	5	2	5	36	7	50
1960 (N = 10)	3	2	1	4	3	2	4	1	4	40	7	70
1962 (N = 13)	4	0	2	5	1	4	3	4	6	46	4	33
1965 (N = 19)	6	3	1	9	4	5	5	3	7	37	9	53
Total 138	38 (59%)	26 (41%)	9 (13%)	59 (87%)	31 (46%)	36 (54%)	47 (69%)	21 (31%)	47	34	78	52

NOTE: These data regarding college attendance and place of residence were accurate as of 1973 when they were collected.

[a]Top and bottom of class were figured differently (for no reason other than inconsistency in data collection techniques). For 1947 to 1956, I included students in the top and bottom third of their class; for 1960–1965, I included every other student in the class, starting with the top ranked student. The actual Ns are 1947, 24; 1948, 25; 1949, 22; 1950, 33; 1951, 27; 1956, 22; 1960, 19; 1962, 25; 1965, 37. These years were selected because of availability of data.

[b]"Mansfield area" includes the town and countryside in a twenty-five mile area around and including Mansfield school district.

[c]Totals for this and several other years (1956, 1962) do not equal the stated N because of incomplete data on some of the graduates.

TABLE 24

Postsecondary Education and Place of Residence of Graduating Classes, 1967–72

Year	Class Size N	Postsecondary Education N	Postsecondary Education %	Noncollege Postsecondary Dropped Out (DO)	Noncollege Postsecondary Attending (A)	Noncollege Postsecondary Completed (C)	Junior College DO	Junior College A	Junior College C	College DO	College A	College C	Army	College Town	Current Place of Residence — Mansfield & Mansfield area[a] N	Mansfield area[a] %	Mansfield[b] N	Mansfield[b] %
1967	44	18	41	0	0	3	0	1	0	2	2	10	3	3	20	45	6	30
1968	46	22	48	0	0	2	2	0	0	1	2	15	1	2	30	65	10	33
1969	42	17	40	0	0	0	2	0	1	3	7	4	5	7	23	55	10	43
1970	31	18	58	0	0	1	3	3	1	2	8	0	1	7	17	55	10	59
1971	32	20	62	0	2	0	0	6	0	0	12	0	2	12	13	41	7	54
1972	38	15	39	0	3	0	0	2	0	0	10	0	5	9	22	58	19	86
Total	233	110	47	0	5	6	7	12	2	8	41	29	17	40	125	54	62	50

NOTE: Data are accurate as of 1972.

[a]Mansfield area is defined as in table 23. The column contains *all* graduates who lived in Mansfield or Mansfield areas (the percentages are derived from N/class size).

[b]Mansfield refers to Mansfield school district. The percentages in this column are derived from the number living in the school district as a proportion of the total number of graduates living in the Mansfield area (e.g., for 1967, 6/20; for 1968, 10/30; etc.).

TABLE 25

How Mansfield Educators View Mansfield Community
(N = 22)

Item	Agree %	N	Neither agree nor disagree %	N	Disagree %	N
1. Mansfield is a safe place to live.	95.4	21	4.5	1	—	—
2. People in small towns like Mansfield are better able to live the kind of life they prefer than people in larger towns.	27.2	6	13.6	3	59.0	13
3. One of the most important things in Mansfield is its good school system.	81.8	18	18.1	4	—	—
4. I like living in Mansfield because you know just about everybody and everybody knows you.	40.9	9	36.3	8	22.7	5
5. One of the most important things in Mansfield is its good churches.	68.1	15	31.8	7	—	—
6. If you or your family has some misfortune, you could count on people in Mansfield to help out.	86.3	19	4.5	1	9.1	2
7. To me living in Mansfield is somewhat like being part of one big family.	31.8	7	13.6	3	50.0	11
8. People are no friendlier in Mansfield than they are in larger places.	59.0	13	9.1	2	31.8	7
9. Mansfield is a specially good place to raise children.	59.0	13	18.1	4	22.7	5
10. I basically feel that we are at least as well off as most other towns our size.	68.1	15	4.5	1	18.1	4
11. I wish a person in Mansfield had more privacy.	36.3	8	36.3	8	27.2	6

TABLE 26

How Mansfield's Educators Stand on Contemporary Issues
(N = 22)

Item	Agree %	N	Neither agree nor disagree %	N	Disagree %	N
1. Perhaps most people of working age on welfare could work if they really wanted to.	72.7	16	22.7	5	4.5	1
2. This country would be better off if it had stricter gun laws.	31.8	7	36.3	8	31.8	7
3. Abortion should be legal.	77.2	17	9.1	2	13.6	3
4. We may be very worried about energy problems and the financial situation, but communism is still the number one problem facing the United States.	45.4	10	13.6	3	40.9	9
5. I believe that capital punishment should be abolished.	18.1	4	13.6	3	68.1	15
6. I can't get excited about what's happening around the world. There's too much to worry about at home.	4.5	1	—	—	95.4	21
7. The United States should continue to provide financial aid on a regular basis to foreign countries.	4.5	1	18.1	4	77.2	17
8. I feel the women's lib movement is mostly a good thing.	31.8	7	45.4	10	22.7	5
9. Stanton is not as pleasant a place to live as it used to be.	59.0	13	40.9	9	—	—
10. One thing that should never go out of style is good old-fashioned patriotism.	90.9	20	4.5	1	4.5	1
11. The American way of life can't be beat anywhere in the world.	81.8	18	13.6	3	4.5	1
12. I think it is important that a person believes in God.	95.4	21	4.5	1	—	—

TABLE 27

How Far Mansfield Educators Identify with Mansfield Community
(N = 22)

	Agree		Neither agree nor disagree		Disagree	
	%	N	%	N	%	N
1. I probably feel more at home in Mansfield than I ever could some place outside the Mansfield community.	22.7	5	36.3	8	40.9	9
2. I get mad if I hear somebody insult Mansfield.	72.7	16	18.1	4	9.1	2
3. It wouldn't bother me if, for some reason, the name of our town was changed from Mansfield to some other name.	4.5	1	4.5	1	90.9	20
4. It still makes sense to me to be loyal to one's community.	50.0	11	22.7	5	27.2	6
5. It is important to me what people in Mansfield think of me.	86.3	19	9.1	2	4.5	1
6. It is hard for me to think of living happily in some place other than Mansfield.	13.6	3	13.6	3	72.7	16
7. I wish I could move away from Mansfield right now.	13.6	3	40.9	9	40.9	9
8. Even if I had the opportunity to move from Mansfield, I would prefer to stay here.	31.8	7	36.3	8	18.1	4

TABLE 28

Feelings of Mansfield Groups toward the
Absence of Negroes in Mansfield

	Loss	Gain	Neither loss nor gain	Total
Farmers	0	10	1	11
High school students	8	7	1	16
Grade school students	3	9	0	12
High school teachers	4	5	2	11
Retired persons	2	2	0	4
Factory workers	0	6	0	6
Businessmen	0	3	0	3
Ministers	1	2	1	4
Total	18	44	5	67

TABLE 29

How Mansfield High School Students View Mansfield Community
(N = 157)

	Agree		Neither agree nor disagree		Disagree	
	%	N	%	N	%	N
1. Mansfield is a safe place to live.	78.9	124	15.2	24	5.7	9
2. People in small towns like Mansfield are better able to live the kind of life they prefer than people in larger towns.	57.3	90	24.8	39	17.8	28
3. One of the most important things in Mansfield is its good school system.	36.3	57	25.4	40	37.5	59
4. I like living in Mansfield because you know just about everybody and everybody knows you.	54.1	85	17.8	28	26.7	42
5. One of the most important things in Mansfield is its good churches.	40.1	63	41.4	65	18.4	29
6. If you or your family had some misfortune, you could count on people in Mansfield to help out.	64.9	102	19.7	31	15.2	24
7. To me living in Mansfield is somewhat like being part of one big family.	34.3	54	19.1	30	46.4	73
8. People are no friendlier in Mansfield than they are in large places.	31.2	49	19.1	30	48.4	76
9. Mansfield is a specially good place to raise children.	47.7	75	26.7	42	24.2	38
10. I basically feel that we are at least as well off as most other towns our size.	59.8	94	17.1	27	22.2	35
11. I wish a person in Mansfield had more privacy.	51.5	81	33.7	53	14.0	22

TABLE 30

How Mansfield High School Students Stand on Contemporary Issues
(N = 157)

	Agree		Neither agree nor disagree		Disagree	
	%	N	%	N	%	N
1. Perhaps most people of working age on welfare could work if they really wanted to.	68.1	107	23.5	37	8.2	13
2. This country would be better off if it had stricter gun laws.	25.4	40	35.0	55	38.2	60
3. Abortion should be legal.	46.4	73	21.0	33	31.8	50
4. We may be very worried about energy problems and the financial situation, but communism is still the number one problem facing the U.S.	39.4	62	31.8	50	28.0	44
5. I believe that capital punishment should be abolished.	28.6	45	22.9	36	47.7	75
6. I can't get excited about what's happening around the world. There's too much to worry about at home.	15.9	25	26.1	41	57.9	91
7. The United States should continue to provide financial aid on a regular basis to foreign countries.	17.1	27	31.8	50	50.9	80
8. I feel the women's lib movement is mostly a good thing.	26.7	42	29.2	46	43.9	69
9. Stanton is not as pleasant a place to live as it used to be.	64.9	102	25.4	40	8.2	13
10. One thing that should never go out of style is good old-fashioned patriotism.	61.1	96	30.3	48	7.6	12
11. The American way of life can't be beat anywhere in the world.	61.7	97	23.5	37	14.0	22
12. I think it is important that a person believes in God.	82.8	130	13.3	21	3.1	5

TABLE 31

How Far Mansfield High School Students
Identify with Mansfield Community
(N = 157)

	Agree		Neither agree nor disagree		Disagree	
	%	N	%	N	%	N
1. I probably feel more at home in Mansfield than I ever could some place outside the Mansfield community.	46.4	73	14.0	22	39.4	62
2. I get mad if I hear somebody insult Mansfield.	73.8	116	21.6	34	4.4	7
3. It wouldn't bother me if, for some reason, the name of our town was changed from Mansfield to some other name.	21.6	34	18.4	29	59.8	94
4. It still makes sense to me to be loyal to one's community.	59.8	94	11.4	18	28.6	45
5. It is important to me what people in Mansfield think of me.	57.3	90	31.8	50	10.1	16
6. It is hard for me to think of living happily in some place other than Mansfield.	22.9	36	22.2	35	54.7	86
7. I wish I could move away from Mansfield right now.	22.2	35	25.4	40	44.5	70
8. Even if I had the opportunity to move from Mansfield, I would prefer to stay here.	33.7	53	24.2	38	41.4	65

TABLE 32

Alienation of Mansfielders Compared with That of a National Sample

Item[a]	Population Sampled	Agree	Neither agree nor disagree	Disagree
1. Nothing is worthwhile anymore.	Mansfield students	8.2%	23.5%	68.1%
	Mansfield adults	15.0	7.9	74.4
	U.S. adults	43.3	—	55.9
2. People can't be trusted.	Mansfield students	25.4	28.6	41.3
	Mansfield adults	17.5	12.5	67.3
	U.S. adults	56.1	4.3	39.5
3. I can count on someone to help me when I'm in real trouble.	Mansfield students	64.7	19.7	15.2
	Mansfield adults	75.2	9.1%	14.2
	U.S. adults	24.0%	—	75.1%

NOTE: For Mansfield adults N = 239; for Mansfield students N = 157. The national sample N of 1,484 is taken from the N.O.R.C. publication, *National Data Program for the Social Sciences*.

[a]Item 1 is from the N.O.R.C. publication cited above, July 1974:44; item 2, July 1975:75; item 3, July 1974:46. The wording of N.O.R.C. items and mine is almost identical. I asked additional questions on the alienation dimension but could not find comparative data that would put them in perspective. For example, "I'm satisfied with the respect I get from other people"—87.8 percent of the adults and 71.0 percent of the students agreed; "I feel somewhat apart from people even when I'm among friends"—59.7 percent of the adults and 57.2 percent of the students disagreed.

Appendix B: Sample Tests

American History Tests

Revolutionary Period

1. Discuss the British three-fold plan of 1777 and why it failed and why this failure was important to the colonists. (six points)

2. List the three major sections of fighting in the continental war. Underneath these listings indicate the turning battles and the plan. (ten points)

3. What was the reasoning used by Thomas Paine in his document *Common Sense*? (two points)

4. What were the two stipulations of France before they would fight on our side and what convinced them to do so? (three points)

5. Trace one party back to its origin and tell what issues and what groups separated it from the corresponding parties. (eight points)

6. What are the three principles or theories of government that are expounded in the Declaration of Independence? (three points)

7. Give the significance of the following: (ten points)
    Common Sense
    Saratoga
    John Paul Jones's defeat of the British
    The "olive branch" offered by England in 1778
    Yorktown

Civil War Period

1. Discuss four events that will prove that the Civil War and the idea of secession or state's rights did not start in 1861 but had been fermenting for a number of years.

2. List the advantages and disadvantages of your side before the Civil War.

3. Discuss the statement the war was fought in the East, but won in the West.

4. Discuss briefly the three reconstruction plans and tell what was the actual plan that was implemented.

5. Write an essay discussing the battles and generals of the Civil War that you feel were vital in the ultimate outcome of your side. You must use several battles and the more supporting information will determine your grade.

English Test: Julius Caesar

On the lines at the left of each number write the letter of the statement which completes the sentence most correctly.

_____ 1. Flavius and Marullus went about the streets of Rome disrobing the images of Caesar and driving the vulgar from the streets in order to:

   a. make way for Pompey's triumphal procession
   b. check Caesar's growing popularity
   c. maintain the solemnity befitting the Lupercal

_____ 2. Cassius did not go to the public ceremony on the day of the Lupercal because:

   a. he found the opportunity he'd been waiting for to "Whet Brutus against Caesar"
   b. Brutus had plucked him by the sleeve and bade him refuse to witness Caesar's crowning
   c. Caesar had rebuked him in public for never smiling

_____ 3. The bargain which Casca made with Cassius when they met on the street during a thunderstorm was:

   a. to throw a paper in at Brutus' window
   b. to win Brutus to the cause of the conspiracy
   c. to wait at Pompey's porch and watch for a chance to kill Caesar

_____ 4. About Caesar's desire to be king, Brutus made up his mind thus:

   a. since Rome already suffered from a petty insurrection, it was best to strike at the cause
   b. since you could not tell to what lengths his lust for power would go, it was best to assassinate him as a preventive measure
   c. since certain Romans had decided against Caesar's right to live, it was not right for Brutus to question their decision

_____ 5. Caesar was persuaded to go to the Senate House in spite of his wife's fear by:

   a. Brutus
   b. Trebonius
   c. Decius

_____ 6. *Immediately* after Caesar's death, Mark Antony:

    a. fled to his house and sent a message to Octavius describing the things in Rome

    b. kneeled at Caesar's body and spoke an eloquent farewell

    c. sent a message to Brutus, promising allegiance and asking only for an explanation of why Caesar deserved to die

_____ 7. Mark Antony's speech at Caesar's funeral turned out to be a justification of:

    a. Caesar's doubts that Mark Antony was true friend

    b. Brutus' faith that the cause of the conspiracy would suffer none from allowing Caesar's body full ceremonial rites

    c. Cassius' fears that Antony would use the opportunity to inflame the mob against the conspiracy . . .

True or False

_____ 1. Cassius regarded Caesar an unworthy person of all the honors heaped upon him.

_____ 2. Brutus was troubled about the present state of Rome or, more specifically, Caesar's power even before Cassius approached him.

_____ 3. Caesar was not suspicious of Cassius.

_____ 4. Caesar dealt kindly with those who opposed him.

_____ 5. Others besides Cassius regarded Brutus as necessary to the success of the conspiracy.

_____ 6. Brutus saw no way to protect Rome except to kill Caesar.

_____ 7. Brutus did not believe that the cause of the conspiracy was just.

_____ 8. At the end of their conversation, Caesar was not willing to change his plans because of his wife's dream.

_____ 9. Cassius was more uneasy before the killing than Brutus was.

_____10. Cassius believed it was best to let Antony live . . .

Biology Test

1. Life begins as a _____, a fusion of the _____ and the _____ cells.

2. The knowledge contained in the above cell that insures a complete individual of the same kind, generation after generation, is called

   _____.

3. A series of organized changes that a dividing cell undergoes is called

   _____.

4. The primary purpose of this process is to insure a complete set of _____ for each new cell.

5. These structures contain the genetic material _____.

6. This material can have the important properties of determining the heredity of an organism only if it is intact from the _____ cell to the _____ cell.

7. A change in a tiny part of the DNA is known as a _____.

8. The fact that the hereditary material can change has, along with time, caused _____.

9. If the changed organism was better able to live in its environment, it _____, if not it _____.

10. _____ is the process by which chromosome numbers are reduced or halved.

11. When the _____ number of chromosomes from the egg combines with the _____ number from the sperm, this provides for a mixing of hereditary materials from each parent in the _____ and results in a better adapted offspring.

12. The hypothesis that we accept today concerning the passage of DNA is:

13. This resulted in the formation of a chemical and physical model of the DNA molecule called the _____ _____ model.

14. This theory of heredity includes the idea that a part of the DNA molecule is called a _____, which brings about the formation of an _____, that brings about and controls a specific chemical reaction.

15. The four nucleotides involved in DNA are:

Notes

Chapter 1

1. See, for example, ERIC (1969); Gehlen (1969); Photiadis and Schwarzeller (1970); and U.S. Department of Agriculture (1971).

2. As noted later, the names of all places and persons have been changed. There are at least eight real Mansfields in the United States and one Mansfield Center. None of them, of course, is the site of my research.

3. Over the years, as rural communities and their schools have occupied a smaller and smaller niche in American life, political power and public interest, concern, and money have understandably shifted toward urban areas and their enormous problems. Research has followed this shift, so that in the 1967–72 period the *Education Index* listed only 32 studies under the headings *rural education, rural high schools,* and *rural schools,* down from 284 under the same headings in the 1929–32 period.

4. But it must be emphasized that a community, by the fact that it is able to link persons in communal terms, must also exclude others who, indeed, may reject these very terms. These places of comfort and security for some are achieved and maintained at a definite cost to others. An examination of the benefits of community therefore must take account of its costs.

5. Undoubtedly, another investigator could find another study in Mansfield, one that focused on the outsiders and the unresponsiveness of local people and institutions to their needs and outlook. I did not so much choose to ignore them as I preferred to write about the mainstream, dominant in numbers and in most other ways.

6. Mansfielders are fully capable of rejecting a group based on a single criterion —black Americans, for example. Such groups do not happen to live in Mansfield.

7. Community has an abundance of definitions. Freilich began with Hillery's "area of agreement—persons in social interaction within a geographic area . . . having one or more additional ties" and progressed toward an operational definition (1963:118)—"people in relatively high-frequency interaction, exchanging information at a set of related centers, and practicing and developing local-interaction culture based on past information shared" (1963:127). I prefer MacIver and Page's definition because it captures the *sense* of community which I believe transforms a collectivity into a community, and it establishes the point of community locus. This is important because communities like Mansfield have fairly definite geographical boundaries.

8. This term is comparable to Litwak and Meyer's "local community." "For our purposes," they write, "the core component of the 'local community' of any particular school consists of families of children who attend it and their immediate neighbors. . . . there is always a geographic aspect" (1974:1). But I do not

assume that proximity to a school is sufficient for a family to be considered part of the support community. Moreover, there need not be a geographic basis to a local community, as they define it, in that private schools may serve families who are quite removed from the location of the school their children attend. Perhaps Litwak and Meyers mean to refer only to public schools. Their definition does suggest another group—one simply composed of all parents who send their children to a school. They are taxpayers, but they need not compose a support community or a subgroup, as these terms are used here.

9. The four collectivities of community, support community, subgroup, and taxpayer may appear in many possible combinations, but this is tangential to my study.

Chapter 2

1. These are township, not school district, figures; the township, with a population of 1,818 is almost coterminous with the school district. School district figures are not available.

2. These, too, are township, not school district figures. The shift is necessitated by the availability of data in the census tracts.

3. After nearly twenty years of deep involvement in Mansfield's public life, Matthews departed for Colorado, his Mansfield contact thereafter confined to his subscription to the *Times*. In 1918, six years after his departure, he wrote to his successor to congratulate him for "spanking the obstructionists on the village board" who opposed paving and other "progressive movements." He apologized for not being able to be there in person to resist the "anti Matthews forces and help the cause of fighting for a greater Mansfield."

4. Ad for revival meeting in the *Mansfield Times* (January 1908):

KEEP IN SIGHT

this invitation to attend Evangelical Church Revival

THEMES

WHAT	Sin? (Wednesday)
	Punishment? (Thursday)
DOES	Salvation? (Saturday)
	God's Effort to Save? (Sunday)
GOD'S	What Man Must Do To Be Saved?
	(7 p.m. Sunday)
WORD	1000 Conversions? (Monday)
	The conversion of a Treasurer?
SAY	(Tuesday)
	The conversion of Saul of Tarsus?
ABOUT	(Wednesday)

QUERIES WELCOME ANY TIME

5. On the face of it, this fact introduces a possible bias to the questionnaire findings. However, we investigated the answers that male and female respondents gave to the items and found no difference of consequence in any scale. The critical factor, if there is one, is not sex; those males and females who volunteered to return their questionnaires hold astonishingly congruent views. Perhaps they would differ significantly from those who received the questionnaire and did not return it; I do not have data on this point.

6. In regard to questions about their community, Mansfielders, in my judgment, are not indifferent. Thus for table 10 I generally interpret their "neither agree nor disagree" responses as indeterminacy. In some cases, they may hide a negative response in this answer category in order to avoid speaking negatively about some aspect of the community—its churches, for example.

7. Interpretations of the extent of community are confounded because there is no single factor which is accepted as *the* indicator of community; it is a complex phenomenon with many dimensions. Thus, to be precise, one might need to specify the dimension one has in mind when speaking of extent. But from the available data, I am content to identify Mansfield as a community and to conclude that it embraces the majority of Mansfielders. The precise limits of its embrace are beyond my focus here.

8. A strong fear of communism is expressed in the classroom transcripts that appear in a later chapter, but a fairly characteristic example of feeling toward communism appears in the June 29, 1945, *Mansfield Times* under the heading, "Babson Talks to Returning Servicemen."

> Most economists are agreed that we should be prepared for trouble any time after 1950. If, after 1950, Russia with the rest of the world suffers from unemployment, we have not much to fear. If, however, when we next have 15,000,000 unemployed, Russia and the communist countries should have no unemployment, then we may see a civil war here.

Furthermore, when a national sample was asked to name the most important problem facing the United States, 89 percent named the high cost of living; only 11 percent mentioned international problems, a category which would contain references to communism (Gallup Opinion Index, 1973:11).

9. Although the response to this question may deny a hidebound isolationist view, the question itself is too gross to allow me to state what Mansfielders actually believe in this regard. Perhaps in their position on involvement in world affairs Mansfielders would join a cross-section of almost 1,500 Americans interviewed in a Roper survey: 66 percent felt it is best to take an active part in world affairs, 30 percent said we should stay out, and 4 percent did not know (N.O.R.C., 1973:5).

10. Many questions in this and the other scales engendered a large proportion —20 percent or more—of "neither agree nor disagree" responses. Given, however, that the percentage of responses in this category ranges from 7.1 percent to 30.5 percent in table 11, for example, I assume that the respondents were generally concerned about the point of the questions asked, but that for a variety of reasons they were unable to agree or disagree about some of them. In the items on abortion, gun laws, and women's lib, uncertainty is likely generated by the fact that a complex, multidimensioned phenomenon is obscured by a too-simple question. Take the case of gun control. There are various kinds of controls that could be employed. Unfortunately, my question is general and does not specify one. But national data show that in towns under 2,500, 62 percent believe that guns should be registered (Gallup Opinion Index, 1974:15). And regarding abortion, one could agree that it should be legal if birth endangers the mother's life or if pregnancy resulted from rape, but illegal in most other instances. So believing, one would feel obliged to select the middle response, neither agree nor disagree. Thus my point is that when the conservative response is less robust than I expected, I cannot conclude that my expectations of a conservative syndrome are incorrect.

11. These subscribers were verified as actual newcomers and leavers from Mansfield's telephone district, which embraces most of the school district.

12. That intimacy exists in Mansfield is undeniable. Feeling about it is generally positive but with a strong strain of ambivalence. To the statement, "I like living in Mansfield because you know just about everybody and everybody knows you," 56 percent of the adult respondents agreed, 19 percent disagreed, and 23 percent neither agreed nor disagreed.

13. The *Mansfield Times* described the Homecoming banquet of 1948:

> The toastmaster than introduced Miss Dorie Clagg who brought greetings from the class of '85, after which there were short but interesting talks by Sarah Ramsey, '01, Cloris Bettweather, '06, Ralph Horn, '10, Burt Sheldon, '16, Fay Harwood, '26, Fred Kling, '28, and Mary Burnside, '30. Each speaker had something distinctive to say and there wasn't a dull moment while the former grads were rolling back the curtains to give the group a glimpse of never-to-be-forgotten days.

14. The characteristics of community identified in the two sections on the sense of community are well established in the literature. They are presented here to document its reality in Mansfield. For further discussion see Moe and Taylor (1942); Gore (1967); Quandt (1970); Stacey (1960); MacIver and Page (1949); Williams (1969); Bell and Newby (1971); Jacob and Toscano (1964); and Rees (1950).

Chapter 3

1. In contrast, seven high school "varsity" basketball games brought out only 1,880 paying fans in 1972 and 2,729 in ten games in 1971.

2. There is one nonathletic example. The dramatic coach is paid $100.00 per play.

3. In 1973, the average student-teacher ratio in the country was 1 to 21.4.

4. *Reader's Digest* has a subsidiary which sells candy as part of its education division. One of its salesmen explained that his company views candy sales as an opportunity for students to learn to meet and deal with the public, to organize sales, and to handle money. In fact, he says, candy sales are under the business education department of some high schools.

5. That a potential for the opposing sentiment exists can be seen in an item from the July 10, 1946, *Mansfield Times*:

> In Saturday's election the voters in the village . . . will vote . . . as to whether they accept the outlying territory. . . . So far as known there is no organized effort in the village to oppose the merger. It has been reported, however, that there are some in the rural areas hard at work against the consolidation. There is only one purpose in consolidation and that is to create a better . . . school for the coming generation. . . . Authorities in education regard consolidation . . . to be a progressive step in rural education.

6. For a contrary picture from various time periods, see Sims (1912), Moe and Taylor (1942), and Select Committee (1971). Perhaps the fluctuation in Mansfield is due to changing economic conditions.

7. Because a local minister urged his congregation to express their disapproval, there was a greater response to this goal than to the others. The formulators of the goal intended no sanction of evolutionary theory and, indeed, the teaching

of the subject in biology (see chap. 6) does not warrant the concern found in the responses. Here is a sampling of the responses:

> I am opposed to the teaching of any science that would reflect the origin of man as anything but the direct creation of God. Any other teaching would be in direct opposition to the teaching of the Bible and the teaching of the churches in this school district (*Citizen*).

> In a survey taken during February 1970, with all churches of this school district participating, the following information was reported. Seventy-four percent reported they attended one of the churches. Only 12.7 percent reported they had no preference at all. Four percent were not contacted. This survey reflects that 83.3 percent of the citizens of this school district attends or prefers a church in this community. Therefore I believe in order for school to best serve the majority of the citizens it would not teach subjects that are in direct opposition of what the students are taught in the home and in their respective churches (*Citizen*).

> Do not approve if this encompasses teaching evolution (*Teacher*).

> I don't think we have enough of this. Most kids only take one year of science because they are afraid of chemistry with all the formulas, and physics is complicated. I think we should have some more about man like botany and zoology is about plants and animals (*Student*).

8. One version of this goal also included other "areas of concern": "Loyalty, patriotism, and non-discriminatory behavior," but they were omitted from the version submitted to the state office.

9. By writing directly to local superintendents I obtained the "Goals for To-morrow" from ten school districts and did a content analysis of their statements.

Chapter 4

1. After Mr. Tate's death, the assemblies were replaced by a daily announcement that teachers read to the newly organized ten-minute home room. It is these announcements that are included in chapter 7.

2. Schools have existed in Mansfield for over ninety years, but Mansfield has had a unified elementary and secondary school system with one school board for only twenty years. Farmers and natives also dominated its earlier dual school system.

3. Recently, a new and zealous policeman ticketed an old and distinguished Mansfield native for illegal parking. The ticket caused much talk in town. Mr. Hastings always parks his car in the same place and since it is considered his parking place, illegal or not, it is unthinkable to ticket him.

4. The superintendent, in a letter accompanying a school board agenda sent to board members, made a sardonic reference to certain adults in the community. He called them "specialists." They are usually young, college-educated, nonnative residents who attend meetings and urge consideration of some ideas involving change.

5. In the dialogue that follows, the voices are those of board members, the superintendent, or the grade school or high school principal. The content will usually indicate whether a board member or educator is speaking, though occasionally the speaker is identified.

6. All three interviews have been edited. The staccato effect produced by the short questions and answers is natural. These are nearly verbatim accounts.

Chapter 5

1. This is a neighborhood type of institution which serves, though not exclusively, small-town graduates from the central part of the state.

2. I have no data about Mansfield's teachers either to support or to refute Tamblyn's (1971:19) observation that since the more "aggressive and ambitious [rural-born teachers] seek their first teaching assignment elsewhere, those who remain to teach in rural schools are likely to be less adventurous and less ambitious." The dictum, of course, could be applied to rural people in general, excluding farmers.

3. According to a 1971 Gallup Poll (1972:17) taken in communities of 2,500 or less, 64 percent of the respondents were satisfied with their children's education, 26 percent were not, and 10 percent did not know. Comparable statistics for the nation as a whole were 60, 20 and 12 percent. I cite these figures with diffidence since, unlike Gallup election polls, I have no way to determine their accuracy for the groups they are supposed to represent. Moreover, in my own survey I did not ask if people in Mansfield were pleased with their children's education, but if they thought the school system was one of the most important things in Mansfield. This is a more demanding question; thus a positive answer requires a more positive assessment of schooling than the Gallup Poll question requires.

Chapter 6

1. To capture the life of the classroom, my research assistants and I observed and taped teachers and students at work in various subjects and at various grade levels, collected student papers and tests, and interviewed students to obtain their reactions to their classroom experience. The excerpts included here are not meant to be the basis for judgments about the quality of teaching at MHS. In fact, the excerpts are basically drawn from teachers who are among the most energetic, intelligent, and committed ones in the high school. The intent of this chapter is to document what a student is likely to hear when he goes to class at Mansfield High School, the emphasis being on value orientations. Lessons from this chapter were selected in terms of readability and their capacity to capture the flavor and the affective disposition of the teachers included here. Special emphasis was given to English, biology, and U.S. history because they are required subjects.

2. The tape recorder, good in its place, misses much of importance in the classroom. Simultaneous with the above discussion, the following exchange took place:

> "Will you marry Jerry?"
> "Not for a couple of years, at least."
> "Why not now?"
> "Because my mom'd kill me if I left school."
> "No, she wouldn't."
> "She sure would. She'd leave nothing left of me to get married."
> "Is Jerry still in school?"
> "No, he quit."

3. As in the case of the sophomore English transcripts, the edited (that is, shortened) transcripts below are taken from several different class sessions.

Chapter 7

1. Barker and Gump (1964:198) estimate that approximately 80 percent of the behavior settings in the schools they studied involved nonacademic activities.

2. How far school districts will be forced to go in times of economic hardship may be revealed by the combination of inflation and reduced state appropriations which characterizes the present period. It will be interesting to observe what aspects of the school experience remain secure in a time of financial hardship. A recent issue of the *Champaign News Gazette* reported that a number of schools, because of failed referenda, had cut back or were threatening to eliminate athletics (January 8, 1974:14).

3. These announcements are read in a ten-minute home room. Formerly they were read aloud each morning by the superintendent to all students assembled in the gymnasium.

4. That is, neither my research assistants nor I were present to record what happened; we recorded and the results were unpromising; no program or agenda was available; nor was it written up in the school newspaper.

5. Small towns often do not have much going on which merits reporting, so when school is closed there is a real dearth of publishable items and the *Times* resorts more heavily than it ordinarily does to filler pieces from news agencies. Throughout the school year, the *Mansfield Times* reports on both major and minor school events, thereby informing most Mansfielders of all ages about school affairs, including the weekly lunch menu, highlights of school board meetings, names of honor roll students, facts of money-raising drives, winners of school awards, club events, and athletic team scores.

6. FHA members in this project were asked during a free period to talk about their "grandmothers," older Mansfield women who, like the girls, volunteered to be part of a grandchild-grandmother relationship.

Chapter 8

1. For what is still perhaps the most exhaustive study of this age group see Coleman (1961).

2. Students who became diarists responded, generally, either to an invitation appearing in *Tiger Tidings*, the student newspaper, or to a personal request. The usual criticisms apply to results obtained from such an unsystematic sample. The alternative, however—selecting students at random and then bringing pressure on them to cooperate—might have produced more representative results, but it would have served to offend and alienate those whose voluntary, willing cooperation I needed and whose ease with my presence had to be taken for granted. The trade-off of voluntary responses and acceptance for possibly more representative results still seems warranted, especially since the information obtained from the diaries can be corroborated by other means. I indicated to students that I needed the type of information contained in diaries to understand more fully their lives as students. Students accepted my invitation to keep a diary because they liked being helpful and they liked the idea of keeping one. Also, it became a "thing to do"—students were attracted by others who had agreed to keep one. I urged them to write for at least one week. The diary keepers received these instructions:

1. Keeping a diary is completely voluntary. Nobody should do one unless he wants to.

2. The diaries are necessary for our study because we feel it is important to understand what students experience, both in school and out of school, and to appreciate what they think and how they feel about their experiences.

3. So, what should you write in your diary? The everyday sorts of things that happen to you. What kind of experiences are we interested in? All kinds— funny, sad, interesting, strange, dull, exciting, serious, happy, worrisome, fearful.

A total of twenty-seven students, twenty-one females and six males, fairly well distributed over all grades, volunteered to keep a diary. As the results show, each adopted a somewhat different style in terms of what they wrote, the frankness of their language, the intimacy of the subject matter, and the length of daily entries. In general, the diary volunteers had above-average grades, participated actively in school affairs, were popular, and were from moderately well-to-do families. I have no reason to think that what happens in the lives of the diary writers and their perception of what happens differs markedly from what happens in the lives of non–diary writers.

The diaries included here were selected because they seemed to articulate student life well and naturally and because they were interesting. All have been edited by changing names, places, and events so that they do not identify the writer. To enhance readability, I omitted full days and parts of days that were redundant. Otherwise, the diaries were left in the language of the writers, just as they wrote them. The ideal was to get naturalistic expression from each writer; of course, this was not fully possible. Some students wrote self-consciously, with restraint, unable to forget that their accounts would have an audience beyond themselves. Nonetheless, those included here have a rich, revealing quality that aptly illuminates Mansfield's student peer culture. Whether they would have written differently had they been writing only for themselves, I do not know.

3. See Hauben (1972) for a diary written in another time and place.

4. Cusick (1973) documents the peripheral nature of academic activities in a high school student's life.

5. This assumption was confirmed by MHS graduates who read this chapter in manuscript form.

6. The Hechingers (1962) write with great concern about the teen-age culture and its influence on American society.

Chapter 9

1. Unlike the diaries, which are drawn from a small, voluntary group, these are drawn from almost all students in an entire graduating class interviewed during their study hall periods. They are responses essentially to two questions: "How do you feel about having gone to school at Mansfield High School?" and "How do you feel about graduating?"

2. Since 1970, when MHS's Honor Society received its charter, an average of three to four students have been inducted each year; based on the number of students in class, a total of nine to ten students could have been eligible.

3. A Mansfield student, now a college graduate living out of the area, described going to college in a way that suggests the difference going away can make in terms of adaptation to different settings:

During my first year of college it was like being in a different pond. I camouflaged and fit into that pond very easily. The pond got bigger. I could fit in just as easily as I could in Mansfield. I definitely was not trapped in Mansfield. But I do think people in Mansfield lead a very sheltered life. If they've never been away, they have no idea what the other half of the world looks like.

Chapter 10

1. Margaret Stacey (1960) attempts to show that the alternatives are not either the security of traditional small communities or the disorder of nontraditional settings. John Holt, however, makes an unqualified plea for the rewards of traditional community (1970:xvii).

2. Compare Vidich and Bensman's Springdale (1968).

3. A major connection between Mansfield's survival and its schools is the very presence of the school in Mansfield proper, with its centripetal impact on parents: people tend to shop where their children attend school.

4. Cronin makes a similar observation in his discussion of urban schools: "Thus one can argue for the selection of teachers and principals not by impersonal 'professional' criteria alone but by subjective criteria, too" (1973:208).

5. Literature on the curriculum of rural schools has fluctuated widely on the issue of adaptation: should rural schools reflect rural life or should they be like urban schools? John Drosick (Select Committee, 1971:6393) believes that "a good program in a rural school is a good program in an urban school." In fact, the issue of adaptation and survival bears more on who is teaching than on what is taught, more on the adolescent culture than the choice of algebra textbooks. An examination of Mansfield's curriculum would not reveal how closely Mansfield High School is adapted to Mansfield.

6. The community school concept invited a very substantial effort to adapt the school consciously to community realities. Note Everett (1938). For the waning of the community school movement see Gividen (1963).

7. For example, I sent my questionnaire to an MHS graduating class of the late 1940s and got close to 100 percent returns from them. The following reactions are based on twenty-six responses from persons in that class living outside Mansfield school district. Forty-two percent believe that people in small towns like Mansfield are better able to live the kind of life they prefer than urban people; 61.4 percent believe people in small towns are friendlier than those living in larger places; and 61.4 percent agreed that Mansfield is a specially good place to raise children. One leaver wrote, "I would not go back because it is much too small and uninteresting and dead." She now lives nine miles away in a town of 2,000! One man wrote, in terms that seem to fit many, that he left because of his need to find work, but he "never felt that growing up elsewhere could have been more enjoyable or beneficial."

8. The data in table 32 are not fully persuasive, but they tend to confirm my sense of Mansfield's low level of alienation, particularly among mainstream Mansfielders as against non-Mansfielders.

9. See also Nisbet: "Surely the outstanding characteristic of contemporary thought on man and society is the preoccupation with personal alienation and cultural disintegration" (1962:3).

10. See Fein's (1971) excellent book for further discussion of universalism and the relationship between school and community.

11. It is always easier to point out the hazards of a dilemma than to construct policy which avoids the hazards. Compare Cronin (1973:208).

12. Sidney is a central Illinois village of 900. Facing the loss of its only school, a K–6 institution, its residents reacted vigorously to their school board's decision:

A caravan of about 75 cars stretched from Sidney to Philo . . . and they were all going to the . . . Board meeting. At the meeting the School Board was confronted with 250 angry people. (*Champaign News Gazette*, Feb. 27, 1976:3).

In a letter to the editor several villagers wrote:

We, residents of Sidney, are not a bunch of violent radicals as some people are leading you to believe, but some very concerned citizens that happen to feel that our children and the growth of our town are very important to us (*Champaign News Gazette*, April 2, 1976:5).

13. Mansfielders also express opposing positions:

I tell you, I've got a lot of relations that graduated from Mansfield. Most of them have gone to college. They said Mansfield is not that good a system because when you get out there amongst the world, a lot of those kids are from bigger schools that offer more.

14. In the February 1975 issue of *Illinois Education News*, a state publication, the executive director or president of the Illinois Federation of Teachers, Illinois Education Association, Illinois Association of School Boards, and Illinois Association of School Administrators prepared statements on school district reorganization. None referred to the school's relationship to its community as a factor to take account of in reorganization. The Illinois Education Association's views on reorganization are characteristic of approaches that ignore the community. It recommends that school districts should have at least fifteen hundred students with a minimum of one hundred students in each high school graduation class (IEN, 1975:2).

15. Jessica Weber, observing that the concept "Bigger is better" is open to question, wrote,

Giantism is the triumph of the big over the small: of huge corporations over small businesses, of immense government structures over neighborhoods, of agribusiness over the family farm. Many educators have come to a similar conclusion, and the result is the rural school movement, a nationwide phenomenon (1975:6).

See also Stans (1972:3).

16. In the spring of 1976 white South Bostonians organized to patrol their neighborhood. One marshal said, "We might look like animals . . . but these people [South Bostonians] need a strong defense for peace of mind. They think they're losing everything" (*Newsweek*, May 24, 1976:30). Some days before this report appeared, Ron Nessen, President Ford's press secretary, said that Ford wanted the Supreme Court to "explore alternative solutions [to busing] that would be less destructive to community life."

17. The bilingual-bicultural school example presents a major problem to its support community not shared by its counterpart in places like Mansfield. When such schools are located in cities, they are controlled centrally, not by the support community. Moreover, as relatively recent claimants of educational prerogatives, the Latino community in the north has had limited opportunity to shape the school by and in its own interests. Also, the community may be heterogeneous to the

point that the school gets very mixed messages about which realities it should reflect and reinforce.

18. Burger's observation about the Amish may be appropriate for a Supreme Court pronouncement, but it skirts the critical fact of the case. Religious beliefs are central to the survival of the Amish as a group and a community. Because religion has constitutional protection in the First Amendment, Amish particularism is protected. Other groups, lacking a religious foundation, do not have constitutional sanction for maintaining their exclusiveness. However, is there any warrant for religion's being the only acceptable basis for protection of a culturally exclusive group? I think not.

19. Nations, like communities, can also be exclusive, if not hostile to subgroups within their boundaries. Both are essential to the well-being of individuals and groups they encompass. The political disintegration of new states and the social chaos in areas with profoundly hostile groups, like Northern Ireland, Cyprus, and Lebanon, testifies to the essential need for national integration. And both offer limited goods, not worth having at any price. It is a reciprocal matter: neither community nor nation should define its ideals in disregard of the welfare of the other.

20. They, too, probably censor in the sense of disallowing certain reading material (on fundamentalism, for example) to be used in school. More than disallowing, however, the Kanawha County protagonists prefer a classroom climate that is more closed than open regarding the examination of ideas. It is this difference in climate that may constitute the important difference in an issue too complex to elaborate further here.

21. A. D. Luke's testimony before the Select Committee on Equal Educational Opportunity (1971:6371–78) speaks to this point.

22. F. A. Rodgers (1975) discusses the pre-integration high school in North Carolina. He concludes that desegregation not only caused many black educators to lose their jobs and students to lose opportunities to "reinforce positive self-concepts," but the black community lost a critical factor for promoting its political and social activities (1975:91). Rodgers's doubt about the outcome of the 1954 Supreme Court decision suggests that one may question whether or not national ideals should take priority over local community gains and losses.

23. For further discussion of communities and their survival see Gallaher (1967).

24. As Nisbet reminds us, "The quest for community will not be denied, for it springs from some powerful needs of human nature—needs for a clear sense of cultural purpose, membership, status, and continuity" (1962:73).

25. Several recent newspaper articles aptly convey this tension. Merle Good observes:

> I write from a part of unmelted America, where one can stand in the shade of a maple on the edge of an open field of growing crops and breathe clear air, and hear neither plane nor trucks for the better part of a morning. Things are different here. The soil is respected and friendships are for life. People know their neighbors and few lock their houses at night. . . . Modern progress . . . has some basic flaws. . . . I realize that this tension is not unique in our [Amish] people. The Irish face it. Blacks who are now searching out roots can't escape it. . . . Destruction of the tongues and eyes and tastes of the tribal community. Bite, gulp, dissolve. Gone modern (1977:2).

In strong and striking contrast, Roland Dewolk responds to his perception of the small community.

I refuse to take it anymore. I refuse to see another television commercial or program in which the virtues of small town life are practically deified. . . . Listen America: It just ain't so! Six years ago I spent the junior year of my high school days in a small (population 7000) town. . . . My history teacher taught the class that Hitler lost World War II because God had put into his mind to open a two-front war. . . . I was taunted and threatened because I once said marijuana should be legalized and the war in Viet Nam was wrong (1977:2).

26. Note Diane Ravitch's case for uncertainty about which "community" (of the several possible ones) a child may be part of and her consequent preference for a universalistic outlook in schools—the "common humanity of . . . pupils" (Ravitch, 1974:402). If one's locus of study is the comparative discord of New York, then comity stands forth as a solution; if one begins with the accord of Mansfield, then support for diversity is appealing.

27. Milton Mayer would attest to the presence of my blinders: "My wistfulness commends the community's care to me, but the most I seem to be able to manage is a prayer for the faith, hope, and love that reduces my hostility to its indifference" (1975:6). Mayer believes "community is a sentimental concept."

28. Sidey (1976) believes there is a resurgence of small-town life, of places where people can regain identity.

References

Barker, Roger and Gump, Paul. 1964. *Big School, Small School.* Stanford: Stanford University Press.

Bartlett, Kay. 1977. "School Book Banning Ignites Controversy." *Champaign* (Ill.) *News Gazette*, Feb. 20.

Bell, Colin and Newby, Howard, eds. 1972. *Community Studies.* New York: Praeger Publishers.

Coleman, James S. 1961. *The Adolescent Society.* New York: The Free Press.

Commager, Henry S. 1973. "Only the Federal Government." *Today's Education* 62:47–48.

Cronin, Joseph. 1973. *The Control of Urban Schools.* New York: The Free Press.

Cusick, Phillip A. 1973. *Inside High School.* New York: Holt, Rinehart and Winston.

Dewolk, Roland. 1977. "Backwoods Paradise? I'll Take the City Any Day." *Caravan*, Mar. 16.

E.R.I.C. 1969. "The Changing Rural Scene." Las Cruces, N.M.: ERIC Clearinghouse on Rural Education and Small Schools.

Everett, Samuel, ed. 1938. *The Community School.* New York: D. Appleton-Century Co.

Fein, Leonard J. 1971. *The Ecology of the Public Schools: An Inquiry into Community Control.* New York: Pegasus.

Freilich, Morris. 1963. "Toward an Operational Definition of Community." *Rural Sociology* 28:117–27.

Fried, Marc. 1963. "Grieving for a Lost Home." In *The Urban Condition*, edited by Leonard Duhl. New York: Basic Books.

Gallaher, Art, Jr. 1967. "The Little Community in the United States." In *Change in the Small Community*, edited by William J. Gore and Leroy Hodapp. New York: Friendship Press.

Gallup, George. 1971. *Gallup Opinion Index*, No. 100.

Gehlen, Frieda L. 1969. *The Political Aspects of Small Towns and Rural Schools.* Las Cruces, N.M.: ERIC Clearinghouse on Rural Education and Rural Schools.

Gividen, Noble J. 1963. *High School Education for Rural Youth.* Washington, D.C.: National Committee for Children and Youth.

Good, Merle. 1977. "Amish Not Backward, But Ahead of Their Time." *Caravan*, Mar. 16.

Gore, William J. 1967. "An Overview of Social Science Perspectives toward a Small Town. In *Change in the Small Community*, edited by William J. Gore and Leroy Hodapp. New York: Friendship Press.

Hauben, Daniel. 1972. "Diary." In *High School*, edited by Ronald Gross and Paul Osterman. New York: Simon and Schuster.

Hechinger, Grace, and Hechinger, Fred. 1964. *Teen-Age Tyranny*. New York: Fawcett World Library.

Holt, John. 1970. Introduction to *My Country School Diary*, by Julia Gordon. New York: Dell Publishing Co.

Homans, George C. 1950. *The Human Group*. New York: Harcourt, Brace and Co.

"The Issue Is: School District Reorganization." 1975. *Illinois Education News* 4:2 and passim.

Jacob, P. E., and Toscano, J. V., eds. 1964. *The Integration of Political Communities*. Philadelphia: J. B. Lippincott Co.

Keim, Albert, ed. 1975. *Compulsory Education and the Amish*. Boston: Beacon Press.

Klein, Joe. 1975. "The Boston Busing Crisis." *Rolling Stone* 198:32.

Litwak, Eugene, and Meyer, Henry J. 1974. *School, Family, and Neighborhood: The Theory and Practice of School-Community Relations*. New York: Columbia University Press.

MacIver, Robert M., and Page, Charles H. 1949. *Society: An Introductory Analysis*. New York: Rinehart and Co.

Mayer, Milton. 1975. "Community Anyone?" *Center Magazine* 8:4–7.

Moe, Edward O. and Taylor, C. C. 1942. *Culture of a Contemporary Rural Community: Irwin, Iowa*. Washington, D.C.: U.S. Department of Agriculture.

National Opinion Research Center. 1973–74. *National Data Program for the Social Sciences*. Ann Arbor, Mich.: Interuniversity Consortium for Political Research.

————. 1974–75. Ibid.

Nisbet, Robert. 1962. *Community and Power*. New York: Oxford University Press.

Photiadis, I. D., and Schwarzweller, H. K., eds. 1970. *Change in Rural Appalachia*. Philadelphia: University of Pennsylvania Press.

Pierson, George W. 1973. *The Moving American*. New York: Alfred A. Knopf.

Quandt, Jean. 1970. *From the Small Town to the Great Community*. New Brunswick, N.J.: Rutgers University Press.

Ravitch, Diane. 1974. *The Great School Wars*. New York: Basic Books.

Rees, A. 1950. *Life in a Welsh Countryside*. Cardiff: University of Wales Press.

Rodgers, Fred A. 1975. *The Black High School and Its Community*. Lexington, Mass.: Lexington Books.

Select Committee on Equal Educational Opportunity. 1971. *Education in Rural America*, pt. 15. Washington, D.C.: U.S. Government Printing Office.

Sidey, Hugh. 1976. "Our Country and the Search for Community. *Today's Education* 65: 18–21.

Sims, N. L. 1912. "A Hoosier Village." M.A. Thesis, Columbia University.

Stacey, Margaret. 1960. *Tradition and Change: A Study of Banbury*. London: Oxford University Press.

Stans, Patricia. 1972. "Issues in Rural Education: Consolidation." ERIC/CRESS *Newsletter* 7:3.

Tamblyn, Lewis R. 1971. *Rural Education in the United States*. Washington, D.C.: Rural Education Association.

United States Bureau of the Census. 1890–1970. *U.S. Census of Population*. Washington, D.C.: U.S. Government Printing Office.

United States Department of Agriculture. 1971. *The Economic and Social Condition of Rural America in the 1970s*. Washington, D.C.: Economic Development Division.

Vidich, Arthur J., and Bensman, Joseph. 1958. *Small Town in Mass Society*. Garden City, N.Y.: Doubleday.

Weber, Jessica C. 1975. "Rural Schools: An Option." *Illinois Education News* 4:6–7.

Williams, William M. 1969. "Gosforth and the Outside World." In *The Community: A Comparative Perspective*, edited by Robert M. French. Itasca, Ill.: F. E. Peacock Publishers.

Index

Academic standards. *See* Students; Teachers
Adaptation, 198, 247 n.5
Adopted Grandmother, 136–37
Agriculture: changes in, 42–43; farming, 62; importance in Mansfield, 9
Alienation, 200, 247 n.8, 247 n.9; of Mansfielders compared, 233
Amish, 204–5, 249 n.18
Athletics: basketball, 115, 141–42, 164–65; football, 140–41; importance in Mansfield High School, 142–43, 153–54, 166, 183; interest in Mansfield, 18, 45; track, 141. *See also* Football
Auburn, 64, 169–170, 181–82, 188

Belonging, 193, 206
Bilingual-bicultural studies, 203–4, 206, 248–49 n.17
Biology, 117–21
Black literature, 72, 101, 183
Bradlow, 19, 182
Brenton, 19, 170, 182

Chorus, 116–17
Communism, 111–15
Community: 239 n.4, 241 n.7, 242 n.14; ambivalence toward, 32–33; defined, 6, 239 n.7; psychological boundaries of, 34; sense of in Mansfield, 26–39, 194; survival of in Mansfield, 206–9
Community maintenance: costs of, *see* Local control; and the nation, 201, 205, 208, 249 n.22; and the school board, 61–62, 70–71, 197; and schooling, 37–38, 64, 143, 147, 192, 195–96, 205, 208–9, 247 n.3, 148 n.14
Consolidation, 46, 49, 53, 63–65, 93, 97, 194, 202, 242 n.5, 248 n.12
Cruising, 89, 150, 152
Current Events, 111–15

Diaries, 151–173; instructions for, 245–46 n.2; themes, 151
Drugs: alcohol, 152–53, 157, 159, 162, 172; marijuana, 152–53

English, 51, 106–11, 184–85, 194
Ethos: defined, 193. *See also* Mansfield
Evolution, theory of, 118–22, 242–43 n.7
Extracurricular activities: academic-oriented, 127; athletic, 140–43; career guidance, 144–47; character building, 136–38; fund raising, 138–40, 224; Homecoming, 131–33; ideologically oriented, 128–31; importance at Mansfield High School, 126–27, 146–49, 195; pep and spirit, 133–35
Fieldwork in Mansfield: anonymity, 4; nature of, 1–4, 7; origin of, 2–3
Football, 45, 89, 183, 194
Fund raising, 50, 139–40
Future Farmers of America, 127
Future Homemakers of America, 127, 133–37, 150

Girls' Athletic Association, 137–38, 162
Guidance: educational, 143; vocational, 144–47, 185

Homecoming, 90, 131–33, 242 n.13

Intimacy, 36–37, 206, 242 n.12
Island Trees, New York, 207, 209

Kanawha County schools, 204, 206, 209, 249 n.20
Kentuckians, 21, 25–26
Kinship, 27

Local control: dilemmas of, 199–203, 207; importance of in Mansfield, 8, 195, 198, 209

Mansfield: centennial, 38; coal mining in, 40–41; economic status, 42–43, 217; ethos, 193; history, 14–26, 39–42; migration pattern, 31–32, 54–55; nature of, 10–13, 211–13; psychological boundaries of, *see* Community; stability, 214–15; survival of, 41–44

255